The Collected Poems of

W.B. Yeats

Om Books International

This edition first published in 2023 by

Om Books International

Corporate and Editorial Office
A-12, Sector 64, Noida 201 301
Uttar Pradesh, India
Phone: +91 120 477 4100
Email: editorial@ombooks.com
Website: www.ombooksinternational.com

Sales Office
107, Ansari Road, Darya Ganj,
New Delhi 110 002, India
Phone: +91 11 4000 9000
Email: sales@ombooks.com
Website: www.ombooks.com

ISBN: 978-81-960447-7-0

Printed in India

10 9 8 7 6 5 4 3 2 1

William Butler Yeats (1865–1939) is one of Ireland's most revered poets and playwrights. His work has been widely circulated and anthologised.

Yeats was born in Dublin, Ireland, on 13 June 1865 but moved to Chiswick, London, in 1867 due to his father's career as a lawyer and did not return to Ireland until 1881, where he studied at the Metropolitan School of Art. It was here that he met fellow poet George Russell who shared his interest in mysticism. In 1885, Yeats had his first poems published in the *Dublin University Review*, in 1887 he returned with his family to Chiswick, and 1890 saw him along with Ernest Rhys form the Rhymers' Club, a group of poets who would meet in Fleet Street, London, during 1891–94. Along with playwright Lady Gregory, he founded the Irish Theatre, which later became the Abbey Theatre.

The Nobel Prize for literature was awarded to him in 1923. In his literary career, he wrote many poems, plays, short stories and articles which covered many aspects from folklore to politics. He was also the editor of the controversial *Oxford Book of Modern Verse 1892–1935* (1936).

W.B. Yeats died in 1939 in Roquebrune-Cap-Martin, France, but his coffin was later moved to Ireland.

CONTENTS

LYRICAL

CROSSWAYS—1889

The Rose—1893

THE WIND AMONG THE REEDS—1899

IN THE SEVEN WOODS—1904

THE GREEN HELMET AND OTHER POEMS—1910

RESPONSIBILITIES—1914

THE WILD SWANS AT COOLE—1919

MICHAEL ROBARTES AND THE DANCER—1921

THE TOWER—1928

THE WINDING STAIR AND OTHER POEMS—1933

FROM A FULL MOON IN MARCH—1933

LAST POEMS - 1936—1939

NARRATIVE AND DRAMATIC

THE WANDERINGS OF OISIN—1889

THE OLD AGE OF QUEEN MAEVE—1903

BAILE AND AILLINN—1903

THE SHADOWY WATERS—1906

THE TWO KINGS—1914

THE GIFT OF HARUN AL-RASHID—1923

LYRICAL

CROSSWAYS
1889

The Song of the Happy Shepherd

The woods of Arcady are dead,
And over is their antique joy;
Of old the world on dreaming fed;
Grey Truth is now her painted toy;
Yet still she turns her restless head:
But O, sick children of the world,
Of all the many changing things
In dreary dancing past us whirled,
To the cracked tune that Chronos sings,
Words alone are certain good.
Where are now the warring kings,
Word be-mockers? — By the Rood
Where are now the warring kings?
An idle word is now their glory,
By the stammering schoolboy said,
Reading some entangled story:
The kings of the old time are dead;
The wandering earth herself may be
Only a sudden flaming word,
In clanging space a moment heard,
Troubling the endless reverie.

Then nowise worship dusty deeds,
Nor seek, for this is also sooth,
To hunger fiercely after truth,
Lest all thy toiling only breeds
New dreams, new dreams; there is no truth
Saving in thine own heart. Seek, then,

No learning from the starry men,
Who follow with the optic glass
The whirling ways of stars that pass —
Seek, then, for this is also sooth,
No word of theirs — the cold star-bane
Has cloven and rent their hearts in twain,
And dead is all their human truth.
Go gather by the humming sea
Some twisted, echo-harbouring shell,
And to its lips thy story tell,
And they thy comforters will be,
Rewarding in melodious guile
Thy fretful words a little while,
Till they shall singing fade in ruth
And die a pearly brotherhood;
For words alone are certain good:
Sing, then, for this is also sooth.

I must be gone: there is a grave
Where daffodil and lily wave,
And I would please the hapless faun,
Buried under the sleepy ground,
With mirthful songs before the dawn.
His shouting days with mirth were crowned;
And still I dream he treads the lawn,
Walking ghostly in the dew,
Pierced by my glad singing through,
My songs of old earth's dreamy youth:
But ah! she dreams not now; dream thou!
For fair are poppies on the brow:
Dream, dream, for this is also sooth.

The Sad Shepherd

There was a man whom Sorrow named his friend,
And he, of his high comrade Sorrow dreaming,
Went walking with slow steps along the gleaming
And humming sands, where windy surges wend:
And he called loudly to the stars to bend
From their pale thrones and comfort him, but they

Among themselves laugh on and sing alway:
And then the man whom Sorrow named his friend
Cried out, *Dim sea, hear my most piteous story*!
The sea swept on and cried her old cry still,
Rolling along in dreams from hill to hill.
He fled the persecution of her glory
And, in a far-off, gentle valley stopping,
Cried all his story to the dewdrops glistening.
But naught they heard, for they are always listening,
The dewdrops, for the sound of their own dropping.
And then the man whom Sorrow named his friend
Sought once again the shore, and found a shell,
And thought, *I will my heavy story tell*
Till my own words, re-echoing, shall send
Their sadness through a hollow, pearly heart;
And my own tale again for me shall sing,
And my own whispering words be comforting,
And lo! *my ancient burden may depart.*
Then he sang softly nigh the pearly rim;
But the sad dweller by the sea-ways lone
Changed all he sang to inarticulate moan
Among her wildering whirls, forgetting him.

The Cloak, the Boat And the Shoes

'What do you make so fair and bright?'

'I make the cloak of Sorrow:
O lovely to see in all men's sight
Shall be the cloak of Sorrow,
In all men's sight.'

'What do you build with sails for flight?'

'I build a boat for Sorrow:
O swift on the seas all day and night
Saileth the rover Sorrow,
All day and night.'

'What do you weave with wool so white?'

'I weave the shoes of Sorrow:
Soundless shall be the footfall light
In all men's ears of Sorrow,
Sudden and light.'

Anashuya And Vijaya

A little Indian temple in the Golden Age. Around it a garden; around that the forest. Anashuya, the young priestess, kneeling within the temple.

Anashuya. Send peace on all the lands and flickering corn. —
O, may tranquillity walk by his elbow
When wandering in the forest, if he love
No other. — Hear, and may the indolent flocks
Be plentiful. — And if he love another,
May panthers end him. — Hear, and load our king
With wisdom hour by hour. — May we two stand,
When we are dead, beyond the setting suns,
A little from the other shades apart,
With mingling hair, and play upon one lute.

Vijaya (*entering and throwing* a *lily at her*). Hail! hail, my Anashuya.

Anashuya. No: be still.
I, priestess of this temple, offer up
prayers for the land.

Vijaya. *I* will wait here, Amrita.

Anashuya. By mighty Brahma's ever-rustling robe,
Who is Amrita? Sorrow of all sorrows!
Another fills your mind.

Vijaya. My mother's name.

Anashuya (*sings, coming out of the temple*).

A sad, sad *thought went by me slowly:*
Sigh, O *you little stars!* O *sigh and shake your blue apparel!*
The sad, sad thought has *gone from me now wholly:*
Sing, O you *little stars!* O *sing and raise your rapturous carol*
To mighty Brahma, be *who made you many* as *the sands,*
And laid you on *the gates* of *evening with his quiet hands.*
(*sits down on the steps of the temple.*)

Vijaya, I have brought my evening rice;
The sun has laid his chin on the grey wood,
Weary, with all his poppies gathered round him.

Vijaya. The hour when Kama, full of sleepy laughter,
Rises, and showers abroad his fragrant arrows,
Piercing the twilight with their murmuring barbs.

Anashuya. See how the sacred old flamingoes come,
Painting with shadow all the marble steps:
Aged and wise, they seek their wonted perches
Within the temple, devious walking, made
To wander by their melancholy minds.
Yon tall one eyes my supper; chase him away,
Far, far away. I named him after you.
He is a famous fisher; hour by hour
He ruffles with his bill the minnowed streams.
Ah! there he snaps my rice. I told you so.
Now cuff him off. He's off! A kiss for you,
Because you saved my rice. Have you no thanks?

Vijaya (*sings*). *Sing you* of *her,* O *first few stars,*
Whom Brahma, touching with his finger, praises, for you hold
The van of *wandering quiet; ere you be too calm and old,*
Sing, turning in your cars,
Sing, till you raise your hands and sigh, and from your car-heads peer,
With all your whirling hair, and drop many an azure tear.

Anashuya. What know the pilots of the stars of tears?

Vijaya. Their faces are all worn, and in their eyes
Flashes the fire of sadness, for they see
The icicles that famish all the North,

Where men lie frozen in the glimmering snow;
And in the flaming forests cower the lion
And lioness, with all their whimpering cubs;
And, ever pacing on the verge of things,
The phantom, Beauty, in a mist of tears;
While we alone have round us woven woods,
And feel the softness of each other's hand,
Amrita, while —

Anashuya (*going away from him*).
Ah me! you love another,
(*Bursting into tears.*)
And may some sudden dreadful ill befall her!

Vijaya. I loved another; now I love no other.
Among the mouldering of ancient woods
You live, and on the village border she,
With her old father the blind wood-cutter;
I saw her standing in her door but now.

Anashuya. Vijaya, swear to love her never more.

Vijaya. Ay, ay.

Anashuya. Swear by the parents of the gods,
Dread oath, who dwell on sacred Himalay,
On the far Golden peak; enormous shapes,
Who still were old when the great sea was young;
On their vast faces mystery and dreams;
Their hair along the mountains rolled and filled
From year to year by the unnumbered nests
Of aweless birds, and round their stirless feet
The joyous flocks of deer and antelope,
Who never hear the unforgiving hound.
Swear!

Vijaya. By the parents of the gods, I swear.

Anashuya (*sings*). I *have forgiven,* O *new star*!
Maybe you have not heard of us, you have come forth so *newly,*

You hunter of the fields afar!
Ah, you will know my loved one by his hunter's arrows truly,
Shoot on him shafts of quietness, that he may ever keep
A lonely laughter, and may kiss his hands to me in sleep.

Farewell, Vijaya. Nay, no word, no word;
I, priestess of this temple, offer up
Prayers for the land.

(*Vijaya goes.*)

O Brahma, guard in sleep
The merry lambs and the complacent kine,
The flies below the leaves, and the young mice
In the tree roots, and all the sacred flocks
Of red flamingoes; and my love, Vijaya;
And may no restless fay with fidget finger
Trouble his sleeping: give him dreams of me.

The Indian upon God

I passed along the water's edge below the humid trees,
My spirit rocked in evening light, the rushes round my knees,
My spirit rocked in sleep and sighs; and saw the moorfowl pace
All dripping on a grassy slope, and saw them cease to chase
Each other round in circles, and heard the eldest speak:
Who holds the world between His bill and made us strong or weak
Is an undying moorfowl, and He lives beyond the sky.
The rains are from His dripping wing, the moonbeams from His eye.
I passed a little further on and heard a lotus talk:
Who made the world and ruleth it, He hangeth on a stalk,
For I am in His image made, and all this tinkling tide
Is but a sliding drop of rain between His petals wide.
A little way within the gloom a roebuck raised his eyes
Brimful of starlight, and he said: *The Stamper of the Skies,*
He is a gentle roebuck; for how else, I pray, could He
Conceive a thing so sad and soft, a gentle thing like me?
I passed a little further on and heard a peacock say:
Who made the grass and made the worms and made my feathers gay,

He is a monstrous peacock, and He waveth all the night
His languid tail above us, lit with myriad spots of ilight.

The Indian to His Love

The island dreams under the dawn
And great boughs drop tranquillity;
The peahens dance on a smooth lawn,
A parrot sways upon a tree,
Raging at his own image in the enamelled sea.

Here we will moor our lonely ship
And wander ever with woven hands,
Murmuring softly lip to lip,
Along the grass, along the sands,
Murmuring how far away are the unquiet lands:

How we alone of mortals are
Hid under quiet boughs apart,
While our love grows an Indian star,
A meteor of the burning heart,
One with the tide that gleams, the wings that gleam and dart,

The heavy boughs, the burnished dove
That moans and sighs a hundred days:
How when we die our shades will rove,
When eve has hushed the feathered ways,
With vapoury footsole by the water's drowsy blaze.

The Falling of the Leaves

Autumn is over the long leaves that love us,
And over the mice in the barley sheaves;
Yellow the leaves of the rowan above us,
And yellow the wet wild-strawberry leaves.

The hour of the waning of love has beset us,
And weary and worn are our sad souls now;
Let us part, ere the season of passion forget us,
With a kiss and a tear on thy drooping brow.

Ephemera

'Your eyes that once were never weary of mine
Are bowed in sorrow under pendulous lids,
Because our love is waning.'
And then she:
'Although our love is waning, let us stand
By the lone border of the lake once more,
Together in that hour of gentleness
When the poor tired child, Passion, falls asleep:
How far away the stars seem, and how far
Is our first kiss, and ah, how old my heart!'
Pensive they paced along the faded leaves,
While slowly he whose hand held hers replied:
'Passion has often worn our wandering hearts.'

The woods were round them, and the yellow leaves
Fell like faint meteors in the gloom, and once
A rabbit old and lame limped down the path;
Autumn was over him: and now they stood
On the lone border of the lake once more:
Turning, he saw that she had thrust dead leaves
Gathered in silence, dewy as her eyes,
In bosom and hair.
'Ah, do not mourn,' he said,
'That we are tired, for other loves await us;
Hate on and love through unrepining hours.
Before us lies eternity; our souls
Are love, and a continual farewell.'

The Madness of King Goll

I sat on cushioned otter-skin,
My word was law from Ith to Emain,
And shook at Inver Amergin
The hearts of the world-troubling seamen,
And drove tumult and war away
From girl and boy and man and beast;
The fields grew fatter day by day,

The wild fowl of the air increased;
And every ancient Ollave said,
While he bent down his fading head.
'He drives away the Northern cold.'
They will not hush, the leaves a-flutter round me, the beech leaves old.

I sat and mused and drank sweet wine;
A herdsman came from inland valleys,
Crying, the pirates drove his swine
To fill their dark-beaked hollow galleys.
I called my battle-breaking men
And my loud brazen battle-cars
From rolling vale and rivery glen;
And under the blinking of the stars
Fell on the pirates by the deep,
And hurled them in the gulph of sleep:
These hands won many a torque of gold.
They will not hush, the leaves a-flutter round me, the beech leaves old.

But slowly, as I shouting slew
And trampled in the bubbling mire,
In my most secret spirit grew
A whirling and a wandering fire:
I stood: keen stars above me shone,
Around me shone keen eyes of men:
I laughed aloud and hurried on
By rocky shore and rushy fen;
I laughed because birds fluttered by,
And starlight gleamed, and clouds flew high,
And rushes waved and waters rolled.
They will not hush, the leaves a-flutter round me, the beech leaves old.

And now I wander in the woods
When summer gluts the golden bees,
Or in autumnal solitudes
Arise the leopard-coloured trees;
Or when along the wintry strands

The cormorants shiver on their rocks;
I wander on, and wave my hands,
And sing, and shake my heavy locks.
The grey wolf knows me; by one ear
I lead along the woodland deer;
The hares run by me growing bold.
They will not hush, the leaves a-flutter round me, the beech leaves old.

I came upon a little town
That slumbered in the harvest moon,
And passed a-tiptoe up and down,
Murmuring, to a fitful tune,
How I have followed, night and day,
A tramping of tremendous feet,
And saw where this old tympan lay
Deserted on a doorway seat,
And bore it to the woods with me;
Of some inhuman misery
Our married voices wildly trolled.
They will not hush, the leaves a-flutter round me, the beech leaves old.

I sang how, when day's toil is done,
Orchil shakes out her long dark hair
That hides away the dying sun
And sheds faint odours through the air:
When my hand passed from wire to wire
It quenched, with sound like falling dew
The whirling and the wandering fire;
But lift a mournful ulalu,
For the kind wires are torn and still,
And I must wander wood and hill
Through summer's heat and winter's cold.
They will not hush, the leaves a-flutter round me, the beech leaves old.

The Stolen Child

Where dips the rocky highland
Of Sleuth Wood in the lake,
There lies a leafy island
Where flapping herons wake
The drowsy water-rats;
There we've hid our faery vats,
Full of berries
And of reddest stolen cherries.
Come away, O human child!
To the waters and the wild
With a faery, hand in hand,
For the world's more full of weeping than you can understand.

Where the wave of moonlight glosses
The dim grey sands with light,
Far off by furthest Rosses
We foot it all the night,
Weaving olden dances,
Mingling hands and mingling glances
Till the moon has taken flight;
To and fro we leap
And chase the frothy bubbles,
While the world is full of troubles
And is anxious in its sleep.
Come away, O human child!
To the waters and the wild
With a faery, hand in hand,
For the world's more full of weeping than you can understand.

Where the wandering water gushes
From the hills above Glen-Car,
In pools among the rushes
That scarce could bathe a star,
We seek for slumbering trout
And whispering in their ears
Give them unquiet dreams;
Leaning softly out
From ferns that drop their tears

Over the young streams.
Come away, O human child!
To the waters and the wild
With a faery, hand in hand,
For the world's more full of weeping than you can understand.

Away with us he's going,
The solemn-eyed:
He'll hear no more the lowing
Of the calves on the warm hillside
Or the kettle on the hob
Sing peace into his breast,
Or see the brown mice bob
Round and round the oatmeal-chest.
For he comes, the human child,
To the waters and the wild
With a faery, hand in hand,
From a world more full of weeping than he can understand.

To an Isle in the Water

Shy one, shy one,
Shy one of my heart,
She moves in the firelight
Pensively apart.

She carries in the dishes,
And lays them in a row.
To an isle in the water
With her would I go.

She carries in the candles,
And lights the curtained room,
Shy in the doorway
And shy in the gloom;

And shy as a rabbit,
Helpful and shy.
To an isle in the water
With her would I fly.

Down by the Salley Gardens

Down by the salley gardens my love and I did meet;
She passed the salley gardens with little snow-white feet.
She bid me take love easy, as the leaves grow on the tree;
But I, being young and foolish, with her would not agree.

In a field by the river my love and I did stand,
And on my leaning shoulder she laid her snow-white hand.
She bid me take life easy, as the grass grows on the weirs;
But I was young and foolish, and now am full of tears.

The Meditation of the Old Fisherman

You waves, though you dance by my feet like children at play,
Though you glow and you glance, though you purr and you dart;
In the Junes that were warmer than these are, the waves were
more gay,
When I was a boy with never a crack in my heart.

The herring are not in the tides as they were of old;
My sorrow! for many a creak gave the creel in the cart
That carried the take to Sligo town to be sold,
When I was a boy with never a crack in my heart.

And ah, you proud maiden, you are not so fair when his oar
Is heard on the water, as they were, the proud and apart,
Who paced in the eve by the nets on the pebbly shore,
When I *was* a boy *with never* a *crack in my heart.*

The Ballad of Father O'Hart

Good Father John O'Hart
In penal days rode out
To a shoneen who had free lands
And his own snipe and trout.

In trust took he John's lands;
Sleiveens were all his race;
And he gave them as dowers to his daughters,
And they married beyond their place.

But Father John went up,
And Father John went down;
And he wore small holes in his shoes,
And he wore large holes in his gown.

All loved him, only the shoneen,
Whom the devils have by the hair,
From the wives, and the cats, and the children,
To the birds in the white of the air.

The birds, for he opened their cages
As he went up and down;
And he said with a smile, 'Have peace now';
And he went his way with a frown.

But if when anyone died
Came keeners hoarser than rooks,
He bade them give over their keening;
For he was a man of books.

And these were the works of John,
When, weeping score by score,
People came into Colooney;
For he'd died at ninety-four.

There was no human keening;
The birds from Knocknarea
And the world round Knocknashee
Came keening in that day.

The young birds and old birds
Came flying, heavy and sad;
Keening in from Tiraragh,
Keening from Ballinafad;

Keening from Inishmurray.
Nor stayed for bite or sup;
This way were all reproved
Who dig old customs up.

The Ballad of Moll Magee

Come round me, little childer;
There, don't fling stones at me
Because I mutter as I go;
But pity Moll Magee.

My man was a poor fisher
With shore lines in the say;
My work was saltin' herrings
The whole of the long day.

And sometimes from the saltin' shed
I scarce could drag my feet,
Under the blessed moonlight,
Along the pebbly street.

I'd always been but weakly,
And my baby was just born;
A neighbour minded her by day,
I minded her till morn.

I lay upon my baby;
Ye little childer dear,
I looked on my cold baby
When the morn grew frosty and clear.

A weary woman sleeps so hard!
My man grew red and pale,
And gave me money, and bade me go
To my own place, Kinsale.

He drove me out and shut the door.
And gave his curse to me;

I went away in silence,
No neighbour could I see.

The windows and the doors were shut,
One star shone faint and green,
The little straws were turnin' round
Across the bare boreen.

I went away in silence:
Beyond old Martin's byre
I saw a kindly neighbour
Blowin' her mornin' fire.

She drew from me my story —
My money's all used up,
And still, with pityin', scornin' eye,
She gives me bite and sup.

She says my man will surely come
And fetch me home agin;
But always, as I'm movin' round,
Without doors or within,

Pilin' the wood or pilin' the turf,
Or goin' to the well,
I'm thinkin' of my baby
And keenin' to mysel'.

And sometimes I am sure she knows
When, openin' wide His door,
God lights the stats, His candles,
And looks upon the poor.

So now, ye little childer,
Ye won't fling stones at me;
But gather with your shinin' looks
And pity Moll Magee.

The Ballad of the Foxhunter

'Lay me in a cushioned chair;
Carry me, ye four,
With cushions here and cushions there,
To see the world once more.

'To stable and to kennel go;
Bring what is there to bring;
Lead my Lollard to and fro,
Or gently in a ring.

'Put the chair upon the grass:
Bring Rody and his hounds,
That I may contented pass
From these earthly bounds.'

His eyelids droop, his head falls low,
His old eyes cloud with dreams;
The sun upon all things that grow
Falls in sleepy streams.

Brown Lollard treads upon the lawn,
And to the armchair goes,
And now the old man's dreams are gone,
He smooths the long brown nose.

And now moves many a pleasant tongue
Upon his wasted hands,
For leading aged hounds and young
The huntsman near him stands.

'Huntsmam Rody, blow the horn,
Make the hills reply.'
The huntsman loosens on the morn
A gay wandering cry.

Fire is in the old man's eyes,
His fingers move and sway,
And when the wandering music dies
They hear him feebly say,

'Huntsman Rody, blow the horn,
Make the hills reply.'
'I cannot blow upon my horn,
I can but weep and sigh.'

Servants round his cushioned place
Are with new sorrow wrung;
Hounds are gazing on his face,
Aged hounds and young.

One blind hound only lies apart
On the sun-smitten grass;
He holds deep commune with his heart:
The moments pass and pass;

The blind hound with a mournful din
Lifts slow his wintry head;
The servants bear the body in;
The hounds wail for the dead.

THE ROSE
1893

To the Rose upon the Rood of Time

Red Rose, proud Rose, sad Rose of all my days!
Come near me, while I sing the ancient ways:
Cuchulain battling with the bitter tide;
The Druid, grey, wood-nurtured, quiet-eyed,
Who cast round Fergus dreams, and ruin untold;
And thine own sadness, whereof stars, grown old
In dancing silver-sandalled on the sea,
Sing in their high and lonely melody.
Come near, that no more blinded by man's fate,
I find under the boughs of love and hate,
In all poor foolish things that live a day,
Eternal beauty wandering on her way.

Come near, come near, come near—Ah, leave me still
A little space for the rose-breath to fill!
Lest I no more hear common things that crave;
The weak worm hiding down in its small cave,
The field-mouse running by me in the grass,
And heavy mortal hopes that toil and pass;
But seek alone to hear the strange things said
By God to the bright hearts of those long dead,
And learn to chaunt a tongue men do not know.
Come near; I would, before my time to go,
Sing of old Eire and the ancient ways:
Red Rose, proud Rose, sad Rose of all my days.

Fergus and the Druid

Fergus. This whole day have I followed in the rocks,
And you have changed and flowed from shape to shape,
First as a raven on whose ancient wings
Scarcely a feather lingered, then you seemed
A weasel moving on from stone to stone,
And now at last you wear a human shape,
A thin grey man half lost in gathering night.

Druid. What would you, king of the proud Red Branch kings?

Fergus. This would I say, most wise of living souls:
Young subtle Conchubar sat close by me
When I gave judgment, and his words were wise,
And what to me was burden without end,
To him seemed easy, so I laid the crown
Upon his head to cast away my sorrow.

Druid. What would you, king of the proud Red Branch kings?

Fergus. A king and proud! and that is my despair.
I feast amid my people on the hill,
And pace the woods, and drive my chariot-wheels
In the white border of the murmuring sea;
And still I feel the crown upon my head.

Druid. What would you, Fergus?

Fergus. Be no more a king
But learn the dreaming wisdom that is yours.

Druid. Look on my thin grey hair and hollow cheeks
And on these hands that may not lift the sword,
This body trembling like a wind-blown reed.
No woman's loved me, no man sought my help.

Fergus. A king is but a foolish labourer
Who wastes his blood to be another's dream.

Druid. Take, if you must, this little bag of dreams;
Unloose the cord, and they will wrap you round.

Fergus. I see my life go drifting like a river
From change to change; I have been many things —
A green drop in the surge, a gleam of light
Upon a sword, a fir-tree on a hill,
An old slave grinding at a heavy quern,
A king sitting upon a chair of gold —
And all these things were wonderful and great;
But now I have grown nothing, knowing all.
Ah! Druid, Druid, how great webs of sorrow
Lay hidden in the small slate-coloured thing!

Cuchulain's Fight with the Sea

A man came slowly from the setting sun,
To Emer, raddling raiment in her dun,
And said, 'I am that swineherd whom you bid
Go watch the road between the wood and tide,
But now I have no need to watch it more.'

Then Emer cast the web upon the floor,
And raising arms all raddled with the dye,
Parted her lips with a loud sudden cry.

That swineherd stared upon her face and said,
'No man alive, no man among the dead,
Has won the gold his cars of battle bring.'

'But if your master comes home triumphing
Why must you blench and shake from foot to crown?'

Thereon he shook the more and cast him down
Upon the web-heaped floor, and cried his word:
'With him is one sweet-throated like a bird.'

'You dare me to my face,' and thereupon
She smote with raddled fist, and where her son

Herded the cattle came with stumbling feet,
And cried with angry voice, 'It is not meet
To idle life away, a common herd.'

'I have long waited, mother, for that word:
But wherefore now?'

'There is a man to die;
You have the heaviest arm under the sky.'

'Whether under its daylight or its stars
My father stands amid his battle-cars.'

'But you have grown to be the taller man.'

'Yet somewhere under starlight or the sun
My father stands.'

'Aged, worn out with wars
On foot. on horseback or in battle-cars.'

'I only ask what way my journey lies,
For He who made you bitter made you wise.'

'The Red Branch camp in a great company
Between wood's rim and the horses of the sea.
Go there, and light a camp-fire at wood's rim;
But tell your name and lineage to him
Whose blade compels, and wait till they have found
Some feasting man that the same oath has bound.'

Among those feasting men Cuchulain dwelt,
And his young sweetheart close beside him knelt,
Stared on the mournful wonder of his eyes,
Even as Spring upon the ancient skies,
And pondered on the glory of his days;
And all around the harp-string told his praise,
And Conchubar, the Red Branch king of kings,
With his own fingers touched the brazen strings.

At last Cuchulain spake, 'Some man has made
His evening fire amid the leafy shade.
I have often heard him singing to and fro,
I have often heard the sweet sound of his bow.
Seek out what man he is.'

One went and came.
'He bade me let all know he gives his name
At the sword-point, and waits till we have found
Some feasting man that the same oath has bound.'

Cuchulain cried, 'I am the only man
Of all this host so bound from childhood on!'

After short fighting in the leafy shade,
He spake to the young man, 'Is there no maid
Who loves you, no white arms to wrap you round,
Or do you long for the dim sleepy ground,
That you have come and dared me to my face?'

'The dooms of men are in God's hidden place,'

'Your head a while seemed like a woman's head
That I loved once.'
Again the fighting sped,
But now the war-rage in Cuchulain woke,
And through that new blade's guard the old blade broke,
And pierced him.
'Speak before your breath is done.'

'Cuchulain I, mighty Cuchulain's son.'

'I put you from your pain. I can no more.'

While day its burden on to evening bore,
With head bowed on his knees Cuchulain stayed;
Then Conchubar sent that sweet-throated maid,
And she, to win him, his grey hair caressed;
In vain her arms, in vain her soft white breast.
Then Conchubar, the subtlest of all men,

Ranking his Druids round him ten by ten,
Spake thus: 'Cuchulain will dwell there and brood
For three days more in dreadful quietude,
And then arise, and raving slay us all.
Chaunt in his ear delusions magical,
That he may fight the horses of the sea.'
The Druids took them to their mystery,
And chaunted for three days.
Cuchulain stirred,
Stared on the horses of the sea, and heard
The cars of battle and his own name cried;
And fought with the invulnerable tide.

The Rose of the World

Who dreamed that beauty passes like a dream?
For these red lips, with all their mournful pride,
Mournful that no new wonder may betide,
Troy passed away in one high funeral gleam,
And Usna's children died.

We and the labouring world are passing by:
Amid men's souls, that waver and give place
Like the pale waters in their wintry race,
Under the passing stars, foam of the sky,
Lives on this lonely face.

Bow down, archangels, in your dim abode:
Before you were, or any hearts to beat,
Weary and kind one lingered by His seat;
He made the world to be a grassy road
Before her wandering feet.

The Rose of Peace

If Michael, leader of God's host
When Heaven and Hell are met,
Looked down on you from Heaven's door-post
He would his deeds forget.

Brooding no more upon God's wars
In his divine homestead,
He would go weave out of the stars
A chaplet for your head.

And all folk seeing him bow down,
And white stars tell your praise,
Would come at last to God's great town,
Led on by gentle ways;

And God would bid His warfare cease,
Saying all things were well;
And softly make a rosy peace,
A peace of Heaven with Hell.

The Rose of Battle

Rose of all Roses, Rose of all the World!
The tall thought-woven sails, that flap unfurled
Above the tide of hours, trouble the air,
And God's bell buoyed to be the water's care;
While hushed from fear, or loud with hope, a band
With blown, spray-dabbled hair gather at hand,
Turn if you may from battles never done,
I call, as they go by me one by one,
Danger no refuge holds, and war no peace,
For him who hears love sing and never cease,
Beside her clean-swept hearth, her quiet shade:
But gather all for whom no love hath made
A woven silence, or but came to cast
A song into the air, and singing passed
To smile on the pale dawn; and gather you
Who have sought more than is in rain or dew,
Or in the sun and moon, or on the earth,
Or sighs amid the wandering, starry mirth,
Or comes in laughter from the sea's sad lips,
And wage God's battles in the long grey ships.
The sad, the lonely, the insatiable,
To these Old Night shall all her mystery tell;

God's bell has claimed them by the little cry
Of their sad hearts, that may not live nor die.

Rose of all Roses, Rose of all the World!
You, too, have come where the dim tides are hurled
Upon the wharves of sorrow, and heard ring
The bell that calls us on; the sweet far thing.
Beauty grown sad with its eternity
Made you of us, and of the dim grey sea.
Our long ships loose thought-woven sails and wait,
For God has bid them share an equal fate;
And when at last, defeated in His wars,
They have gone down under the same white stars,
We shall no longer hear the little cry
Of our sad hearts, that may not live nor die.

A Faery Song

Sung by the people of Faery over Diarmuid and Grania, in their bridal sleep under a Cromlech.

We who are old, old and gay,
O so old!
Thousands of years, thousands of years,
If all were told:

Give to these children, new from the world,
Silence and love;
And the long dew-dropping hours of the night,
And the stars above:

Give to these children, new from the world,
Rest far from men.
Is anything better, anything better?
Tell us it then:

Us who are old, old and gay,
O so old!
Thousands of years, thousands of years,
If all were told.

The Lake Isle of Innisfree

I will arise and go now, and go to Innisfree,
And a small cabin build there, of clay and wattles made;
Nine bean-rows will I have there, a hive for the honey-bee,
And live alone in the bee-loud glade.

And I shall have some peace there, for peace comes dropping
    slow,
Dropping from the veils of the morning to where the cricket
    sings;
There midnight's all a glimmer, and noon a purple glow,
And evening full of the linnet's wings.

I will arise and go now, for always night and day
I hear lake water lapping with low sounds by the shore;
While I stand on the roadway, or on the pavements grey,
I hear it in the deep heart's core.

A Cradle Song

The angels are stooping
Above your bed;
They weary of trooping
With the whimpering dead.

God's laughing in Heaven
To see you so good;
The Sailing Seven
Are gay with His mood.

I sigh that kiss you,
For I must own
That I shall miss you
When you have grown.

The Pity of Love

A pity beyond all telling
Is hid in the heart of love:
The folk who are buying and selling,
The clouds on their journey above,
The cold wet winds ever blowing,
And the shadowy hazel grove
Where mouse-grey waters are flowing,
Threaten the head that I love.

The Sorrow of Love

The brawling of a sparrow in the eaves,
The brilliant moon and all the milky sky,
And all that famous harmony of leaves,
Had blotted out man's image and his cry.

A girl arose that had red mournful lips
And seemed the greatness of the world in tears,
Doomed like Odysseus and the labouring ships
And proud as Priam murdered with his peers;

Arose, and on the instant clamorous eaves,
A climbing moon upon an empty sky,
And all that lamentation of the leaves,
Could but compose man's image and his cry.

When You Are Old

When you are old and grey and full of sleep,
And nodding by the fire, take down this book,
And slowly read, and dream of the soft look
Your eyes had once, and of their shadows deep;

How many loved your moments of glad grace,
And loved your beauty with love false or true,
But one man loved the pilgrim soul in you,
And loved the sorrows of your changing face;

And bending down beside the glowing bars,
Murmur, a little sadly, how Love fled
And paced upon the mountains overhead
And hid his face amid a crowd of stars.

The White Birds

I would that we were, my beloved, white birds on the foam of
the sea!
We tire of the flame of the meteor, before it can fade and flee;
And the flame of the blue star of twilight, hung low on the rim
of the sky,
Has awaked in our hearts, my beloved, a sadness that may not
die.

A weariness comes from those dreamers, dew-dabbled, the lily
and rose;
Ah, dream not of them, my beloved, the flame of the meteor
that goes,
Or the flame of the blue star that lingers hung low in the fall of
the dew:
For I would we were changed to white birds on the wandering
foam: I and you!

I am haunted by numberless islands, and many a Danaan
shore,
Where Time would surely forget us, and Sorrow come near us
no more;
Soon far from the rose and the lily and fret of the flames would
we be,
Were we only white birds, my beloved, buoyed out on the
foam of the sea!

A Dream of Death

I dreamed that one had died in a strange place
Near no accustomed hand,
And they had nailed the boards above her face,
The peasants of that land,
Wondering to lay her in that solitude,
And raised above her mound
A cross they had made out of two bits of wood,
And planted cypress round;
And left her to the indifferent stars above
Until I carved these words:
She was more beautiful than thy first love,
But now lies under boards.

The Countess Cathleen in Paradise

All the heavy days are over;
Leave the body's coloured pride
Underneath the grass and clover,
With the feet laid side by side.

Bathed in flaming founts of duty
She'll not ask a haughty dress;
Carry all that mournful beauty
To the scented oaken press.

Did the kiss of Mother Mary
Put that music in her face?
Yet she goes with footstep wary,
Full of earth's old timid grace.

'Mong the feet of angels seven
What a dancer glimmering!
All the heavens bow down to Heaven,
Flame to flame and wing to wing.

Who Goes with Fergus?

Who will go drive with Fergus now,
And pierce the deep wood's woven shade,
And dance upon the level shore?
Young man, lift up your russet brow,
And lift your tender eyelids, maid,
And brood on hopes and fear no more.

And no more turn aside and brood
Upon love's bitter mystery;
For Fergus rules the brazen cars,
And rules the shadows of the wood,
And the white breast of the dim sea
And all dishevelled wandering stars.

The Man Who Dreamed of Faeryland

He stood among a crowd at Drumahair;
His heart hung all upon a silken dress,
And he had known at last some tenderness,
Before earth took him to her stony care;
But when a man poured fish into a pile,
It seemed they raised their little silver heads,
And sang what gold morning or evening sheds
Upon a woven world-forgotten isle
Where people love beside the ravelled seas;
That Time can never mar a lover's vows
Under that woven changeless roof of boughs:
The singing shook him out of his new ease.

He wandered by the sands of Lissadell;
His mind ran all on money cares and fears,
And he had known at last some prudent years
Before they heaped his grave under the hill;
But while he passed before a plashy place,
A lug-worm with its grey and muddy mouth
Sang that somewhere to north or west or south
There dwelt a gay, exulting, gentle race

Under the golden or the silver skies;
That if a dancer stayed his hungry foot
It seemed the sun and moon were in the fruit:
And at that singing he was no more wise.

He mused beside the well of Scanavin,
He mused upon his mockers: without fail
His sudden vengeance were a country tale,
When earthy night had drunk his body in;
But one small knot-grass growing by the pool
Sang where — unnecessary cruel voice —
Old silence bids its chosen race rejoice,
Whatever ravelled waters rise and fall
Or stormy silver fret the gold of day,
And midnight there enfold them like a fleece
And lover there by lover be at peace.
The tale drove his fine angry mood away.

He slept under the hill of Lugnagall;
And might have known at last unhaunted sleep
Under that cold and vapour-turbaned steep,
Now that the earth had taken man and all:
Did not the worms that spired about his bones
proclaim with that unwearied, reedy cry
That God has laid His fingers on the sky,
That from those fingers glittering summer runs
Upon the dancer by the dreamless wave.
Why should those lovers that no lovers miss
Dream, until God burn Nature with a kiss?
The man has found no comfort in the grave.

The Dedication to a Book of Stories Selected from the Irish Novelists

There was a green branch hung with many a bell
When her own people ruled this tragic Eire;
And from its murmuring greenness, calm of Faery,
A Druid kindness, on all hearers fell.

It charmed away the merchant from his guile,
And turned the farmer's memory from his cattle,
And hushed in sleep the roaring ranks of battle:
And all grew friendly for a little while.

Ah, Exiles wandering over lands and seas,
And planning, plotting always that some morrow
May set a stone upon ancestral Sorrow!
I also bear a bell-branch full of ease.

I tore it from green boughs winds tore and tossed
Until the sap of summer had grown weary!
I tore it from the barren boughs of Eire,
That country where a man can be so crossed;

Can be so battered, badgered and destroyed
That he's a loveless man: gay bells bring laughter
That shakes a mouldering cobweb from the rafter;
And yet the saddest chimes are best enjoyed.

Gay bells or sad, they bring you memories
Of half-forgotten innocent old places:
We and our bitterness have left no traces
On Munster grass and Connemara skies

The Lamentation of the Old Pensioner

Although I shelter from the rain
Under a broken tree,
My chair was nearest to the fire
In every company
That talked of love or politics,
Ere Time transfigured me.

Though lads are making pikes again
For some conspiracy,
And crazy rascals rage their fill
At human tyranny,
My contemplations are of Time
That has transfigured me.

There's not a woman turns her face
Upon a broken tree,
And yet the beauties that I loved
Are in my memory;
I spit into the face of Time
That has transfigured me.

The Ballad of Father Gilligan

The old priest Peter Gilligan
Was weary night and day;
For half his flock were in their beds
Or under green sods lay.

Once, while he nodded in a chair,
At the moth-hour of the eve
Another poor man sent for him,
And he began to grieve.

'I have no rest, nor joy, nor peace,
For people die and die;
And after cried he, 'God forgive!
My body spake not I!'

He knelt, and leaning on the chair
He prayed and fell asleep;
And the moth-hour went from the fields,
And stars began to peep.

They slowly into millions grew,
And leaves shook in the wind;
And God covered the world with shade,
And whispered to mankind.

Upon the time of sparrow-chirp
When the moths came once more,
The old priest Peter Gilligan
Stood upright on the floor.

'Mavrone, mavrone! The man has died
While I slept on the chair.'
He roused his horse out of its sleep
And rode with little care.

He rode now as he never rode,
By rocky lane and fen;
The sick man's wife opened the door,
'Father! you come again!'

'And is the poor man dead?' he cried.
'He died an hour ago.'
The old priest Peter Gilligan
In grief swayed to and fro.

'When you were gone, he turned and died,
As merry as a bird.'
The old priest Peter Gilligan
He knelt him at that word.

'He Who hath made the night of stars
For souls who tire and bleed,
Sent one of this great angels down,
To help me in my need.

'He Who is wrapped in purple robes,
With planets in His care
Had pity on the least of things
Asleep upon a chair.'

The Two Trees

Beloved, gaze in thine own heart,
The holy tree is growing there;
From joy the holy branches start,
And all the trembling flowers they bear.
The changing colours of its fruit
Have dowered the stars with merry light;
The surety of its hidden root

Has planted quiet in the night;
The shaking of its leafy head
Has given the waves their melody,
And made my lips and music wed,
Murmuring a wizard song for thee.
There the Loves a circle go,
The flaming circle of our days,
Gyring, spiring to and fro
In those great ignorant leafy ways;
Remembering all that shaken hair
And how the winged sandals dart,
Thine eyes grow full of tender care:
Beloved, gaze in thine own heart.

Gaze no more in the bitter glass
The demons, with their subtle guile.
Lift up before us when they pass,
Or only gaze a little while;
For there a fatal image grows
That the stormy night receives,
Roots half hidden under snows,
Broken boughs and blackened leaves.
For all things turn to barrenness
In the dim glass the demons hold,
The glass of outer weariness,
Made when God slept in times of old.
There, through the broken branches, go
The ravens of unresting thought;
Flying, crying, to and fro,
Cruel claw and hungry throat,
Or else they stand and sniff the wind,
And shake their ragged wings; alas!
Thy tender eyes grow all unkind:
Gaze no more in the bitter glass.

To Some I Have Talked with by the Fire

While I wrought out these fitful Danaan rhymes,
My heart would brim with dreams about the times
When we bent down above the fading coals
And talked of the dark folk who live in souls
Of passionate men, like bats in the dead trees;
And of the wayward twilight companies
Who sigh with mingled sorrow and content,
Because their blossoming dreams have never bent
Under the fruit of evil and of good:
And of the embattled flaming multitude
Who rise, wing above wing, flame above flame,
And, like a storm, cry the Ineffable Name,
And with the clashing of their sword-blades make
A rapturous music, till the morning break
And the white hush end all but the loud beat
Of their long wings, the flash of their white feet.

To Ireland in the Coming Times

Know, that I would accounted be
True brother of a company
That sang, to sweeten Ireland's wrong,
Ballad and story, rann and song;
Nor be I any less of them,
Because the red-rose-bordered hem
Of her, whose history began
Before God made the angelic clan,
Trails all about the written page.
When Time began to rant and rage
The measure of her flying feet
Made Ireland's heart begin to beat;
And Time bade all his candles flare
To light a measure here and there;
And may the thoughts of Ireland brood
Upon a measured quietude.

Nor may I less be counted one
With Davis, Mangan, Ferguson,
Because, to him who ponders well,
My rhymes more than their rhyming tell
Of things discovered in the deep,
Where only body's laid asleep.
For the elemental creatures go
About my table to and fro,
That hurry from unmeasured mind
To rant and rage in flood and wind;
Yet he who treads in measured ways
May surely barter gaze for gaze.
Man ever journeys on with them
After the red-rose-bordered hem.
Ah, faeries, dancing under the moon,
A Druid land, a Druid tune!

While still I may, I write for you
The love I lived, the dream I knew.
From our birthday, until we die,
Is but the winking of an eye;
And we, our singing and our love,
What measurer Time has lit above,
And all benighted things that go
About my table to and fro,
Are passing on to where may be,
In truth's consuming ecstasy,
No place for love and dream at all;
For God goes by with white footfall.
I cast my heart into my rhymes,
That you, in the dim coming times,
May know how my heart went with them
After the red-rose-bordered hem.

THE WIND AMONG THE REEDS
1899

The Hosting of the Sidhe

The host is riding from Knocknarea
And over the grave of Clooth-na-Bare;
Caoilte tossing his burning hair,
And Niamh calling *Away, come away:*
Empty your heart of its mortal dream.
The winds awaken, the leaves whirl round,
Our cheeks are pale, our hair is unbound,
Our breasts are heaving, our eyes are agleam,
Our arms are waving, our lips are apart;
And if any gaze on our rushing band,
We come between him and the deed of his hand,
We come between him and the hope of his heart.
The host is rushing 'twixt night and day,
And where is there hope or deed as fair?
Caoilte tossing his burning hair,
And Niamh calling Away, come away.

The Everlasting Voices

O sweet everlasting Voices, be still;
Go to the guards of the heavenly fold
And bid them wander obeying your will,
Flame under flame, till Time be no more;
Have you not heard that our hearts are old,
That you call in birds, in wind on the hill,
In shaken boughs, in tide on the shore?
O sweet everlasting Voices, be still.

The Moods

Time drops in decay,
Like a candle burnt out,
And the mountains and woods
Have their day, have their day;
What one in the rout
Of the fire-born moods
Has fallen away?

The Lover Tells of the Rose in His Heart

All things uncomely and broken, all things worn out and old,
The cry of a child by the roadway, the creak of a lumbering
 cart,
The heavy steps of the ploughman, splashing the wintry
 mould,
Are wronging your image that blossoms a rose in the deeps of
 my heart.

The wrong of unshapely things is a wrong too great to be told;
I hunger to build them anew and sit on a green knoll apart,
With the earth and the sky and the water, re-made, like a
 casket of gold
For my dreams of your image that blossoms a rose in the deeps
 of my heart.

The Host of the Air

O'Driscoll drove with a song
The wild duck and the drake
From the tall and the tufted reeds
Of the drear Hart Lake.

And he saw how the reeds grew dark
At the coming of night-tide,
And dreamed of the long dim hair
Of Bridget his bride.

He heard while he sang and dreamed
A piper piping away,
And never was piping so sad,
And never was piping so gay.

And he saw young men and young girls
Who danced on a level place,
And Bridget his bride among them,
With a sad and a gay face.

The dancers crowded about him
And many a sweet thing said,
And a young man brought him red wine
And a young girl white bread.

But Bridget drew him by the sleeve
Away from the merry bands,
To old men playing at cards
With a twinkling of ancient hands.

The bread and the wine had a doom,
For these were the host of the air;
He sat and played in a dream
Of her long dim hair.

He played with the merry old men
And thought not of evil chance,
Until one bore Bridget his bride
Away from the merry dance.

He bore her away in his arms,
The handsomest young man there,
And his neck and his breast and his arms
Were drowned in her long dim hair.

O'Driscoll scattered the cards
And out of his dream awoke:
Old men and young men and young girls
Were gone like a drifting smoke;

But he heard high up in the air
A piper piping away,
And never was piping so sad,
And never was piping so gay.

The Fish

Although you hide in the ebb and flow
Of the pale tide when the moon has set,
The people of coming days will know
About the casting out of my net,

And how you have leaped times out of mind
Over the little silver cords,
And think that you were hard and unkind,
And blame you with many bitter words.

The Unappeasable Host

The Danaan children laugh, in cradles of wrought gold,
And clap their hands together, and half close their eyes,
For they will ride the North when the ger-eagle flies,
With heavy whitening wings, and a heart fallen cold:
I kiss my wailing child and press it to my breast,
And hear the narrow graves calling my child and me.
Desolate winds that cry over the wandering sea;
Desolate winds that hover in the flaming West;
Desolate winds that beat the doors of Heaven, and beat
The doors of Hell and blow there many a whimpering ghost;
O heart the winds have shaken, the unappeasable host
Is comelier than candles at Mother Mary's feet.

Into the Twilight

Out-worn heart, in a time out-worn,
Come clear of the nets of wrong and right;
Laugh, heart, again in the grey twilight,
Sigh, heart, again in the dew of the morn.

Your mother Eire is aways young,
Dew ever shining and twilight grey;
Though hope fall from you and love decay,
Burning in fires of a slanderous tongue.

Come, heart, where hill is heaped upon hill:
For there the mystical brotherhood
Of sun and moon and hollow and wood
And river and stream work out their will;

And God stands winding His lonely horn,
And time and the world are ever in flight;
And love is less kind than the grey twilight,
And hope is less dear than the dew of the morn.

The Song of Wandering Aengus

I went out to the hazel wood,
Because a fire was in my head,
And cut and peeled a hazel wand,
And hooked a berry to a thread;
And when white moths were on the wing,
And moth-like stars were flickering out,
I dropped the berry in a stream
And caught a little silver trout.

When I had laid it on the floor
I went to blow the fire aflame,
But something rustled on the floor,
And someone called me by my name:
It had become a glimmering girl
With apple blossom in her hair
Who called me by my name and ran
And faded through the brightening air.

Though I am old with wandering
Through hollow lands and hilly lands,
I will find out where she has gone,
And kiss her lips and take her hands;

And walk among long dappled grass,
And pluck till time and times are done,
The silver apples of the moon,
The golden apples of the sun.

The Song of the Old Mother

I rise in the dawn, and I kneel and blow
Till the seed of the fire flicker and glow;
And then I must scrub and bake and sweep
Till stars are beginning to blink and peep;
And the young lie long and dream in their bed
Of the matching of ribbons for bosom and head,
And their day goes over in idleness,
And they sigh if the wind but lift a tress:
While I must work because I am old,
And the seed of the fire gets feeble and cold.

The Heart of the Woman

O what to me the little room
That was brimmed up with prayer and rest;
He bade me out into the gloom,
And my breast lies upon his breast.

O what to me my mother's care,
The house where I was safe and warm;
The shadowy blossom of my hair
Will hide us from the bitter storm.

O hiding hair and dewy eyes,
I am no more with life and death,
My heart upon his warm heart lies,
My breath is mixed into his breath.

The Lover Mourns for the Loss of Love

Pale brows, still hands and dim hair,
I had a beautiful friend
And dreamed that the old despair
Would end in love in the end:
She looked in my heart one day
And saw your image was there;
She has gone weeping away.

He Mourns for the Change That Has Come upon Him And His Beloved, And Longs for the End of the World

Do you not hear me calling, white deer with no horns?
I have been changed to a hound with one red ear;
I have been in the Path of Stones and the Wood of Thorns,
For somebody hid hatred and hope and desire and fear
Under my feet that they follow you night and day.
A man with a hazel wand came without sound;
He changed me suddenly; I was looking another way;
And now my calling is but the calling of a hound;
And Time and Birth and Change are hurrying by.
I would that the Boar without bristles had come from the West
And had rooted the sun and moon and stars out of the sky
And lay in the darkness, grunting, and turning to his rest

He Bids His Beloved Be at Peace

I hear the Shadowy Horses, their long manes a-shake,
Their hoofs heavy with tumult, their eyes glimmering white;
The North unfolds above them clinging, creeping night,
The East her hidden joy before the morning break,
The West weeps in pale dew and sighs passing away,
The South is pouring down roses of crimson fire:
O vanity of Sleep, Hope, Dream, endless Desire,
The Horses of Disaster plunge in the heavy clay:
Beloved, let your eyes half close, and your heart beat
Over my heart, and your hair fall over my breast,
Drowning love's lonely hour in deep twilight of rest,
And hiding their tossing manes and their tumultuous feet.

He Reproves the Curlew

O curlew, cry no more in the air,
Or only to the water in the West;
Because your crying brings to my mind
passion-dimmed eyes and long heavy hair
That was shaken out over my breast:
There is enough evil in the crying of wind.

He Remembers Forgotten Beauty

When my arms wrap you round I press
My heart upon the loveliness
That has long faded from the world;
The jewelled crowns that kings have hurled
In shadowy pools, when armies fled;
The love-tales wrought with silken thread
By dreaming ladies upon cloth
That has made fat the murderous moth;
The roses that of old time were
Woven by ladies in their hair,
The dew-cold lilies ladies bore
Through many a sacred corridor
Where such grey clouds of incense rose
That only God's eyes did not close:
For that pale breast and lingering hand
Come from a more dream-heavy land,
A more dream-heavy hour than this;
And when you sigh from kiss to kiss
I hear white Beauty sighing, too,
For hours when all must fade like dew.
But flame on flame, and deep on deep,
Throne over throne where in half sleep,
Their swords upon their iron knees,
Brood her high lonely mysteries.

A Poet to His Beloved

I bring you with reverent hands
The books of my numberless dreams,

White woman that passion has worn
As the tide wears the dove-grey sands,
And with heart more old than the horn
That is brimmed from the pale fire of time:
White woman with numberless dreams,
I bring you my passionate rhyme.

He Gives His Beloved Certain Rhymes

Fasten your hair with a golden pin,
And bind up every wandering tress;
I bade my heart build these poor rhymes:
It worked at them, day out, day in,
Building a sorrowful loveliness
Out of the battles of old times.

You need but lift a pearl-pale hand,
And bind up your long hair and sigh;
And all men's hearts must burn and beat;
And candle-like foam on the dim sand,
And stars climbing the dew-dropping sky,
Live but to light your passing feet.

To His Heart, Bidding It Have No Fear

Be you still, be you still, trembling heart;
Remember the wisdom out of the old days:
Him who trembles before the flame and the flood,
And the winds that blow through the starry ways,
Let the starry winds and the flame and the flood
Cover over and hide, for he has no part
With the lonely, majestical multitude.

The Cap and Bells

The jester walked in the garden:
The garden had fallen still;
He bade his soul rise upward
And stand on her window-sill.

It rose in a straight blue garment,
When owls began to call:
It had grown wise-tongued by thinking
Of a quiet and light footfall;

But the young queen would not listen;
She rose in her pale night-gown;
She drew in the heavy casement
And pushed the latches down.

He bade his heart go to her,
When the owls called out no more;
In a red and quivering garment
It sang to her through the door.

It had grown sweet-tongued by dreaming
Of a flutter of flower-like hair;
But she took up her fan from the table
And waved it off on the air.

'I have cap and bells,' he pondered,
'I will send them to her and die';
And when the morning whitened
He left them where she went by.

She laid them upon her bosom,
Under a cloud of her hair,
And her red lips sang them a love-song
Till stars grew out of the air.

She opened her door and her window
And the heart and the soul came through,
To her right hand came the red one,
To her left hand came the blue.

They set up a noise like crickets,
A chattering wise and sweet,
And her hair was a folded flower
And the quiet of love in her feet.

The Valley of the Black Pig

The dews drop slowly and dreams gather: unknown spears
Suddenly hurtle before my dream-awakened eyes,
And then the clash of fallen horsemen and the cries
Of unknown perishing armies beat about my ears.
We who still labour by the cromlech on the shore,
The grey calm on the hill, when day sinks drowned in dew,
Being weary of the world's empires, bow down to you,
Master of the still stars and of the flaming door.

The Lover Asks Forgiveness Because of His Many Moods

If this importunate heart trouble your peace
With words lighter than air,
Or hopes that in mere hoping flicker and cease;
Crumple the rose in your hair;
And cover your lips with odorous twilight and say,
'O Hearts of wind-blown flame!
O Winds, older than changing of night and day,
That murmuring and longing came
From marble cities loud with tabors of old
In dove-grey faery lands;
From battle-banners, fold upon purple fold,
Queens wrought with glimmering hands;
That saw young Niamh hover with love-lorn face
Above the wandering tide;
And lingered in the hidden desolate place
Where the last Phoenix died,
And wrapped the flames above his holy head;
And still murmur and long:
O piteous Hearts, changing till change be dead
In a tumultuous song':
And cover the pale blossoms of your breast
With your dim heavy hair,
And trouble with a sigh for all things longing for rest
The odorous twilight there.

He Tells of a Valley Full of Lovers

I dreamed that I stood in a valley, and amid sighs,
For happy lovers passed two by two where I stood;
And I dreamed my lost love came stealthily out of the wood
With her cloud-pale eyelids falling on dream-dimmed eyes:
I cried in my dream *O women bid the young men lay*
Their heads on your knees, and drown their eyes with your hair,
Or remembering hers they will find no other face fair
Till all the valleys of the world have been withered away.

He Tells of the Perfect Beauty

O cloud-pale eyelids, dream-dimmed eyes,
The poets labouring all their days
To build a perfect beauty in rhyme
Are overthrown by a woman's gaze
And by the unlabouring brood of the skies:
And therefore my heart will bow, when dew
Is dropping sleep, until God burn time,
Before the unlabouring stars and you.

He Hears the Cry of the Sedge

I wander by the edge
Of this desolate lake
Where wind cries in the sedge:
Until the axle break
That keeps the stars in their round,
And hands hurl in the deep
The banners of East and West,
And the girdle of light is unbound,
Your breast will not lie by the breast
Of your beloved in sleep.

He Thinks of Those Who Have Spoken Evil of His Beloved

Half close your eyelids, loosen your hair,
And dream about the great and their pride;

They have spoken against you everywhere,
But weigh this song with the great and their pride;
I made it out of a mouthful of air,
Their children's children shall say they have lied.

The Blessed

Cumhal called out, bending his head,
Till Dathi came and stood,
With a blink in his eyes, at the cave-mouth,
Between the wind and the wood.

And Cumhal said, bending his knees,
'I have come by the windy way
To gather the half of your blessedness
And learn to pray when you pray.

'I can bring you salmon out of the streams
And heron out of the skies.'
But Dathi folded his hands and smiled
With the secrets of God in his eyes.

And Cumhal saw like a drifting smoke
All manner of blessed souls,
Women and children, young men with books,
And old men with croziers and stoles.

'Praise God and God's Mother,' Dathi said,
'For God and God's Mother have sent
The blessedest souls that walk in the world
To fill your heart with content.'

'And which is the blessedest,' Cumhal said,
'Where all are comely and good?
Is it these that with golden thuribles
Are singing about the wood?'

'My eyes are blinking,' Dathi said,
'With the secrets of God half blind,
But I can see where the wind goes
And follow the way of the wind;

'And blessedness goes where the wind goes,
And when it is gone we are dead;
I see the blessedest soul in the world
And he nods a drunken head.

'O blessedness comes in the night and the day
And whither the wise heart knows;
And one has seen in the redness of wine
The Incorruptible Rose,

'That drowsily drops faint leaves on him
And the sweetness of desire,
While time and the world are ebbing away
In twilights of dew and of fire.'

The Secret Rose

Far-off, most secret, and inviolate Rose,
Enfold me in my hour of hours; where those
Who sought thee in the Holy Sepulchre,
Or in the wine-vat, dwell beyond the stir
And tumult of defeated dreams; and deep
Among pale eyelids, heavy with the sleep
Men have named beauty. Thy great leaves enfold
The ancient beards, the helms of ruby and gold
Of the crowned Magi; and the king whose eyes
Saw the pierced Hands and Rood of elder rise
In Druid vapour and make the torches dim;
Till vain frenzy awoke and he died; and him
Who met Fand walking among flaming dew
By a grey shore where the wind never blew,
And lost the world and Emer for a kiss;
And him who drove the gods out of their liss,
And till a hundred morns had flowered red
Feasted, and wept the barrows of his dead;
And the proud dreaming king who flung the crown
And sorrow away, and calling bard and clown
Dwelt among wine-stained wanderers in deep woods:
And him who sold tillage, and house, and goods,

And sought through lands and islands numberless years,
Until he found, with laughter and with tears,
A woman of so shining loveliness
That men threshed corn at midnight by a tress,
A little stolen tress. I, too, await
The hour of thy great wind of love and hate.
When shall the stars be blown about the sky,
Like the sparks blown out of a smithy, and die?
Surely thine hour has come, thy great wind blows,
Far-off, most secret, and inviolate Rose?

Maid Quiet

Where has Maid Quiet gone to,
Nodding her russet hood?
The winds that awakened the stars
Are blowing through my blood.
O how could I be so calm
When she rose up to depart?
Now words that called up the lightning
Are hurtling through my heart.

The Travail of Passion

When the flaming lute-thronged angelic door is wide;
When an immortal passion breathes in mortal clay;
Our hearts endure the scourge, the plaited thorns, the way
Crowded with bitter faces, the wounds in palm and side,
The vinegar-heavy sponge, the flowers by Kedron stream;
We will bend down and loosen our hair over you,
That it may drop faint perfume, and be heavy with dew,
Lilies of death-pale hope, roses of passionate dream.

The Lover Pleads with His Friend for Old Friends

Though you are in your shining days,
Voices among the crowd
And new friends busy with your praise,

Be not unkind or proud,
But think about old friends the most:
Time's bitter flood will rise,
Your beauty perish and be lost
For all eyes but these eyes.

The Lover Speaks to the Hearers of His Songs in Coming Days

O women, kneeling by your altar-rails long hence,
When songs I wove for my beloved hide the prayer,
And smoke from this dead heart drifts through the violet air
And covers away the smoke of myrrh and frankincense;
Bend down and pray for all that sin I wove in song,
Till the Attorney for Lost Souls cry her sweet cry,
And.call to my beloved and me: 'No longer fly
Amid the hovering, piteous, penitential throng.'

The Poet Pleads with the Elemental Powers

The Powers whose name and shape no living creature knows
Have pulled the Immortal Rose;
And though the Seven Lights bowed in their dance and wept,
The Polar Dragon slept,
His heavy rings uncoiled from glimmering deep to deep:
When will he wake from sleep?

Great Powers of falling wave and wind and windy fire,
With your harmonious choir
Encircle her I love and sing her into peace,
That my old care may cease;
Unfold your flaming wings and cover out of sight
The nets of day and night.

Dim powers of drowsy thought, let her no longer be
Like the pale cup of the sea,
When winds have gathered and sun and moon burned dim
Above its cloudy rim;
But let a gentle silence wrought with music flow
Whither her footsteps go.

He Wishes His Beloved Were Dead

Were you but lying cold and dead,
And lights were paling out of the West,
You would come hither, and bend your head,
And I would lay my head on your breast;
And you would murmur tender words,
Forgiving me, because you were dead:
Nor would you rise and hasten away,
Though you have the will of the wild birds,
But know your hair was bound and wound
About the stars and moon and sun:
O would, beloved, that you lay
Under the dock-leaves in the ground,
While lights were paling one by one.

He Wishes for the Cloths of Heaven

Had I the heavens' embroidered cloths,
Enwrought with golden and silver light,
The blue and the dim and the dark cloths
Of night and light and the half-light,
I would spread the cloths under your feet:
But I, being poor, have only my dreams;
I have spread my dreams under your feet;
Tread softly because you tread on my dreams.

He Thinks of His Past Greatness When a Part of the Constellations of Heaven

I have drunk ale from the Country of the Young
And weep because I know all things now:
I have been a hazel-tree, and they hung
The Pilot Star and the Crooked Plough
Among my leaves in times out of mind:
I became a rush that horses tread:
I became a man, a hater of the wind,
Knowing one, out of all things, alone, that his head

May not lie on the breast nor his lips on the hair
Of the woman that he loves, until he dies.
O beast of the wilderness, bird of the air,
Must I endure your amorous cries?

The Fiddler of Dooney

When I play on my fiddle in Dooney,
Folk dance like a wave of the sea;
My cousin is priest in Kilvarnet,
My brother in Mocharabuiee.

I passed my brother and cousin:
They read in their books of prayer;
I read in my book of songs
I bought at the Sligo fair.

When we come at the end of time
To Peter sitting in state,
He will smile on the three old spirits,
But call me first through the gate;

For the good are always the merry,
Save by an evil chance,
And the merry love the fiddle,
And the merry love to dance:

And when the folk there spy me,
They will all come up to me,
With 'Here is the fiddler of Dooney!'
And dance like a wave of the sea.

IN THE SEVEN WOODS
1904

In the Seven Woods

I have heard the pigeons of the Seven Woods
Make their faint thunder, and the garden bees
Hum in the lime-tree flowers; and put away
The unavailing outcries and the old bitterness
That empty the heart. I have forgot awhile
Tara uprooted, and new commonness
Upon the throne and crying about the streets
And hanging its paper flowers from post to post,
Because it is alone of all things happy.
I am contented, for I know that Quiet
Wanders laughing and eating her wild heart
Among pigeons and bees, while that Great Archer,
Who but awaits His hour to shoot, still hangs
A cloudy quiver over Parc-na-lee.

The Arrow

I thought of your beauty, and this arrow,
Made out of a wild thought, is in my marrow.
There's no man may look upon her, no man,
As when newly grown to be a woman,
Tall and noble but with face and bosom
Delicate in colour as apple blossom.
This beauty's kinder, yet for a reason
I could weep that the old is out of season.

The Folly of Being Comforted

One that is ever kind said yesterday:
'Your well-beloved's hair has threads of grey,
And little shadows come about her eyes;
Time can but make it easier to be wise
Though now it seems impossible, and so
All that you need is patience.'
Heart cries, 'No,
I have not a crumb of comfort, not a grain.
Time can but make her beauty over again:
Because of that great nobleness of hers
The fire that stirs about her, when she stirs,
Burns but more clearly. O she had not these ways
When all the wild Summer was in her gaze.'

O heart! O heart! if she'd but turn her head,
You'd know the folly of being comforted.

Old Memory

O thought, fly to her when the end of day
Awakens an old memory, and say,
'Your strength, that is so lofty and fierce and kind,
It might call up a new age, calling to mind
The queens that were imagined long ago,
Is but half yours: he kneaded in the dough
Through the long years of youth, and who would have thought
It all, and more than it all, would come to naught,
And that dear words meant nothing?' But enough,
For when we have blamed the wind we can blame love;
Or, if there needs be more, be nothing said
That would be harsh for children that have strayed.

Never Give All the Heart

Never give all the heart, for love
Will hardly seem worth thinking of
To passionate women if it seem
Certain, and they never dream
That it fades out from kiss to kiss;
For everything that's lovely is
But a brief, dreamy, kind delight.
O never give the heart outright,
For they, for all smooth lips can say,
Have given their hearts up to the play.
And who could play it well enough
If deaf and dumb and blind with love?
He that made this knows all the cost,
For he gave all his heart and lost.

The Withering of the Boughs

I cried when the moon was murmuring to the birds:
'Let peewit call and curlew cry where they will,
I long for your merry and tender and pitiful words,
For the roads are unending, and there is no place to my mind.'
The honey-pale moon lay low on the sleepy hill,
And I fell asleep upon lonely Echtge of streams.
No boughs have withered because of the wintry wind;
The boughs have withered because I have told them my, dreams.

I know of the leafy paths that the witches take
Who come with their crowns of pearl and their spindles of wool,
And their secret smile, out of the depths of the lake;
I know where a dim moon drifts, where the Danaan kind
Wind and unwind their dances when the light grows cool
On the island lawns, their feet where the pale foam gleams.
No boughs have withered because of the wintry wind;
The boughs have withered because I have told them my dreams.

I know of the sleepy country, where swans fly round
Coupled with golden chains, and sing as they fly.

A king and a queen are wandering there, and the sound
Has made them so happy and hopeless, so deaf and so blind
With wisdom, they wander till all the years have gone by;
I know, and the curlew and peewit on Echtge of streams.
No boughs have withered because of the wintry wind;
The boughs have withered because I have told them my dreams.

Adam's Curse

We sat together at one summer's end,
That beautiful mild woman, your close friend,
And you and I, and talked of poetry.
I said, 'A line will take us hours maybe;
Yet if it does not seem a moment's thought,
Our stitching and unstitching has been naught.
Better go down upon your marrow-bones
And scrub a kitchen pavement, or break stones
Like an old pauper, in all kinds of weather;
For to articulate sweet sounds together
Is to work harder than all these, and yet
Be thought an idler by the noisy set
Of bankers, schoolmasters, and clergymen
The martyrs call the world.'

And thereupon
That beautiful mild woman for whose sake
There's many a one shall find out all heartache
On finding that her voice is sweet and low
Replied, 'To be born woman is to know —
Although they do not talk of it at school —
That we must labour to be beautiful.'

I said, 'It's certain there is no fine thing
Since Adam's fall but needs much labouring.
There have been lovers who thought love should be
So much compounded of high courtesy
That they would sigh and quote with learned looks
precedents out of beautiful old books;
Yet now it seems an idle trade enough.'

We sat grown quiet at the name of love;
We saw the last embers of daylight die,
And in the trembling blue-green of the sky
A moon, worn as if it had been a shell
Washed by time's waters as they rose and fell
About the stars and broke in days and years.

I had a thought for no one's but your ears:
That you were beautiful, and that I strove
To love you in the old high way of love;
That it had all seemed happy, and yet we'd grown
As weary-hearted as that hollow moon.

Red Hanrahan's Song about Ireland

The old brown thorn-trees break in two high over Cummen
    Strand,
Under a bitter black wind that blows from the left hand;
Our courage breaks like an old tree in a black wind and dies,
But we have hidden in our hearts the flame out of the eyes
Of Cathleen, the daughter of Houlihan.

The wind has bundled up the clouds high over Knocknarea,
And thrown the thunder on the stones for all that Maeve can say.
Angers that are like noisy clouds have set our hearts abeat;
But we have all bent low and low and kissed the quiet feet
Of Cathleen, the daughter of Houlihan.

The yellow pool has overflowed high up on Clooth-na-Bare,
For the wet winds are blowing out of the clinging air;
Like heavy flooded waters our bodies and our blood;
But purer than a tall candle before the Holy Rood
Is Cathleen, the daughter of Houlihan.

The Old Men Admiring Themselves in the Water

I heard the old, old men say,
'Everything alters,
And one by one we drop away.'
They had hands like claws, and their knees
Were twisted like the old thorn-trees
By the waters.
I heard the old, old men say,
'All that's beautiful drifts away
Like the waters.'

Under the Moon

I have no happiness in dreaming of Brycelinde,
Nor Avalon the grass-green hollow, nor Joyous Isle,
Where one found Lancelot crazed and hid him for a while;
Nor Ulad, when Naoise had thrown a sail upon the wind;
Nor lands that seem too dim to be burdens on the heart:
Land-under-Wave, where out of the moon's light and the sun's
Seven old sisters wind the threads of the long-lived ones,
Land-of-the-Tower, where Aengus has thrown the gates apart,
And Wood-of-Wonders, where one kills an ox at dawn,
To find it when night falls laid on a golden bier.
Therein are many queens like Branwen and Guinevere;
And Niamh and Laban and Fand, who could change to an
otter or fawn,
And the wood-woman, whose lover was changed to a blue-
eyed hawk;
And whether I go in my dreams by woodland, or dun, or shore,
Or on the unpeopled waves with kings to pull at the oar,
I hear the harp-string praise them, or hear their mournful talk.

Because of something told under the famished horn
Of the hunter's moon, that hung between the night and the
day,
To dream of women whose beauty was folded in dismay,
Even in an old story, is a burden not to be borne.

The Ragged Wood

O hurry where by water among the trees
The delicate-stepping stag and his lady sigh,
When they have looked upon their images
Would none had ever loved but you and I!

Or have you heard that sliding silver-shoed
Pale silver-proud queen-woman of the sky,
When the sun looked out of his golden hood? —
O that none ever loved but you and I!

O hurry to the ragged wood, for there
I will drive all those lovers out and cry —
O my share of the world, O, yellow hair!
No one has ever loved but you and I.

Do Not Love Too Long

Sweetheart, do not love too long:
I loved long and long,
And grew to be out of fashion
Like an old song.

All through the years of our youth
Neither could have known
Their own thought from the other's,
We were so much at one.

But O, in a minute she changed —
O do not love too long,
Or you will grow out of fashion
Like an old song.

The Players Ask For a Blessing on the Psalteries and on Themselves

Three Voices (*together*). Hurry to bless the hands that play,
The mouths that speak, the notes and strings,
O masters of the glittering town!
O! lay the shrilly trumpet down,
Though drunken with the flags that sway
Over the ramparts and the towers,
And with the waving of your wings.

First Voice. Maybe they linger by the way.
One gathers up his purple gown;
One leans and mutters by the wall —
He dreads the weight of mortal hours.

Second Voice. O no, O no! they hurry down
Like plovers that have heard the call.

Third Voice. O kinsmen of the Three in One,
O kinsmen, bless the hands that play.
The notes they waken shall live on
When all this heavy history's done;
Our hands, our hands must ebb away.

Three Voices (*together*). The proud and careless notes live on,
But bless our hands that ebb away.

The Happy Townland

There's many a strong farmer
Whose heart would break in two,
If he could see the townland
That we are riding to;
Boughs have their fruit and blossom
At all times of the year;
Rivers are running over
With red beer and brown beer.
An old man plays the bagpipes

In a golden and silver wood;
Queens, their eyes blue like the ice,
Are dancing in a crowd.

The little fox he murmured,
'O what of the world's bane?'
The sun was laughing sweetly,
The moon plucked at my rein;
But the little red fox murmured,
'O do not pluck at his rein,
He is riding to the townland
That is the world's bane.'

When their hearts are so high
That they would come to blows,
They unhook their heavy swords
From golden and silver boughs;
But all that are killed in battle
Awaken to life again.
It is lucky that their story
Is not known among men,
For O, the strong farmers
That would let the spade lie,
Their hearts would be like a cup
That somebody had drunk dry.

The little fox he murmured,
'O what of the world's bane?'
The sun was laughing sweetly,
The moon plucked at my rein;
But the little red fox murmured,
'O do not pluck at his rein,
He is riding to the townland
That is the world's bane.'

Michael will unhook his trumpet
From a bough overhead,
And blow a little noise
When the supper has been spread.

Gabriel will come from the water
With a fish-tail, and talk
Of wonders that have happened
On wet roads where men walk.
And lift up an old horn
Of hammered silver, and drink
Till he has fallen asleep
Upon the starry brink.

The little fox he murmured,
'O what of the world's bane?'
The sun was laughing sweetly,
The moon plucked at my rein;
But the little red fox murmured.
'O do not pluck at his rein,
He is riding to the townland
That is the world's bane.'

THE GREEN HELMET AND OTHER POEMS

1910

His Dream

I swayed upon the gaudy stem
The butt-end of a steering-oar,
And saw wherever I could turn
A crowd upon a shore.

And though I would have hushed the crowd,
There was no mother's son but said,
'What is the figure in a shroud
Upon a gaudy bed?'

And after running at the brim
Cried out upon that thing beneath
— It had such dignity of limb —
By the sweet name of Death.

Though I'd my finger on my lip,
What could I but take up the song?
And running crowd and gaudy ship
Cried out the whole night long,

Crying amid the glittering sea,
Naming it with ecstatic breath,
Because it had such dignity,
By the sweet name of Death.

A Woman Homer Sung

If any man drew near
When I was young,
I thought, 'He holds her dear,'
And shook with hate and fear.
But O! 'twas bitter wrong
If he could pass her by
With an indifferent eye.

Whereon I wrote and wrought,
And now, being grey,
I dream that I have brought
To such a pitch my thought
That coming time can say,
'He shadowed in a glass
What thing her body was.'

For she had fiery blood
When I was young,
And trod so sweetly proud
As 'twere upon a cloud,
A woman Homer sung,
That life and letters seem
But an heroic dream.

Words

I had this thought a while ago,
'My darling cannot understand
What I have done, or what would do
In this blind bitter land.'

And I grew weary of the sun
Until my thoughts cleared up again,
Remembering that the best I have done
Was done to make it plain;

That every year I have cried, 'At length
My darling understands it all,
Because I have come into my strength,
And words obey my call';

That had she done so who can say
What would have shaken from the sieve?
I might have thrown poor words away
And been content to live.

No Second Troy

Why should I blame her that she filled my days
With misery, or that she would of late
Have taught to ignorant men most violent ways,
Or hurled the little streets upon the great,
Had they but courage equal to desire?
What could have made her peaceful with a mind
That nobleness made simple as a fire,
With beauty like a tightened bow, a kind
That is not natural in an age like this,
Being high and solitary and most stern?
Why, what could she have done, being what she is?
Was there another Troy for her to burn?

Reconciliation

Some may have blamed you that you took away
The verses that could move them on the day
When, the ears being deafened, the sight of the eyes blind
With lightning, you went from me, and I could find
Nothing to make a song about but kings,
Helmets, and swords, and half-forgotten things
That were like memories of you—but now
We'll out, for the world lives as long ago;
And while we're in our laughing, weeping fit,
Hurl helmets, crowns, and swords into the pit.
But, dear, cling close to me; since you were gone,
My barren thoughts have chilled me to the bone.

King and No King

'Would it were anything but merely voice!'
The No King cried who after that was King,
Because he had not heard of anything
That balanced with a word is more than noise;
Yet Old Romance being kind, let him prevail
Somewhere or somehow that I have forgot,
Though he'd but cannon — Whereas we that had thought
To have lit upon as clean and sweet a tale
Have been defeated by that pledge you gave
In momentary anger long ago;
And I that have not your faith, how shall I know
That in the blinding light beyond the grave
We'll find so good a thing as that we have lost?
The hourly kindness, the day's common speech,
The habitual content of each with each
Men neither soul nor body has been crossed.

Peace

Ah, that Time could touch a form
That could show what Homer's age
Bred to be a hero's wage.
'Were not all her life but storm
Would not painters paint a form
Of such noble lines,' I said,
'Such a delicate high head,
All that sternness amid charm,
All that sweetness amid strength?'
Ah, but peace that comes at length,
Came when Time had touched her form.

Against Unworthy Praise

O heart, be at peace, because
Nor knave nor dolt can break
What's not for their applause,

Being for a woman's sake.
Enough if the work has seemed,
So did she your strength renew,
A dream that a lion had dreamed
Till the wilderness cried aloud,
A secret between you two,
Between the proud and the proud.
What, still you would have their praise!
But here's a haughtier text,
The labyrinth of her days
That her own strangeness perplexed;
And how what her dreaming gave
Earned slander, ingratitude,
From self-same dolt and knave;
Aye, and worse wrong than these.
Yet she, singing upon her road,
Half lion, half child, is at peace.

The Fascination of What's Difficult

The fascination of what's difficult
Has dried the sap out of my veins, and rent
Spontaneous joy and natural content
Out of my heart. There's something ails our colt
That must, as if it had not holy blood
Nor on Olympus leaped from cloud to cloud,
Shiver under the lash, strain, sweat and jolt
As though it dragged road metal. My curse on plays
That have to be set up in fifty ways,
On the day's war with every knave and dolt,
Theatre business, management of men.
I swear before the dawn comes round again
I'll find the stable and pull out the bolt.

A Drinking Song

Wine comes in at the mouth
And love comes in at the eye;

That's all we shall know for truth
Before we grow old and die.
I lift the glass to my mouth,
I look at you, and I sigh.

The Coming of Wisdom with Time

Though leaves are many, the root is one;
Through all the lying days of my youth
I swayed my leaves and flowers in the sun;
Now I may wither into the truth.

On Hearing That the Students of Our New University Have Joined the Agitation against Immoral Literature

Where, where but here have Pride and Truth,
That long to give themselves for wage,
To shake their wicked sides at youth
Restraining reckless middle-age?

To a Poet, Who Would Have Me Praise Certain Bad Poets, Imitators of His and Mine

You say, as I have often given tongue
In praise of what another's said or sung,
'Twere politic to do the like by these;
But was there ever dog that praised his fleas?

The Mask

'Put off that mask of burning gold
With emerald eyes.'
'O no, my dear, you make so bold
To find if hearts be wild and wise,
And yet not cold.'

'I would but find what's there to find,
Love or deceit.'
'It was the mask engaged your mind,
And after set your heart to beat,
Not what's behind.'

'But lest you are my enemy,
I must enquire.'
'O no, my dear, let all that be;
What matter, so there is but fire
In you, in me?'

Upon a House Shaken by the Land Agitation

How should the world be luckier if this house,
Where passion and precision have been one
Time out of mind, became too ruinous
To breed the lidless eye that loves the sun?
And the sweet laughing eagle thoughts that grow
Where wings have memory of wings, and all
That comes of the best knit to the best? Although
Mean roof-trees were the sturdier for its fall.
How should their luck run high enough to reach
The gifts that govern men, and after these
To gradual Time's last gift, a written speech
Wrought of high laughter, loveliness and ease?

At the Abbey Theatre

(*Imitated from Ronsard*)

Dear Craoibhin Aoibhin, look into our case.
When we are high and airy hundreds say
That if we hold that flight they'll leave the place,
While those same hundreds mock another day
Because we have made our art of common things,
So bitterly, you'd dream they longed to look
All their lives through into some drift of wings.
You've dandled them and fed them from the book

And know them to the bone; impart to us —
We'll keep the secret — a new trick to please.
Is there a bridle for this Proteus
That turns and changes like his draughty seas?
Or is there none, most popular of men,
But when they mock us, that we mock again?

These Are the Clouds

These are the clouds about the fallen sun,
The majesty that shuts his burning eye:
The weak lay hand on what the strong has done,
Till that be tumbled that was lifted high
And discord follow upon unison,
And all things at one common level lie.
And therefore, friend, if your great race were run
And these things came, so much the more thereby
Have you made greatness your companion,
Although it be for children that you sigh:
These are the clouds about the fallen sun,
The majesty that shuts his burning eye.

At Galway Races

There where the course is,
Delight makes all of the one mind,
The riders upon the galloping horses,
The crowd that closes in behind:
We, too, had good attendance once,
Hearers and hearteners of the work;
Aye, horsemen for companions,
Before the merchant and the clerk
Breathed on the world with timid breath.
Sing on: somewhere at some new moon,
We'll learn that sleeping is not death,
Hearing the whole earth change its tune,
Its flesh being wild, and it again
Crying aloud as the racecourse is,
And we find hearteners among men
That ride upon horses.

A Friend's Illness

Sickness brought me this
Thought, in that scale of his:
Why should I be dismayed
Though flame had burned the whole
World, as it were a coal,
Now I have seen it weighed
Against a soul?

All Things Can Tempt Me

All things can tempt me from this craft of verse:
One time it was a woman's face, or worse —
The seeming needs of my fool-driven land;
Now nothing but comes readier to the hand
Than this accustomed toil. When I was young,
I had not given a penny for a song
Did not the poet sing it with such airs
That one believed he had a sword upstairs;
Yet would be now, could I but have my wish,
Colder and dumber and deafer than a fish.

Brown Penny

I whispered, 'I am too young,'
And then, 'I am old enough';
Wherefore I threw a penny
To find out if I might love.
'Go and love, go and love, young man,
If the lady be young and fair.'
Ah, penny, brown penny, brown penny,
I am looped in the loops of her hair.

O love is the crooked thing,
There is nobody wise enough
To find out all that is in it,
For he would be thinking of love

Till the stars had run away
And the shadows eaten the moon.
Ah, penny, brown penny, brown penny,
One cannot begin it too soon.

RESPONSIBILITIES
1914

'In dreams begin responsibilities.'

Old Play

'How am I fallen from myself, for a long time now
I have not seen the Prince of Chang in my dreams.'

Khoung-Fou-Tseu

Pardon, old fathers, if you still remain
Somewhere in ear-shot for the story's end,
Old Dublin merchant 'free of the ten and four'
Or trading out of Galway into Spain;
Old country scholar, Robert Emmet's friend,
A hundred-year-old memory to the poor;
Merchant and scholar who have left me blood
That has not passed through any huckster's loin,
Soldiers that gave, whatever die was cast:
A Butler or an Armstrong that withstood
Beside the brackish waters of the Boyne
James and his Irish when the Dutchman crossed;
Old merchant skipper that leaped overboard
After a ragged hat in Biscay Bay;
You most of all, silent and fierce old man,
Because the daily spectacle that stirred
My fancy, and set my boyish lips to say,
'Only the wasteful virtues earn the sun';
Pardon that for a barren passion's sake,
Although I have come close on forty-nine,
I have no child, I have nothing but a book,
Nothing but that to prove your blood and mine.

The Grey Rock

Poets with whom I learned my trade,
Companions of the Cheshire Cheese,
Here's an old story I've re-made,
Imagining 'twould better please
Your ears than stories now in fashion,
Though you may think I waste my breath
Pretending that there can be passion
That has more life in it than death,
And though at bottling of your wine
Old wholesome Goban had no say;
The moral's yours because it's mine.

When cups went round at close of day —
Is not that how good stories run? —
The gods were sitting at the board
In their great house at Slievenamon.
They sang a drowsy song, Or snored,
For all were full of wine and meat.
The smoky torches made a glare
On metal Goban 'd hammered at,
On old deep silver rolling there
Or on some still unemptied cup
That he, when frenzy stirred his thews,
Had hammered out on mountain top
To hold the sacred stuff he brews
That only gods may buy of him.

Now from that juice that made them wise
All those had lifted up the dim
Imaginations of their eyes,
For one that was like woman made
Before their sleepy eyelids ran
And trembling with her passion said,
'Come out and dig for a dead man,
Who's burrowing somewhere in the ground
And mock him to his face and then
Hollo him on with horse and hound,
For he is the worst of all dead men.'

We should be dazed and terror-struck,
If we but saw in dreams that room,
Those wine-drenched eyes, and curse our luck
That emptied all our days to come.
I knew a woman none could please,
Because she dreamed when but a child
Of men and women made like these;
And after, when her blood ran wild,
Had ravelled her own story out,
And said, 'In two or in three years
I needs must marry some poor lout,'
And having said it, burst in tears.

Since, tavern comrades, you have died,
Maybe your images have stood,
Mere bone and muscle thrown aside,
Before that roomful or as good.
You had to face your ends when young —
'Twas wine or women, or some curse —
But never made a poorer song
That you might have a heavier purse,
Nor gave loud service to a cause
That you might have a troop of friends,
You kept the Muses' sterner laws,
And unrepenting faced your ends,
And therefore earned the right — and yet
Dowson and Johnson most I praise —
To troop with those the world's forgot,
And copy their proud steady gaze.

'The Danish troop was driven out
Between the dawn and dusk,' she said;
'Although the event was long in doubt,
Although the King of Ireland's dead
And half the kings, before sundown
All was accomplished.
'When this day
Murrough, the King of Ireland's son,
Foot after foot was giving way,
He and his best troops back to back

Had perished there, but the Danes ran,
Stricken with panic from the attack,
The shouting of an unseen man;
And being thankful Murrough found,
Led by a footsole dipped in blood
That had made prints upon the ground,
Where by old thorn-trees that man stood;
And though when he gazed here and there,
He had but gazed on thorn-trees, spoke,
'Who is the friend that seems but air
And yet could give so fine a stroke?'
Thereon a young man met his eye,
Who said, 'Because she held me in
Her love, and would not have me die,
Rock-nurtured Aoife took a pin,
And pushing it into my shirt,
Promised that for a pin's sake
No man should see to do me hurt;
But there it's gone; I will not take
The fortune that had been my shame
Seeing, King's son, what wounds you have.'
'Twas roundly spoke, but when night came
He had betrayed me to his grave,
For he and the King's son were dead.
I'd promised him two hundred years,
And when for all I'd done or said —
And these immortal eyes shed tears —
He claimed his country's need was most,
I'd saved his life, yet for the sake
Of a new friend he has turned a ghost.
What does he cate if my heart break?
I call for spade and horse and hound
That we may harry him.' Thereon
She cast herself upon the ground
And rent her clothes and made her moan:
'Why are they faithless when their might
Is from the holy shades that rove
The grey rock and the windy light?
Why should the faithfullest heart most love
The bitter sweetness of false faces?

Why must the lasting love what passes,
Why are the gods by men betrayed?'

But thereon every god stood up
With a slow smile and without sound,
And stretching forth his arm and cup
To where she moaned upon the ground,
Suddenly drenched her to the skin;
And she with Goban's wine adrip,
No more remembering what had been,
Stared at the gods with laughing lip.

I have kept my faith, though faith was tried,
To that rock-born, rock-wandering foot,
And the world's altered since you died,
And I am in no good repute
With the loud host before the sea
That think sword-strokes were better meant
Than lover's music — let that be,
So that the wandering foot's content.

To a Wealthy Man Who Promised a Second Subscription to the Dublin Municipal Gallery If It Were Proved the People Wanted Pictures

You gave, but will not give again
Until enough of Paudeen's pence
By Biddy's halfpennies have lain
To be 'some sort of evidence',
Before you'll put your guineas down,
That things it were a pride to give
Are what the blind and ignorant town
Imagines best to make it thrive.
What cared Duke Ercole, that bid
His mummers to the market-place,
What th' onion-sellers thought or did
So that his plautus set the pace
For the Italian comedies?
And Guidobaldo, when he made
That grammar school of courtesies

Where wit and beauty learned their trade
Upon Urbino's windy hill,
Had sent no runners to and fro
That he might learn the shepherds' will
And when they drove out Cosimo,
Indifferent how the rancour ran,
He gave the hours they had set free
To Michelozzo's latest plan
For the San Marco Library,
Whence turbulent Italy should draw
Delight in Art whose end is peace,
In logic and in natural law
By sucking at the dugs of Greece.

Your open hand but shows our loss,
For he knew better how to live.
Let Paudeens play at pitch and toss,
Look up in the sun's eye and give
What the exultant heart calls good
That some new day may breed the best
Because you gave, not what they would,
But the right twigs for an eagle's nest!

September 1913

What need you, being come to sense,
But fumble in a greasy till
And add the halfpence to the pence
And prayer to shivering prayer, until
You have dried the marrow from the bone?
For men were born to pray and save:
Romantic Ireland's dead and gone,
It's with O'Leary in the grave.

Yet they were of a different kind,
The names that stilled your childish play,
They have gone about the world like wind,
But little time had they to pray
For whom the hangman's rope was spun,
And what, God help us, could they save?

Romantic Ireland's dead and gone,
It's with O'Leary in the grave.

Was it for this the wild geese spread
The grey wing upon every tide;
For this that all that blood was shed,
For this Edward Fitzgerald died,
And Robert Emmet and Wolfe Tone,
All that delirium of the brave?
Romantic Ireland's dead and gone,
It's with O'Leary in the grave.

Yet could we turn the years again,
And call those exiles as they were
In all their loneliness and pain,
You'd cry, 'Some woman's yellow hair
Has maddened every mother's son':
They weighed so lightly what they gave.
But let them be, they're dead and gone,
They're with O'Leary in the grave.

To a Friend Whose Work Has Come to Nothing

Now all the truth is out,
Be secret and take defeat
From any brazen throat,
For how can you compete,
Being honour bred, with one
Who, were it proved he lies,
Were neither shamed in his own
Nor in his neighbours' eyes?
Bred to a harder thing
Than Triumph, turn away
And like a laughing string
Whereon mad fingers play
Amid a place of stone,
Be secret and exult,
Because of all things known
That is most difficult.

Paudeen

Indignant at the fumbling wits, the obscure spite
Of our old Paudeen in his shop, I stumbled blind
Among the stones and thorn-trees, under morning light;
Until a curlew cried and in the luminous wind
A curlew answered; and suddenly thereupon I thought
That on the lonely height where all are in God's eye,
There cannot be, confusion of our sound forgot,
A single soul that lacks a sweet crystalline cry.

To a Shade

If you have revisited the town, thin Shade,
Whether to look upon your monument
(I wonder if the builder has been paid)
Or happier-thoughted when the day is spent
To drink of that salt breath out of the sea
When grey gulls flit about instead of men,
And the gaunt houses put on majesty:
Let these content you and be gone again;
For they are at their old tricks yet.

A man
Of your own passionate serving kind who had brought
In his full hands what, had they only known,
Had given their children's children loftier thought,
Sweeter emotion, working in their veins
Like gentle blood, has been driven from the place,
And insult heaped upon him for his pains,
And for his open-handedness, disgrace;
Your enemy, an old foul mouth, had set
The pack upon him.

Go, unquiet wanderer,
And gather the Glasnevin coverlet
About your head till the dust stops your ear,
The time for you to taste of that salt breath
And listen at the corners has not come;
You had enough of sorrow before death —
Away, away! You are safer in the tomb.

When Helen Lived

We have cried in our despair
That men desert,
For some trivial affair
Or noisy, insolent sport,
Beauty that we have won
From bitterest hours;
Yet we, had we walked within
Those topless towers
Where Helen waked with her boy,
Had given but as the rest
Of the men and women of Troy,
A word and a jest.

On Those That Hated 'The Playboy of the Western World', 1907

Once, when midnight smote the air,
Eunuchs ran through Hell and met
On every crowded street to stare
Upon great Juan riding by:
Even like these to rail and sweat
Staring upon his sinewy thigh.

The Three Beggars

'Though to my feathers in the wet,
I have stood here from break of day.
I have not found a thing to eat,
For only rubbish comes my way.
Am I to live on lebeen-lone?'
Muttered the old crane of Gort.
'For all my pains on lebeen-lone?'

King Guare walked amid his court
The palace-yard and river-side
And there to three old beggars said,

'You that have wandered far and wide
Can ravel out what's in my head.
Do men who least desire get most,
Or get the most who most desire?'
A beggar said, 'They get the most
Whom man or devil cannot tire,
And what could make their muscles taut
Unless desire had made them so?'
But Guare laughed with secret thought,
'If that be true as it seems true,
One of you three is a rich man,
For he shall have a thousand pounds
Who is first asleep, if but he can
Sleep before the third noon sounds.'
And thereon, merry as a bird
With his old thoughts, King Guare went
From river-side and palace-yard
And left them to their argument.
'And if I win,' one beggar said,
'Though I am old I shall persuade
A pretty girl to share my bed';
The second: 'I shall learn a trade';
The third: 'I'll hurry' to the course
Among the other gentlemen,
And lay it all upon a horse';
The second: 'I have thought again:
A farmer has more dignity.'
One to another sighed and cried:
The exorbitant dreams of beggary,
That idleness had borne to pride,
Sang through their teeth from noon to noon;
And when the second twilight brought
The frenzy of the beggars' moon
None closed his blood-shot eyes but sought
To keep his fellows from their sleep;
All shouted till their anger grew
And they were whirling in a heap.

They mauled and bit the whole night through;
They mauled and bit till the day shone;

They mauled and bit through all that day
And till another night had gone,
Or if they made a moment's stay
They sat upon their heels to rail,,
And when old Guare came and stood
Before the three to end this tale,
They were commingling lice and blood
'Time's up,' he cried, and all the three
With blood-shot eyes upon him stared.
'Time's up,' he cried, and all the three
Fell down upon the dust and snored.

'Maybe I shall be lucky yet,
Now they are silent,' said the crane.
'Though to my feathers in the wet
I've stood as I were made of stone
And seen the rubbish run about,
It's certain there are trout somewhere
And maybe I shall take a trout
but I do not seem to care.'

The Three Hermits

Three old hermits took the air
By a cold and desolate sea,
First was muttering a prayer,
Second rummaged for a flea;
On a windy stone, the third,
Giddy with his hundredth year,
Sang unnoticed like a bird:
'Though the Door of Death is near
And what waits behind the door,
Three times in a single day
I, though upright on the shore,
Fall asleep when I should pray.'
So the first, but now the second:
'We're but given what we have earned
When all thoughts and deeds are reckoned,
So it's plain to be discerned

That the shades of holy men
Who have failed, being weak of will,
Pass the Door of Birth again,
And are plagued by crowds, until
They've the passion to escape.'
Moaned the other, 'They are thrown
Into some most fearful shape.'
But the second mocked his moan:
'They are not changed to anything,
Having loved God once, but maybe
To a poet or a king
Or a witty lovely lady.'
While he'd rummaged rags and hair,
Caught and cracked his flea, the third,
Giddy with his hundredth year,
Sang unnoticed like a bird.

Beggar to Beggar Cried

'Time to put off the world and go somewhere
And find my health again in the sea air,'
Beggar to beggar cried, being frenzy-struck,
'And make my soul before my pate is bare.-

'And get a comfortable wife and house
To rid me of the devil in my shoes,'
Beggar to beggar cried, being frenzy-struck,
'And the worse devil that is between my thighs.'

And though I'd marry with a comely lass,
She need not be too comely — let it pass,'
Beggar to beggar cried, being frenzy-struck,
'But there's a devil in a looking-glass.'

'Nor should she be too rich, because the rich
Are driven by wealth as beggars by the itch,'
Beggar to beggar cried, being frenzy-struck,
'And cannot have a humorous happy speech.'

'And there I'll grow respected at my ease,
And hear amid the garden's nightly peace.'
Beggar to beggar cried, being frenzy-struck,
'The wind-blown clamour of the barnacle-geese.'

Running to Paradise

As I came over Windy Gap
They threw a halfpenny into my cap.
For I am running to Paradise;
And all that I need do is to wish
And somebody puts his hand in the dish
To throw me a bit of salted fish:
And there the king is but as the beggar.

My brother Mourteen is worn out
With skelping his big brawling lout,
And I am running to Paradise;
A poor life, do what he can,
And though he keep a dog and a gun,
A serving-maid and a serving-man:
And there the king is but as the beggar.

Poor men have grown to be rich men,
And rich men grown to be poor again,
And I am running to Paradise;
And many a darling wit's grown dull
That tossed a bare heel when at school,
Now it has filled an old sock full:
And there the king is but as the beggar.

The wind is old and still at play
While I must hurry upon my way.
For I am running to Paradise;
Yet never have I lit on a friend
To take my fancy like the wind
That nobody can buy or bind:
And there the king is but as the beggar.

The Hour before Dawn

A cursing rogue with a merry face,
A bundle of rags upon a crutch,
Stumbled upon that windy place
Called Cruachan, and it was as much
As the one sturdy leg could do
To keep him upright while he cursed.
He had counted, where long years ago
Queen Maeve's nine Maines had been nursed,
A pair of lapwings, one old sheep,
And not a house to the plain's edge,
When close to his right hand a heap
Of grey stones and a rocky ledge
Reminded him that he could make.
If he but shifted a few stones,
A shelter till the daylight broke.

But while he fumbled with the stones
They toppled over; 'Were it not
I have a lucky wooden shin
I had been hurt'; and toppling brought
Before his eyes, where stones had been,
A dark deep hollow in the rock.
He gave a gasp and thought to have fled,
Being certain it was no right rock
Because an ancient history said
Hell Mouth lay open near that place,
And yet stood still, because inside
A great lad with a beery face
Had tucked himself away beside
A ladle and a tub of beer,
And snored, no phantom by his look.
So with a laugh at his own fear
He crawled into that pleasant nook.

'Night grows uneasy near the dawn
Till even I sleep light; but who
Has tired of his own company?
What one of Maeve's nine brawling sons

Sick of his grave has wakened me?
But let him keep his grave for once
That I may find the sleep I have lost.'

'What care I if you sleep or wake?
But I'll have no man call me ghost.'

'Say what you please, but from daybreak
I'll sleep another century.'

'And I will talk before I sleep
And drink before I talk.'

                                        And he
Had dipped the wooden ladle deep
Into the sleeper's tub of beer
Had not the sleeper started up.

'Before you have dipped it in the beer
I dragged from Goban's mountain-top
I'll have assurance that you are able
To value beer; no half-legged fool
Shall dip his nose into my ladle
Merely for stumbling on this hole
In the bad hour before the dawn.'

'Why beer is only beer.'
                                        'But say
"I'll sleep until the winter's gone,
Or maybe to Midsummer Day,"
And drink and you will sleep that length.'

'I'd like to sleep till winter's gone
Or till the sun is in his strength.
This blast has chilled me to the bone.'

'I had no better plan at first.
I thought to wait for that or this;
Maybe the weather was accursed
Or I had no woman there to kiss;

So slept for half a year or so;
But year by year I found that less
Gave me such pleasure I'd forgo
Even a half-hour's nothingness,
And when at one year's end I found
I had not waked a single minute,
I chose this burrow under ground.
I'll sleep away all time within it:
My sleep were now nine centuries
But for those mornings when I find
The lapwing at their foolish cries
And the sheep bleating at the wind
As when I also played the fool.'

The beggar in a rage began
Upon his hunkers in the hole,
'It's plain that you are no right man
To mock at everything I love
As if it were not worth, the doing.
I'd have a merry life enough
If a good Easter wind were blowing,
And though the winter wind is bad
I should not be too down in the mouth
For anything you did or said
If but this wind were in the south.'

'You cry aloud, O would 'twere spring
Or that the wind would shift a point,
And do not know that you would bring,
If time were suppler in the joint,
Neither the spring nor the south wind
But the hour when you shall pass away
And leave no smoking wick behind,
For all life longs for the Last Day
And there's no man but cocks his ear
To know when Michael's trumpet cries
That flesh and bone may disappear,
And souls as if they were but sighs,
And there be nothing but God left;
But, I alone being blessed keep

Like some old rabbit to my cleft
And wait Him in a drunken sleep.'
He dipped his ladle in the tub
And drank and yawned and stretched him out,
The other shouted, 'You would rob
My life of every pleasant thought
And every comfortable thing,
And so take that and that.' Thereon
He gave him a great pummelling,
But might have pummelled at a stone
For all the sleeper knew or cared;
And after heaped up stone on stone,
And then, grown weary, prayed and cursed
And heaped up stone on stone again,
And prayed and cursed and cursed and fled
From Maeve and all that juggling plain,
Nor gave God thanks till overhead
The clouds were brightening with the dawn.

A Song from 'The Player Queen'

My mother dandled me and sang,
'How young it is, how young!'
And made a golden cradle
That on a willow swung.

'He went away,' my mother sang,
'When I was brought to bed,'
And all the while her needle pulled
The gold and silver thread.

She pulled the thread and bit the thread
And made a golden gown,
And wept because she had dreamt that I
Was born to wear a crown.

'When she was got,' my mother sang,
I heard a sea-mew cry,
And saw a flake of the yellow foam
That dropped upon my thigh.'

How therefore could she help but braid
The gold into my hair,
And dream that I should carry
The golden top of care?

The Realists

Hope that you may understand!
What can books of men that wive
In a dragon-guarded land,
paintings of the dolphin-drawn
Sea-nymphs in their pearly wagons
Do, but awake a hope to live
That had gone
With the dragons?

I
The Witch

Toil and grow rich,
What's that but to lie
With a foul witch
And after, drained dry,
To be brought
To the chamber where
Lies one long sought
With despair?

II
The Peacock

What's riches to him
That has made a great peacock
With the pride of his eye?
The wind-beaten, stone-grey,
And desolate Three-rock
Would nourish his whim.
Live he or die

Amid wet rocks and heather,
His ghost will be gay
Adding feather to feather
For the pride of his eye.

The Mountain Tomb

Pour wine and dance if manhood still have pride,
Bring roses if the rose be yet in bloom;
The cataract smokes upon the mountain side,
Our Father Rosicross is in his tomb.

Pull down the blinds, bring fiddle and clarionet
That there be no foot silent in the room
Nor mouth from kissing, nor from wine unwet;
Our Father Rosicross is in his tomb.

In vain, in vain; the cataract still cries;
The everlasting taper lights the gloom;
All wisdom shut into his onyx eyes,
Our Father Rosicross sleeps in his tomb.

I

To a Child Dancing in the Wind

Dance there upon the shore;
What need have you to care
For wind or water's roar?
And tumble out your hair
That the salt drops have wet;
Being young you have not known
The fool's triumph, nor yet
Love lost as soon as won,
Nor the best labourer dead
And all the sheaves to bind.
What need have you to dread
The monstrous crying of wind?

II

Two Years Later

Has no one said those daring
Kind eyes should be more learned?
Or warned you how despairing
The moths are when they are burned,
I could have warned you, but you are young,
So we speak a different tongue.

O you will take what ever is offered
And dream that all the world's a friend,
Suffer as your mother suffered,
Be as broken in the end.
But I am old and you are young,
And I speak a barbarous tongue.

A Memory of Youth

The moments passed as at a play;
I had the wisdom love brings forth;
I had my share of mother-wit,
And yet for all that I could say,
And though I had her praise for it,
A cloud blown from the cut-throat north
Suddenly hid Love's moon away.

Believing every word I said,
I praised her body and her mind
Till pride had made her eyes grow bright,
And pleasure made her cheeks grow red,
And vanity her footfall light,
Yet we, for all that praise, could find
Nothing but darkness overhead.

We sat as silent as a stone,
We knew, though she'd not said a word,
That even the best of love must die,
And had been savagely undone

Were it not that Love upon the cry
Of a most ridiculous little bird
Tore from the clouds his marvellous moon.

Fallen Majesty

Although crowds gathered once if she but showed her face,
And even old men's eyes grew dim, this hand alone,
Like some last courtier at a gypsy camping-place
Babbling of fallen majesty, records what's gone.

The lineaments, a heart that laughter has made sweet,
These, these remain, but I record what's gone. A crowd
Will gather, and not know it walks the very street
Whereon a thing once walked that seemed a burning cloud.

Friends

Now must I these three praise —
Three women that have wrought
What joy is in my days:
One because no thought,
Nor those unpassing cares,
No, not in these fifteen
Many-times-troubled years,
Could ever come between
Mind and delighted mind;
And one because her hand
Had strength that could unbind
What none can understand,
What none can have and thrive,
Youth's dreamy load, till she
So changed me that I live
Labouring in ecstasy.
And what of her that took
All till my youth was gone
With scarce a pitying look?
How could I praise that one?

When day begins to break
I count my good and bad,
Being wakeful for her sake,
Remembering what she had,
What eagle look still shows,
While up from my heart's root
So great a sweetness flows
I shake from head to foot.

The Cold Heaven

Suddenly I saw the cold and rook-delighting heaven
That seemed as though ice burned and was but the more ice,
And thereupon imagination and heart were driven
So wild that every casual thought of that and this
Vanished, and left but memories, that should be out of season
With the hot blood of youth, of love crossed long ago;
And I took all the blame out of all sense and reason,
Until I cried and trembled and rocked to and fro,
Riddled with light. Ah! when the ghost begins to quicken,
Confusion of the death-bed over, is it sent
Out naked on the roads, as the books say, and stricken
By the injustice of the skies for punishment?

That the Night Come

She lived in storm and strife,
Her soul had such desire
For what proud death may bring
That it could not endure
The common good of life,
But lived as 'twere a king
That packed his marriage day
With banneret and pennon,
Trumpet and kettledrum,
And the outrageous cannon,
To bundle time away
That the night come.

An Appointment

Being out of heart with government
I took a broken root to fling
Where the proud, wayward squirrel went,
Taking delight that he could spring;
And he, with that low whinnying sound
That is like laughter, sprang again
And so to the other tree at a bound.
Nor the tame will, nor timid brain,
Nor heavy knitting of the brow
Bred that fierce tooth and cleanly limb
And threw him up to laugh on the bough;
No government appointed him.

The Magi

Now as at all times I can see in the mind's eye,
In their stiff, painted clothes, the pale unsatisfied ones
Appear and disappear in the blue depth of the sky
With all their ancient faces like rain-beaten stones,
And all their helms of silver hovering side by side,
And all their eyes still fixed, hoping to find once more,
Being by Calvary's turbulence unsatisfied,
The uncontrollable mystery on the bestial floor.

The Dolls

A doll in the doll-maker's house
Looks at the cradle and bawls:
'That is an insult to us.'
But the oldest of all the dolls,
Who had seen, being kept for show,
Generations of his sort,
Out-screams the whole shelf: 'Although
There's not a man can report
Evil of this place,
The man and the woman bring

Hither, to our disgrace,
A noisy and filthy thing.'
Hearing him groan and stretch
The doll-maker's wife is aware
Her husband has heard the wretch,
And crouched by the arm of his chair,
She murmurs into his ear,
Head upon shoulder leant:
'My dear, my dear, O dear.
It was an accident.'

A Coat

I made my song a coat
Covered with embroideries
Out of old mythologies
From heel to throat;
But the fools caught it,
Wore it in the world's eyes
As though they'd wrought it.
Song, let them take it,
For there's more enterprise
In walking naked.

Closing Rhyme

While I, that reed-throated whisperer
Who comes at need, although not now as once
A clear articulation in the air,
But inwardly, surmise companions
Beyond the fling of the dull ass's hoof
— Ben Johnson's phrase — and find when June is come
At Kyle-na-no under that ancient roof
A sterner conscience and a friendlier home,
I can forgive even that wrong of wrongs,
Those undreamt accidents that have made me
— Seeing that Fame has perished that long while,
Being but a part of ancient ceremony —
Notorious, till all my priceless things
Are but a post the passing dogs defile.

THE WILD SWANS AT COOLE
1919

The Wild Swans at Coole

The trees are in their autumn beauty,
The woodland paths are dry,
Under the October twilight the water
Mirrors a still sky;
Upon the brimming water among the stones
Are nine-and-fifty swans.

The nineteenth autumn has come upon me
Since I first made my count;
I saw, before I had well finished,
All suddenly mount
And scatter wheeling in great broken rings
Upon their clamorous wings.

I have looked upon those brilliant creatures,
And now my heart is sore.
All's changed since I, hearing at twilight,
The first time on this shore,
The bell-beat of their wings above my head,
Trod with a lighter tread.

Unwearied still, lover by lover,
They paddle in the cold
Companionable streams or climb the air;
Their hearts have not grown old;
Passion or conquest, wander where they will,
Attend upon them still.

But now they drift on the still water,
Mysterious, beautiful;
Among what rushes will they build,
By what lake's edge or pool
Delight men's eyes when I awake some day
To find they have flown away?

In Memory of Major Robert Gregory

Now that we're almost settled in our house
I'll name the friends that cannot sup with us
Beside a fire of turf in th' ancient tower,
And having talked to some late hour
Climb up the narrow winding stairs to bed:
Discoverers of forgotten truth
Or mere companions of my youth,
All, all are in my thoughts to-night being dead.

Always we'd have the new friend meet the old
And we are hurt if either friend seem cold,
And there is salt to lengthen out the smart
In the affections of our heart,
And quarrels are blown up upon that head;
But not a friend that I would bring
This night can set us quarrelling,
For all that come into my mind are dead.

Lionel Johnson comes the first to mind,
That loved his learning better than mankind.
Though courteous to the worst; much falling he
Brooded upon sanctity
Till all his Greek and Latin learning seemed
A long blast upon the horn that brought
A little nearer to his thought
A measureless consummation that he dreamed.

And that enquiring man John Synge comes next,
That dying chose the living world for text
And never could have rested in the tomb

But that, long travelling, he had come
Towards nightfall upon certain set apart
In a most desolate stony place,
Towards nightfall upon a race
Passionate and simple like his heart.

And then I think of old George Pollexfen,
In muscular youth well known to Mayo men
For horsemanship at meets or at racecourses,
That could have shown how pure-bred horses
And solid men, for all their passion, live
But as the outrageous stars incline
By opposition, square and trine;
Having grown sluggish and contemplative.

They were my close companions many a year.
A portion of my mind and life, as it were,
And now their breathless faces seem to look
Out of some old picture-book;
I am accustomed to their lack of breath,
But not that my dear friend's dear son,
Our Sidney and our perfect man,
Could share in that discourtesy of death.

For all things the delighted eye now sees
Were loved by him: the old storm-broken trees
That cast their shadows upon road and bridge;
The tower set on the stream's edge;
The ford where drinking cattle make a stir
Nightly, and startled by that sound
The water-hen must change her ground;
He might have been your heartiest welcomer.

When with the Galway foxhounds he would ride
From Castle Taylor to the Roxborough side
Or Esserkelly plain, few kept his pace;
At Mooneen he had leaped a place
So perilous that half the astonished meet
Had shut their eyes; and where was it
He rode a race without a bit?
And yet his mind outran the horses' feet.

We dreamed that a great painter had been born
To cold Clare rock and Galway rock and thorn,
To that stern colour and that delicate line
That are our secret discipline
Wherein the gazing heart doubles her might.
Soldier, scholar, horseman, he,
And yet he had the intensity
To have published all to be a world's delight.

What other could so well have counselled us
In all lovely intricacies of a house
As he that practised or that understood
All work in metal or in wood,
In moulded plaster or in carven stone?
Soldier, scholar, horseman, he,
And all he did done perfectly
As though he had but that one trade alone.

Some burn damp faggots, others may consume
The entire combustible world in one small room
As though dried straw, and if we turn about
The bare chimney is gone black out
Because the work had finished in that flare.
Soldier, scholar, horseman, he,
As 'twere all life's epitome.
What made us dream that he could comb grey hair?

I had thought, seeing how bitter is that wind
That shakes the shutter, to have brought to mind
All those that manhood tried, or childhood loved
Or boyish intellect approved,
With some appropriate commentary on each;
Until imagination brought
A fitter welcome; but a thought
Of that late death took all my heart for speech.

An Irish Airman Foresees His Death

I know that I shall meet my fate
Somewhere among the clouds above;
Those that I fight I do not hate
Those that I guard I do not love;
My country is Kiltartan Cross,
My countrymen Kiltartan's poor,
No likely end could bring them loss
Or leave them happier than before.
Nor law, nor duty bade me fight,
Nor public men, nor cheering crowds,
A lonely impulse of delight
Drove to this tumult in the clouds;
I balanced all, brought all to mind,
The years to come seemed waste of breath,
A waste of breath the years behind
In balance with this life, this death.

Men Improve with the Years

I am worn out with dreams;
A weather-worn, marble triton
Among the streams;
And all day long I look
Upon this lady's beauty
As though I had found in a book
A pictured beauty,
Pleased to have filled the eyes
Or the discerning ears,
Delighted to be but wise,
For men improve with the years;
And yet, and yet,
Is this my dream, or the truth?
O would that we had met
When I had my burning youth!
But I grow old among dreams,
A weather-worn, marble triton
Among the streams.

The Collar-Bone of a Hare

Would I could cast a sail on the water
Where many a king has gone
And many a king's daughter,
And alight at the comely trees and the lawn,
The playing upon pipes and the dancing,
And learn that the best thing is
To change my loves while dancing
And pay but a kiss for a kiss.

I would find by the edge of that water
The collar-bone of a hare
Worn thin by the lapping of water,
And pierce it through with a gimlet, and stare
At the old bitter world where they marry in churches,
And laugh over the untroubled water
At all who marry in churches,
Through the white thin bone of a hare.

Under the Round Tower

'Although I'd lie lapped up in linen
A deal I'd sweat and little earn
If I should live as live the neighbours,'
Cried the beggar, Billy Byrne;
'Stretch bones till the daylight come
On great-grandfather's battered tomb.'

Upon a grey old battered tombstone
In Glendalough beside the stream,
Where the O'Byrnes and Byrnes are buried,
He stretched his bones and fell in a dream
Of sun and moon that a good hour
Bellowed and pranced in the round tower;

Of golden king and silver lady,
Bellowing up and bellowing round,
Till toes mastered a sweet measure,
Mouth mastered a sweet sound,

Prancing round and prancing up
Until they pranced upon the top.

That golden king and that wild lady
Sang till stars began to fade,
Hands gripped in hands, toes close together,
Hair spread on the wind they made;
That lady and that golden king
Could like a brace of blackbirds sing.

'It's certain that my luck is broken,'
That rambling jailbird Billy said;
'Before nightfall I'll pick a pocket
And snug it in a feather bed.
I cannot find the peace of home
On great-grandfather's battered tomb.'

Solomon to Sheba

Sang Solomon to Sheba,
And kissed her dusky face,
'All day long from mid-day
We have talked in the one place,
All day long from shadowless noon
We have gone round and round
In the narrow theme of love
Like a old horse in a pound.

To Solomon sang Sheba,
Plated on his knees,
'If you had broached a matter
That might the learned please,
You had before the sun had thrown
Our shadows on the ground
Discovered that my thoughts, not it,
Are but a narrow pound.'

Said Solomon to Sheba,
And kissed her Arab eyes,

'There's not a man or woman
Born under the skies
Dare match in learning with us two,
And all day long we have found
There's not a thing but love can make
The world a narrow pound.'

The Living Beauty

I bade, because the wick and oil are spent
And frozen are the channels of the blood,
My discontented heart to draw content
From beauty that is cast out of a mould
In bronze, or that in dazzling marble appears,
Appears, but when we have gone is gone again,
Being more indifferent to our solitude
Than 'twere an apparition. O heart, we are old;
The living beauty is for younger men:
We cannot pay its tribute of wild tears.

A Song

I thought no more was needed
Youth to prolong
Than dumb-bell and foil
To keep the body young.
O who could have foretold
That the heart grows old?

Though I have many words,
What woman's satisfied,
I am no longer faint
Because at her side?
O who could have foretold
That the heart grows old?

I have not lost desire
But the heart that I had;

I thought 'twould burn my body
Laid on the death-bed,
For who could have foretold
That the heart grows old?

To a Young Beauty

Dear fellow-artist, why so free
With every sort of company,
With every Jack and Jill?
Choose your companions from the best;
Who draws a bucket with the rest
Soon topples down the hill.

You may, that mirror for a school,
Be passionate, not bountiful
As common beauties may,
Who were not born to keep in trim
With old Ezekiel's cherubim
But those of Beauvarlet.

I know what wages beauty gives,
How hard a life her servant lives,
Yet praise the winters gone:
There is not a fool can call me friend,
And I may dine at journey's end
With Landor and with Donne.

To a Young Girl

My dear, my dear, I know
More than another
What makes your heart beat so;
Not even your own mother
Can know it as I know,
Who broke my heart for her
When the wild thought,
That she denies

And has forgot,
Set all her blood astir
And glittered in her eyes.

Tom O'Roughley

'Though logic-choppers rule the town,
And every man and maid and boy
Has marked a distant object down,
An aimless joy is a pure joy,'
Or so did Tom O'Roughley say
That saw the surges running by.
'And wisdom is a butterfly
And not a gloomy bird of prey.

'If little planned is little sinned
But little need the grave distress.
What's dying but a second wind?
How but in zig-zag wantonness
Could trumpeter Michael be so brave?'
Or something of that sort he said,
'And if my dearest friend were dead
I'd dance a measure on his grave.'

Shepherd and Goatherd

Shepherd. That cry's from the first cuckoo of the year.
I wished before it ceased.

Goatherd. Nor bird nor beast
Could make me wish for anything this day,
Being old, but that the old alone might die,
And that would be against God's providence.
Let the young wish. But what has brought you here?
Never until this moment have we met
Where my goats browse on the scarce grass or leap
From stone to stone.

Shepherd. I am looking for strayed sheep;
Something has troubled me and in my trouble
I let them stray. I thought of rhyme alone,
For rhyme can beat a measure out of trouble
And make the daylight sweet once more; but when
I had driven every rhyme into its place
The sheep had gone from theirs.

Goatherd. I know right well
What turned so good a shepherd from his charge.

Shepherd. He that was best in every country sport
And every country craft, and of us all
Most courteous to slow age and hasty youth,
Is dead.

Goatherd. The boy that brings my griddle-cake
Brought the bare news.

Shepherd. He had thrown the crook away
And died in the great war beyond the sea.

Goatherd. He had often played his pipes among my hills,
And when he played it was their loneliness,
The exultation of their stone, that died
Under his fingers.

Shepherd. I had it from his mother,
And his own flock was browsing at the door.

Goatherd. How does she bear her grief? There is not a shepherd
But grows more gentle when he speaks her name,
Remembering kindness done, and how can I,
That found when I had neither goat nor grazing
New welcome and old wisdom at her fire
Till winter blasts were gone, but speak of her
Even before his children and his wife?

Shepherd. She goes about her house erect and calm
Between the pantry and the linen-chest,

Or else at meadow or at grazing overlooks
Her labouring men, as though her darling lived,
But for her grandson now; there is no change
But such as I have seen upon her face
Watching our shepherd sports at harvest-time
When her son's turn was over.

Goatherd. Sing your song.
I too have rhymed my reveries, but youth
Is hot to show whatever it has found,
And till that's done can neither work nor wait.
Old goatherds and old goats, if in all else
Youth can excel them in accomplishment,
Are learned in waiting.

Shepherd. You cannot but have seen
That he alone had gathered up no gear,
Set carpenters to work on no wide table,
On no long bench nor lofty milking-shed
As others will, when first they take possession,
But left the house as in his father's time
As though he knew himself, as it were, a cuckoo,
No settled man. And now that he is gone
There's nothing of him left but half a score
Of sorrowful, austere, sweet, lofty pipe tunes.

Goatherd. You have put the thought in rhyme.

Shepherd. I worked all day,
And when 'twas done so little had I done
That maybe 'I am sorry' in plain prose
Had sounded better to your mountain fancy.

(*He sings.*)

'Like the speckled bird that steers
Thousands of leagues oversea,
And runs or a while half-flies
On his yellow legs through our meadows.
He stayed for a while; and we
Had scarcely accustomed our ears

To his speech at the break of day,
Had scarcely accustomed our eyes
To his shape at the rinsing-pool
Among the evening shadows,
When he vanished from ears and eyes.
I might have wished on the day
He came, but man is a fool.'

Goatherd. You sing as always of the natural life,
And I that made like music in my youth
Hearing it now have sighed for that young man
And certain lost companions of my own.

Shepherd. They say that on your barren mountain ridge
You have measured out the road that the soul treads
When it has vanished from our natural eyes;
That you have talked with apparitions.

Goatherd. Indeed
My daily thoughts since the first stupor of youth
Have found the path my goats' feet cannot find.

Shepherd. Sing, for it may be that your thoughts have plucked
Some medicable herb to make our grief
Less bitter.

Goatherd. They have brought me from that ridge
Seed-pods and flowers that are not all wild poppy.

(*Sings.*)

'He grows younger every second
That were all his birthdays reckoned
Much too solemn seemed;
Because of what he had dreamed,
Or the ambitions that he served,
Much too solemn and reserved.
Jaunting, journeying
To his own dayspring,
He unpacks the loaded pern
Of all 'twas pain or joy to learn,

Of all that he had made.
The outrageous war shall fade;
At some old winding whitethorn root
He'll practise on the shepherd's flute,
Or on the close-cropped grass
Court his shepherd lass,
Or put his heart into some game
Till daytime, playtime seem the same;
Knowledge he shall unwind
Through victories of the mind,
Till, clambering at the cradle-side,
He dreams himself his mother's pride,
All knowledge lost in trance
Of sweeter ignorance.'

Shepherd. When I have shut these ewes and this old ram
Into the fold, we'll to the woods and there
Cut out our rhymes on strips of new-torn bark
But put no name and leave them at her door.
To know the mountain and the valley have grieved
May be a quiet thought to wife and mother,
And children when they spring up shoulder-high.

The Scholars

Bald heads forgetful of their sins,
Old, learned, respectable bald heads
Edit and annotate the lines
That young men, tossing on their beds,
Rhymed out in love's despair
To flatter beauty's ignorant ear.
All shuffle there; all cough in ink;
All wear the carpet with their shoes;
All think what other people think;
All know the man their neighbour knows.
Lord, what would they say
Did their Catullus walk that way?

Lines Written in Dejection

When have I last looked on
The round green eyes and the long wavering bodies
Of the dark leopards of the moon?
All the wild witches, those most noble ladies,
For all their broom-sticks and their tears,
Their angry tears, are gone.
The holy centaurs of the hills are vanished;
I have nothing but the embittered sun;
Banished heroic mother moon and vanished,
And now that I have come to fifty years
I must endure the timid sun.

The Dawn

I would be ignorant as the dawn
That has looked down
On that old queen measuring a town
With the pin of a brooch,
Or on the withered men that saw
From their pedantic Babylon
The careless planets in their courses,
The stars fade out where the moon comes.
And took their tablets and did sums;
I would be ignorant as the dawn
That merely stood, rocking the glittering coach
Above the cloudy shoulders of the horses;
I would be — for no knowledge is worth a straw —
Ignorant and wanton as the dawn.

On Woman

May God be praised for woman
That gives up all her mind,
A man may find in no man
A friendship of her kind
That covers all he has brought
As with her flesh and bone,
Nor quarrels with a thought
Because it is not her own.

Though pedantry denies,
It's plain the Bible means
That Solomon grew wise
While talking with his queens.
Yet never could, although
They say he counted grass,
Count all the praises due
When Sheba was his lass,
When she the iron wrought, or
When from the smithy fire
It shuddered in the water:
Harshness of their desire
That made them stretch and yawn,
pleasure that comes with sleep,
Shudder that made them one.
What else He give or keep
God grant me — no, not here,
For I am not so bold
To hope a thing so dear
Now I am growing old,
But when, if the tale's true,
The Pestle of the moon
That pounds up all anew
Brings me to birth again —
To find what once I had
And know what once I have known,
Until I am driven mad,
Sleep driven from my bed.
By tenderness and care.

Pity, an aching head,
Gnashing of teeth, despair;
And all because of some one
perverse creature of chance,
And live like Solomon
That Sheba led a dance.

The Fisherman

Although I can see him still,
The freckled man who goes
To a grey place on a hill
In grey Connemara clothes
At dawn to cast his flies,
It's long since I began
To call up to the eyes
This wise and simple man.
All day I'd looked in the face
What I had hoped 'twould be
To write for my own race
And the reality;
The living men that I hate,
The dead man that I loved,
The craven man in his seat,
The insolent unreproved,
And no knave brought to book
Who has won a drunken cheer,
The witty man and his joke
Aimed at the commonest ear,
The clever man who cries
The catch-cries of the clown,
The beating down of the wise
And great Art beaten down.

Maybe a twelvemonth since
Suddenly I began,
In scorn of this audience,
Imagining a man,
And his sun-freckled face,

And grey Connemara cloth,
Climbing up to a place
Where stone is dark under froth,
And the down-turn of his wrist
When the flies drop in the stream;
A man who does not exist,
A man who is but a dream;
And cried, 'Before I am old
I shall have written him one
poem maybe as cold
And passionate as the dawn.'

The Hawk

'Call down the hawk from the air;
Let him be hooded or caged
Till the yellow eye has grown mild,
For larder and spit are bare,
The old cook enraged,
The scullion gone wild.'

'I will not be clapped in a hood,
Nor a cage, nor alight upon wrist,
Now I have learnt to be proud
Hovering over the wood
In the broken mist
Or tumbling cloud.'

'What tumbling cloud did you cleave,
Yellow-eyed hawk of the mind,
Last evening? that I, who had sat
Dumbfounded before a knave,
Should give to my friend
A pretence of wit.

Memory

One had a lovely face,
And two or three had charm,
But charm and face were in vain
Because the mountain grass
Cannot but keep the form
Where the mountain hare has lain.

Her Praise

She is foremost of those that I would hear praised.
I have gone about the house, gone up and down
As a man does who has published a new book,
Or a young girl dressed out in her new gown,
And though I have turned the talk by hook or crook
Until her praise should be the uppermost theme,
A woman spoke of some new tale she had read,
A man confusedly in a half dream
As though some other name ran in his head.
She is foremost of those that I would hear praised.
I will talk no more of books or the long war
But walk by the dry thorn until I have found
Some beggar sheltering from the wind, and there
Manage the talk until her name come round.
If there be rags enough he will know her name
And be well pleased remembering it, for in the old days,
Though she had young men's praise and old men's blame,
Among the poor both old and young gave her praise.

The People

'What have I earned for all that work,' I said,
'For all that I have done at my own charge?
The daily spite of this unmannerly town,
Where who has served the most is most defamed,
The reputation of his lifetime lost
Between the night and morning. I might have lived,

And you know well how great the longing has been,
Where every day my footfall should have lit
In the green shadow of Ferrara wall;
Or climbed among the images of the past —
The unperturbed and courtly images —
Evening and morning, the steep street of Urbino
To where the Duchess and her people talked
The stately midnight through until they stood
In their great window looking at the dawn;
I might have had no friend that could not mix
Courtesy and passion into one like those
That saw the wicks grow yellow in the dawn;
I might have used the one substantial right
My trade allows: chosen my company,
And chosen what scenery had pleased me best,
Thereon my phoenix answered in reproof,
'The drunkards, pilferers of public funds,
All the dishonest crowd I had driven away,
When my luck changed and they dared meet my face,
Crawled from obscurity, and set upon me
Those I had served and some that I had fed;
Yet never have I, now nor any time,
Complained of the people.'

All I could reply
Was: 'You, that have not lived in thought but deed,
Can have the purity of a natural force,
But I, whose virtues are the definitions
Of the analytic mind, can neither close
The eye of the mind nor keep my tongue from speech.'
And yet, because my heart leaped at her words,
I was abashed, and now they come to mind
After nine years, I sink my head abashed.

His Phoenix

There is a queen in China, or maybe it's in Spain,
And birthdays and holidays such praises can be heard
Of her unblemished lineaments, a whiteness with no stain,

That she might be that sprightly girl trodden by a bird;
And there's a score of duchesses, surpassing womankind,
Or who have found a painter to make them so for pay
And smooth out stain and blemish with the elegance of his mind:
I knew a phoenix in my youth, so let them have their day.

The young men every night applaud their Gaby's laughing eye,
And Ruth St. Denis had more charm although she had poor luck;
From nineteen hundred nine or ten, Pavlova's had the cry
And there's a player in the States who gathers up her cloak
And flings herself out of the room when Juliet would be bride
With all a woman's passion, a child's imperious way,
And there are — but no matter if there are scores beside:
I knew a phoenix in my youth, so let them have their day.

There's Margaret and Marjorie and Dorothy and Nan,
A Daphne and a Mary who live in privacy;
One's had her fill of lovers, another's had but one,
Another boasts, 'I pick and choose and have but two or three.'
If head and limb have beauty and the instep's high and light
They can spread out what sail they please for all I have to say,
Be but the breakers of men's hearts or engines of delight:
I knew a phoenix in my youth, so let them have their day.

There'll be that crowd, that barbarous crowd, through all the
centuries,
And who can say but some young belle may walk and talk men wild
Who is my beauty's equal, though that my heart denies,
But not the exact likeness, the simplicity of a child,
And that proud look as though she had gazed into the burning sun,
And all the shapely body no tittle gone astray.
I mourn for that most lonely thing; and yet God's will be done:
I knew a phoenix in my youth, so let them have their day.

A Thought from Propertius

She might, so noble from head
To great shapely knees
The long flowing line,

Have walked to the altar
Through the holy images
At Pallas Athena's side,
Or been fit spoil for a centaur
Drunk with the unmixed wine.

Broken Dreams

There is grey in your hair.
Young men no longer suddenly catch their breath
When you are passing;
But maybe some old gaffer mutters a blessing
Because it was your prayer
Recovered him upon the bed of death.
For your sole sake — that all heart's ache have known,
And given to others all heart's ache,
From meagre girlhood's putting on
Burdensome beauty — for your sole sake
Heaven has put away the stroke of her doom,
So great her portion in that peace you make
By merely walking in a room.

Your beauty can but leave among us
Vague memories, nothing but memories.
A young man when the old men are done talking
Will say to an old man, 'Tell me of that lady
The poet stubborn with his passion sang us
When age might well have chilled his blood.'

Vague memories, nothing but memories,
But in the grave all, all, shall be renewed.
The certainty that I shall see that lady
Leaning or standing or walking
In the first loveliness of womanhood,
And with the fervour of my youthful eyes,
Has set me muttering like a fool.

You are more beautiful than any one,
And yet your body had a flaw:

Your small hands were not beautiful,
And I am afraid that you will run
And paddle to the wrist
In that mysterious, always brimming lake
Where those that have obeyed the holy law
Paddle and are perfect. Leave unchanged
The hands that I have kissed,
For old sake's sake.

The last stroke of midnight dies.
All day in the one chair
From dream to dream and rhyme to rhyme I have ranged
In rambling talk with an image of air:
Vague memories, nothing but memories.

A Deep-sworn Vow

Others because you did not keep
That deep-sworn vow have been friends of mine;
Yet always when I look death in the face,
When I clamber to the heights of sleep,
Or when I grow excited with wine,
Suddenly I meet your face.

Presences

This night has been so strange that it seemed
As if the hair stood up on my head.
From going-down of the sun I have dreamed
That women laughing, or timid or wild,
In rustle of lace or silken stuff,
Climbed up my creaking stair. They had read
All I had rhymed of that monstrous thing
Returned and yet unrequited love.
They stood in the door and stood between
My great wood lectern and the fire
Till I could hear their hearts beating:
One is a harlot, and one a child

That never looked upon man with desire.
And one, it may be, a queen.

The Balloon of the Mind

Hands, do what you're bid:
Bring the balloon of the mind
That bellies and drags in the wind
Into its narrow shed.

To a Squirrel at Kyle-Na-No

Come play with me;
Why should you run
Through the shaking tree
As though I'd a gun
To strike you dead?
When all I would do
Is to scratch your head
And let you go.

On Being Asked for a War Poem

I think it better that in times like these
A poet's mouth be silent, for in truth
We have no gift to set a statesman right;
He has had enough of meddling who can please
A young girl in the indolence of her youth,
Or an old man upon a winter's night.

In Memory of Alfred Pollexfen

Five-and-twenty years have gone
Since old William Pollexfen
Laid his strong bones down in death
By his wife Elizabeth

In the grey stone tomb he made.
And after twenty years they laid
In that tomb by him and her
His son George, the astrologer;
And Masons drove from miles away
To scatter the Acacia spray
Upon a melancholy man
Who had ended where his breath began.
Many a son and daughter lies
Far from the customary skies,
The Mall and Eades's grammar school,
In London or in Liverpool;
But where is laid the sailor John
That so many lands had known,
Quiet lands or unquiet seas
Where the Indians trade or Japanese?
He never found his rest ashore,
Moping for one voyage more.
Where have they laid the sailor John?
And yesterday the youngest son,
A humorous, unambitious man,
Was buried near the astrologer,
Yesterday in the tenth year
Since he who had been contented long,
A nobody in a great throng,
Decided he would journey home,
Now that his fiftieth year had come,
And 'Mr. Alfred' be again
Upon the lips of common men
Who carried in their memory
His childhood and his family.
At all these death-beds women heard
A visionary white sea-bird
Lamenting that a man should die;
And with that cry I have raised my cry.

Upon a Dying Lady

I

Her Courtesy

With the old kindness, the old distinguished grace,
She lies, her lovely piteous head amid dull red hair
propped upon pillows, rouge on the pallor of her face.
She would not have us sad because she is lying there,
And when she meets our gaze her eyes are laughter-lit,
Her speech a wicked tale that we may vie with her,
Matching our broken-hearted wit against her wit,
Thinking of saints and of Petronius Arbiter.

II

Curtain Artist Bring Her Dolls And Drawings

Bring where our Beauty lies
A new modelled doll, or drawing,
With a friend's or an enemy's
Features, or maybe showing
Her features when a tress
Of dull red hair was flowing
Over some silken dress
Cut in the Turkish fashion,
Or, it may be, like a boy's.
We have given the world our passion,
We have naught for death but toys.

III

She Turns the Dolls' Faces to the Wall

Because to-day is some religious festival
They had a priest say Mass, and even the Japanese,
Heel up and weight on toe, must face the wall
— Pedant in passion, learned in old courtesies,
Vehement and witty she had seemed — ; the Venetian lady
Who had seemed to glide to some intrigue in her red shoes,
Her domino, her panniered skirt copied from Longhi;
The meditative critic; all are on their toes,
Even our Beauty with her Turkish trousers on.
Because the priest must have like every dog his day
Or keep us all awake with baying at the moon,
We and our dolls being but the world were best away.

IV

The End of Day

She is playing like a child
And penance is the play,
Fantastical and wild
Because the end of day
Shows her that some one soon
Will come from the house, and say —
Though play is but half done —
'Come in and leave the play.'

V

Her Race

She has not grown uncivil
As narrow natures would
And called the pleasures evil
Happier days thought good;
She knows herself a woman,
No red and white of a face,
Or rank, raised from a common
Unreckonable race;
And how should her heart fail her
Or sickness break her will
With her dead brother's valour
For an example still?

VI

Her Courage

When her soul flies to the predestined dancing-place
(I have no speech but symbol, the pagan speech I made
Amid the dreams of youth) let her come face to face,
Amid that first astonishment, with Grania's shade,
All but the terrors of the woodland flight forgot
That made her Diarmuid dear, and some old cardinal
Pacing with half-closed eyelids in a sunny spot
Who had murmured of Giorgione at his latest breath —
Aye, and Achilles, Timor, Babar, Barhaim, all
Who have lived in joy and laughed into the face of Death.

VII

Her Friends Bring Her a Christmas Tree

Pardon, great enemy,
Without an angry thought
We've carried in our tree,
And here and there have bought
Till all the boughs are gay,
And she may look from the bed
On pretty things that may
please a fantastic head.
Give her a little grace,
What if a laughing eye
Have looked into your face?
It is about to die.

Ego Dominus Tuus

Hic. On the grey sand beside the shallow stream
Under your old wind-beaten tower, where still
A lamp burns on beside the open book
That Michael Robartes left, you walk in the moon,
And, though you have passed the best of life, still trace,
Enthralled by the unconquerable delusion,
Magical shapes.

Ille. By the help of an image
I call to my own opposite, summon all
That I have handled least, least looked upon.

Hic. And I would find myself and not an image.

Ille. That is our modern hope, and by its light
We have lit upon the gentle, sensitive mind
And lost the old nonchalance of the hand;
Whether we have chosen chisel, pen or brush,
We are but critics, or but half create,
Timid, entangled, empty and abashed,
Lacking the countenance of our friends.

Hic. And yet
The chief imagination of Christendom,
Dante Alighieri, so utterly found himself
That he has made that hollow face of his
More plain to the mind's eye than any face
But that of Christ.

Ille. And did he find himself
Or was the hunger that had made it hollow
A hunger for the apple on the bough
Most out of reach? and is that spectral image
The man that Lapo and that Guido knew?
I think he fashioned from his opposite
An image that might have been a stony face
Staring upon a Bedouin's horse-hair roof
From doored and windowed cliff, or half upturned
Among the coarse grass and the camel-dung.
He set his chisel to the hardest stone.
Being mocked by Guido for his lecherous life,
Derided and deriding, driven out
To climb that stair and eat that bitter bread,
He found the unpersuadable justice, he found
The most exalted lady loved by a man.

Hic. Yet surely there are men who have made their art
Out of no tragic war, lovers of life,
Impulsive men that look for happiness
And sing when they have found it.

Ille. No, not sing,
For those that love the world serve it in action,
Grow rich, popular and full of influence,
And should they paint or write, still it is action:
The struggle of the fly in marmalade.
The rhetorician would deceive his neighbours,
The sentimentalist himself; while art
Is but a vision of reality.
What portion in the world can the artist have
Who has awakened from the common dream
But dissipation and despair?

Hic. And yet
No one denies to Keats love of the world;
Remember his deliberate happiness.

Ille. His art is happy, but who knows his mind?
I see a schoolboy when I think of him,
With face and nose pressed to a sweet-shop window,
For certainly he sank into his grave
His senses and his heart unsatisfied,
And made — being poor, ailing and ignorant,
Shut out from all the luxury of the world,
The coarse-bred son of a livery-stable keeper —
Luxuriant song.

Hic. Why should you leave the lamp
Burning alone beside an open book,
And trace these characters upon the sands?
A style is found by sedentary toil
And by the imitation of great masters.

Ille. Because I seek an image, not a book.
Those men that in their writings are most wise,
Own nothing but their blind, stupefied hearts.
I call to the mysterious one who yet
Shall walk the wet sands by the edge of the stream
And look most like me, being indeed my double,
And prove of all imaginable things
The most unlike, being my anti-self,
And, standing by these characters, disclose
All that I seek; and whisper it as though
He were afraid the birds, who cry aloud
Their momentary cries before it is dawn,
Would carry it away to blasphemous men.

A Prayer on Going into My House

God grant a blessing on this tower and cottage
And on my heirs, if all remain unspoiled,
No table or chair or stool not simple enough

For shepherd lads in Galilee; and grant
That I myself for portions of the year
May handle nothing and set eyes on nothing
But what the great and passionate have used
Throughout so many varying centuries
We take it for the norm; yet should I dream
Sinbad the sailor's brought a painted chest,
Or image, from beyond the Loadstone Mountain,
That dream is a norm; and should some limb of the Devil
Destroy the view by cutting down an ash
That shades the road, or setting up a cottage
Planned in a government office, shorten his life,
Manacle his soul upon the Red Sea bottom.

The Phases of the Moon

An old man cocked his ear upon a bridge;
He and his friend, their faces to the South,
Had trod the uneven road. Their boots were soiled,
Their Connemara cloth worn out of shape;
They had kept a steady pace as though their beds,
Despite a dwindling and late-risen moon,
Were distant still. An old man cocked his ear.

Aherne. What made that Sound?

Robartes. A rat or water-hen
Splashed, or an otter slid into the stream.
We are on the bridge; that shadow is the tower,
And the light proves that he is reading still.
He has found, after the manner of his kind,
Mere images; chosen this place to live in
Because, it may be, of the candle-light
From the far tower where Milton's Platonist
Sat late, or Shelley's visionary prince:
The lonely light that Samuel Palmer engraved,
An image of mysterious wisdom won by toil;
And now he seeks in book or manuscript
What he shall never find.

Aherne. Why should not you
Who know it all ring at his door, and speak
Just truth enough to show that his whole life
Will scarcely find for him a broken crust
Of all those truths that are your daily bread;
And when you have spoken take the roads again?

Robartes. He wrote of me in that extravagant style
He had learnt from pater, and to round his tale
Said I was dead; and dead I choose to be.

Aherne. Sing me the changes of the moon once more;
True song, though speech: 'mine author sung it me.'

Robartes. Twenty-and-eight the phases of the moon,
The full and the moon's dark and all the crescents,
Twenty-and-eight, and yet but six-and-twenty
The cradles that a man must needs be rocked in:
For there's no human life at the full or the dark.
From the first crescent to the half, the dream
But summons to adventure and the man
Is always happy like a bird or a beast;
But while the moon is rounding towards the full
He follows whatever whim's most difficult
Among whims not impossible, and though scarred.
As with the cat-o'-nine-tails of the mind,
His body moulded from within his body
Grows comelier. Eleven pass, and then
Athena takes Achilles by the hair,
Hector is in the dust, Nietzsche is born,
Because the hero's crescent is the twelfth.
And yet, twice born, twice buried, grow he must,
Before the full moon, helpless as a worm.
The thirteenth moon but sets the soul at war
In its own being, and when that war's begun
There is no muscle in the arm; and after,
Under the frenzy of the fourteenth moon,
The soul begins to tremble into stillness,
To die into the labyrinth of itself!

Aherne. Sing out the song; sing to the end, and sing
The strange reward of all that discipline.

Robartes. All thought becomes an image and the soul
Becomes a body: that body and that soul
Too perfect at the full to lie in a cradle,
Too lonely for the traffic of the world:
Body and soul cast out and cast away
Beyond the visible world.

Aherne. All dreams of the soul
End in a beautiful man's or woman's body.

Robartes. Have you not always known it?

Aherne. The song will have it
That those that we have loved got their long fingers
From death, and wounds, or on Sinai's top,
Or from some bloody whip in their own hands.
They ran from cradle to cradle till at last
Their beauty dropped out of the loneliness
Of body and soul.

Robartes. The lover's heart knows that.

Aherne. It must be that the terror in their eyes
Is memory or foreknowledge of the hour
When all is fed with light and heaven is bare.

Robartes. When the moon's full those creatures of the full
Are met on the waste hills by countrymen
Who shudder and hurry by: body and soul
Estranged amid the strangeness of themselves,
Caught up in contemplation, the mind's eye
Fixed upon images that once were thought;
For separate, perfect, and immovable
Images can break the solitude
Of lovely, satisfied, indifferent eyes.

And thereupon with aged, high-pitched voice
Aherne laughed, thinking of the man within,
His sleepless candle and laborious pen.

Robartes. And after that the crumbling of the moon.
The soul remembering its loneliness
Shudders in many cradles; all is changed,
It would be the world's servant, and as it serves,
Choosing whatever task's most difficult
Among tasks not impossible, it takes
Upon the body and upon the soul
The coarseness of the drudge.

Aherne. Before the full
It sought itself and afterwards the world.

Robartes. Because you are forgotten, half out of life,
And never wrote a book, your thought is clear.
Reformer, merchant, statesman, learned man,
Dutiful husband, honest wife by turn,
Cradle upon cradle, and all in flight and all
Deformed because there is no deformity
But saves us from a dream.

Aherne. And what of those
That the last servile crescent has set free?

Robartes. Because all dark, like those that are all light,
They are cast beyond the verge, and in a cloud,
Crying to one another like the bats;
And having no desire they cannot tell
What's good or bad, or what it is to triumph
At the perfection of one's own obedience;
And yet they speak what's blown into the mind;
Deformed beyond deformity, unformed,
Insipid as the dough before it is baked,
They change their bodies at a word.

Ahcrne. And then?

Rohartes. When all the dough has been so kneaded up
That it can take what form cook Nature fancies,
The first thin crescent is wheeled round once more.

Aherne. But the escape; the song's not finished yet.

Robartes. Hunchback and Saint and Fool are the last crescents.
The burning bow that once could shoot an arrow
Out of the up and down, the wagon-wheel
Of beauty's cruelty and wisdom's chatter —
Out of that raving tide — is drawn betwixt
Deformity of body and of mind.

Aherne. Were not our beds far off I'd ring the bell,
Stand under the rough roof-timbers of the hall
Beside the castle door, where all is stark
Austerity, a place set out for wisdom
That he will never find; I'd play a part;
He would never know me after all these years
But take me for some drunken countryman;
I'd stand and mutter there until he caught
'Hunchback and Saint and Fool,' and that they came
Under the three last crescents of the moon.
And then I'd stagger out. He'd crack his wits
Day after day, yet never find the meaning.

And then he laughed to think that what seemed hard
Should be so simple — a bat rose from the hazels
And circled round him with its squeaky cry,
The light in the tower window was put out.

The Cat And the Moon

The cat went here and there
And the moon spun round like a top,
And the nearest kin of the moon,
The creeping cat, looked up.
Black Minnaloushe stared at the moon,
For, wander and wail as he would,
The pure cold light in the sky
Troubled his animal blood.
Minnaloushe runs in the grass
Lifting his delicate feet.

Do you dance, Minnaloushe, do you dance?
When two close kindred meet.
What better than call a dance?
Maybe the moon may learn,
Tired of that courtly fashion,
A new dance turn.
Minnaloushe creeps through the grass
From moonlit place to place,
The sacred moon overhead
Has taken a new phase.
Does Minnaloushe know that his pupils
Will pass from change to change,
And that from round to crescent,
From crescent to round they range?
Minnaloushe creeps through the grass
Alone, important and wise,
And lifts to the changing moon
His changing eyes.

The Saint And the Hunchback

Hunchback. Stand up and lift your hand and bless
A man that finds great bitterness
In thinking of his lost renown.
A Roman Caesar is held down
Under this hump.

Saint. God tries each man
According to a different plan.
I shall not cease to bless because
I lay about me with the taws
That night and morning I may thrash
Greek Alexander from my flesh,
Augustus Caesar, and after these
That great rogue Alcibiades.

Hunchback. To all that in your flesh have stood
And blessed, I give my gratitude,
Honoured by all in their degrees,
But most to Alcibiades.

Two Songs of a Fool

I

A speckled cat and a tame hare
Eat at my hearthstone
And sleep there;
And both look up to me alone
For learning and defence
As I look up to Providence.

I start out of my sleep to think
Some day I may forget
Their food and drink;
Or, the house door left unshut,
The hare may run till it's found
The horn's sweet note and the tooth of the hound.

I bear a burden that might well try
Men that do all by rule,
And what can I
That am a wandering-witted fool
But pray to God that He ease
My great responsibilities?

II

I slept on my three-legged stool by the fire,
The speckled cat slept on my knee;
We never thought to enquire
Where the brown hare might be,
And whether the door were shut.
Who knows how she drank the wind
Stretched up on two legs from the mat,
Before she had settled her mind
To drum with her heel and to leap?
Had I but awakened from sleep
And called her name, she had heard,
It may be, and not have stirred,
That now, it may be, has found
The horn's sweet note and the tooth of the hound.

Another Song of a Fool

This great purple butterfly,
In the prison of my hands,
Has a learning in his eye
Not a poor fool understands.

Once he lived a schoolmaster
With a stark, denying look;
A string of scholars went in fear
Of his great birch and his great book.

Like the clangour of a bell,
Sweet and harsh, harsh and sweet.
That is how he learnt so well
To take the roses for his meat.

The Double Vision of Michael Robartes

I
On the grey rock of Cashel the mind's eye
Has called up the cold spirits that are born
When the old moon is vanished from the sky
And the new still hides her horn.

Under blank eyes and fingers never still
The particular is pounded till it is man.
When had I my own will?
O not since life began.

Constrained, arraigned, baffled, bent and unbent
By these wire-jointed jaws and limbs of wood,
Themselves obedient,
Knowing not evil and good;

Obedient to some hidden magical breath.
They do not even feel, so abstract are they.
So dead beyond our death,
Triumph that we obey.

II

On the grey rock of Cashel I suddenly saw
A Sphinx with woman breast and lion paw.
A Buddha, hand at rest,
Hand lifted up that blest;

And right between these two a girl at play
That, it may be, had danced her life away,
For now being dead it seemed
That she of dancing dreamed.

Although I saw it all in the mind's eye
There can be nothing solider till I die;
I saw by the moon's light
Now at its fifteenth night.

One lashed her tail; her eyes lit by the moon
Gazed upon all things known, all things unknown,
In triumph of intellect
With motionless head erect.

That other's moonlit eyeballs never moved,
Being fixed on all things loved, all things unloved.
Yet little peace he had,
For those that love are sad.

O little did they care who danced between,
And little she by whom her dance was seen
So she had outdanced thought.
Body perfection brought,

For what but eye and ear silence the mind
With the minute particulars of mankind?
Mind moved yet seemed to stop
As 'twere a spinning-top.

In contemplation had those three so wrought
Upon a moment, and so stretched it out
That they, time overthrown,
Were dead yet flesh and bone.

III

I knew that I had seen, had seen at last
That girl my unremembering nights hold fast
Or else my dreams that fly
If I should rub an eye,

And yet in flying fling into my meat
A crazy juice that makes the pulses beat
As though I had been undone
By Homer's Paragon

Who never gave the burning town a thought;
To such a pitch of folly I am brought,
Being caught between the pull
Of the dark moon and the full,

The commonness of thought and images
That have the frenzy of our western seas.
Thereon I made my moan,
And after kissed a stone,

And after that arranged it in a song
Seeing that I, ignorant for so long,
Had been rewarded thus
In Cormac's ruined house.

MICHAEL ROBARTES AND THE DANCER
1921

Michael Robartes And the Dancer

He. Opinion is not worth a rush;
    In this altar-piece the knight,
    Who grips his long spear so to push
    That dragon through the fading light,
    Loved the lady; and it's plain
    The half-dead dragon was her thought,
    That every morning rose again
    And dug its claws and shrieked and fought.
    Could the impossible come to pass
    She would have time to turn her eyes,
    Her lover thought, upon the glass
    And on the instant would grow wise.

She. You mean they argued.

He.   Put it so;
    But bear in mind your lover's wage
    Is what your looking-glass can show,
    And that he will turn green with rage
    At all that is not pictured there.

She. May I not put myself to college?

He. Go pluck Athena by the hair;
    For what mere book can grant a knowledge
    With an impassioned gravity
    Appropriate to that beating breast,
    That vigorous thigh, that dreaming eye?

And may the Devil take the rest.

She. And must no beautiful woman be
Learned like a man?

He. Paul Veronese
And all his sacred company
Imagined bodies all their days
By the lagoon you love so much,
For proud, soft, ceremonious proof
That all must come to sight and touch;
While Michael Angelo's Sistine roof,
His 'Morning' and his 'Night' disclose
How sinew that has been pulled tight,
Or it may be loosened in repose,
Can rule by supernatural right
Yet be but sinew.

She. I have heard said
There is great danger in the body.

He. Did God in portioning wine and bread
Give man His thought or His mere body?

She. My wretched dragon is perplexed.

He. I have principles to prove me right.
It follows from this Latin text
That blest souls are not composite,
And that all beautiful women may
Live in uncomposite blessedness,
And lead us to the like — if they
Will banish every thought, unless
The lineaments that please their view
When the long looking-glass is full,
Even from the foot-sole think it too.

She. They say such different things at school.

Solomon and the Witch

And thus declared that Arab lady:
'Last night, where under the wild moon
On grassy mattress I had laid me,
Within my arms great Solomon,
I suddenly cried out in a strange tongue
Not his, not mine.'
                                        Who understood
Whatever has been said, sighed, sung,
Howled, miau-d, barked, brayed, belled, yelled, cried, crowed,
Thereon replied: 'A cockerel
Crew from a blossoming apple bough
Three hundred years before the Fall,
And never crew again till now,
And would not now but that he thought,
Chance being at one with Choice at last,
All that the brigand apple brought
And this foul world were dead at last.
He that crowed out eternity
Thought to have crowed it in again.
For though love has a spider's eye
To find out some appropriate pain —
Aye, though all passion's in the glance —
For every nerve, and tests a lover
With cruelties of Choice and Chance;
And when at last that murder's over
Maybe the bride-bed brings despair,
For each an imagined image brings
And finds a real image there;
Yet the world ends when these two things,
Though several, are a single light,
When oil and wick are burned in one;
Therefore a blessed moon last night
Gave Sheba to her Solomon.'

'Yet the world stays.'
                                        'If that be so,
Your cockerel found us in the wrong
Although he thought it worth a crow.

Maybe an image is too strong
Or maybe is not strong enough.'

'The night has fallen; not a sound
In the forbidden sacred grove
Unless a petal hit the ground,
Nor any human sight within it
But the crushed grass where we have lain!
And the moon is wilder every minute.
O! Solomon! let us try again.'

An Image from a Past Life

He. Never until this night have I been stirred.
The elaborate starlight throws a reflection
On the dark stream,
Till all the eddies gleam;
And thereupon there comes that scream
From terrified, invisible beast or bird:
Image of poignant recollection.

She. An image of my heart that is smitten through
Out of all likelihood, or reason,
And when at last,
Youth's bitterness being past,
I had thought that all my days were cast
Amid most lovely places; smitten as though
It had not learned its lesson.

He. Why have you laid your hands upon my eyes?
What can have suddenly alarmed you
Whereon 'twere best
My eyes should never rest?
What is there but the slowly fading west,
The river imaging the flashing skies,
All that to this moment charmed you?

She. A sweetheart from another life floats there
As though she had been forced to linger

From vague distress
Or arrogant loveliness,
Merely to loosen out a tress
Among the starry eddies of her hair
Upon the paleness of a finger.

He. But why should you grow suddenly afraid
And start — I at your shoulder —
Imagining
That any night could bring
An image up, or anything
Even to eyes that beauty had driven mad,
But images to make me fonder?

She. Now she has thrown her arms above her head;
Whether she threw them up to flout me,
Or but to find,
Now that no fingers bind,
That her hair streams upon the wind,
I do not know, that know I am afraid
Of the hovering thing night brought me.

Under Saturn

Do not because this day I have grown saturnine
Imagine that lost love, inseparable from my thought
Because I have no other youth, can make me pine;
For how should I forget the wisdom that you brought,
The comfort that you made? Although my wits have gone
On a fantastic ride, my horse's flanks are spurred
By childish memories of an old cross Pollexfen,
And of a Middleton, whose name you never heard,
And of a red-haired Yeats whose looks, although he died
Before my time, seem like a vivid memory.
You heard that labouring man who had served my people. He said
Upon the open road, near to the Sligo quay —
No, no, not said, but cried it out — 'You have come again,
And surely after twenty years it was time to come.'

I am thinking of a child's vow sworn in vain
Never to leave that valley his fathers called their home.

Easter 1916

I have met them at close of day
Coming with vivid faces
From counter or desk among grey
Eighteenth-century houses.
I have passed with a nod of the head
Or polite meaningless words,
Or have lingered awhile and said
Polite meaningless words,
And thought before I had done
Of a mocking tale or a gibe
To please a companion
Around the fire at the club,
Being certain that they and I
But lived where motley is worn:
All changed, changed utterly:
A terrible beauty is born.

That woman's days were spent
In ignorant good will,
Her nights in argument
Until her voice grew shrill.
What voice more sweet than hers
When young and beautiful,
She rode to harriers?
This man had kept a school
And rode our winged horse;
This other his helper and friend
Was coming into his force;
He might have won fame in the end,
So sensitive his nature seemed,
So daring and sweet his thought.
This other man I had dreamed
A drunken, vainglorious lout.
He had done most bitter wrong

To some who are near my heart,
Yet I number him in the song;
He, too, has resigned his part
In the casual comedy;
He, too, has been changed in his turn,
Transformed utterly:
A terrible beauty is born.

Hearts with one purpose alone
Through summer and winter, seem
Enchanted to a stone
To trouble the living stream.
The horse that comes from the road,
The rider, the birds that range
From cloud to tumbling cloud,
Minute by minute change;
A shadow of cloud on the stream
Changes minute by minute;
A horse-hoof slides on the brim,
And a horse plashes within it;
Where long-legged moor-hens dive
And hens to moor-cocks call;
Minute by minute they live:
The stone's in the midst of all.

Too long a sacrifice
Can make a stone of the heart.
O when may it suffice?
That is heaven's part, our part
To murmur name upon name,
As a mother names her child
When sleep at last has come
On limbs that had run wild.
What is it but nightfall?
No, no, not night but death;
Was it needless death after all?
For England may keep faith
For all that is done and said.
We know their dream; enough
To know they dreamed and are dead;

And what if excess of love
Bewildered them till they died?
I write it out in a verse —
MacDonagh and MacBride
And Connolly and Pearse
Now and in time to be,
Wherever green is worn,
Are changed, changed utterly:
A terrible beauty is born.

Sixteen Dead Men

O but we talked at large before
The sixteen men were shot,
But who can talk of give and take,
What should be and what not
While those dead men are loitering there
To stir the boiling pot?

You say that we should still the land
Till Germany's overcome;
But who is there to argue that
Now Pearse is deaf and dumb?
And is their logic to outweigh
MacDonagh's bony thumb?

How could you dream they'd listen
That have an ear alone
For those new comrades they have found,
Lord Edward and Wolfe Tone,
Or meddle with our give and take
That converse bone to bone?

The Rose Tree

'O words are lightly spoken,'
Said Pearse to Connolly,
'Maybe a breath of politic words
Has withered our Rose Tree;

Or maybe but a wind that blows
Across the bitter sea.'

'It needs to be but watered,'
James Connolly replied,
'To make the green come out again
And spread on every side,
And shake the blossom from the bud
To be the garden's pride.'

'But where can we draw water,'
Said Pearse to Connolly,
'When all the wells are parched away?
O plain as plain can be
There's nothing but our own red blood
Can make a right Rose Tree.'

On a Political Prisoner

She that but little patience knew,
From childhood on, had now so much
A grey gull lost its fear and flew
Down to her cell and there alit,
And there endured her fingers' touch
And from her fingers ate its bit.

Did she in touching that lone wing
Recall the years before her mind
Became a bitter, an abstract thing,
Her thought some popular enmity:
Blind and leader of the blind
Drinking the foul ditch where they lie?

When long ago I saw her ride
Under Ben Bulben to the meet,
The beauty of her country-side
With all youth's lonely wildness stirred,
She seemed to have grown clean and sweet
Like any rock-bred, sea-borne bird:

Sea-borne, or balanced on the air
When first it sprang out of the nest
Upon some lofty rock to stare
Upon the cloudy canopy,
While under its storm-beaten breast
Cried out the hollows of the sea.

The Leaders of the Crowd

They must to keep their certainty accuse
All that are different of a base intent;
Pull down established honour; hawk for news
Whatever their loose fantasy invent
And murmur it with bated breath, as though
The abounding gutter had been Helicon
Or calumny a song. How can they know
Truth flourishes where the student's lamp has shone,
And there alone, that have no solitude?
So the crowd come they care not what may come.
They have loud music, hope every day renewed
And heartier loves; that lamp is from the tomb.

Towards Break of Day

Was it the double of my dream
The woman that by me lay
Dreamed, or did we halve a dream
Under the first cold gleam of day?

I thought: 'There is a waterfall
Upon Ben Bulben side
That all my childhood counted dear;
Were I to travel far and wide
I could not find a thing so dear.'
My memories had magnified
So many times childish delight.

I would have touched it like a child
But knew my finger could but have touched
Cold stone and water. I grew wild.
Even accusing Heaven because
It had set down among its laws:
Nothing that we love over-much
Is ponderable to our touch.

I dreamed towards break of day,
The cold blown spray in my nostril.
But she that beside me lay
Had watched in bitterer sleep
The marvellous stag of Arthur,
That lofty white stag, leap
From mountain steep to steep.

Demon And Beast

For certain minutes at the least
That crafty demon and that loud beast
That plague me day and night
Ran out of my sight;
Though I had long perned in the gyre,
Between my hatred and desire.
I saw my freedom won
And all laugh in the sun.

The glittering eyes in a death's head
Of old Luke Wadding's portrait said
Welcome, and the Ormondes all
Nodded upon the wall,
And even Strafford smiled as though
It made him happier to know
I understood his plan.
Now that the loud beast ran
There was no portrait in the Gallery
But beckoned to sweet company,
For all men's thoughts grew clear
Being dear as mine are dear.

But soon a tear-drop started up,
For aimless joy had made me stop
Beside the little lake
To watch a white gull take
A bit of bread thrown up into the air;
Now gyring down and perning there
He splashed where an absurd
Portly green-pated bird
Shook off the water from his back;
Being no more demoniac
A stupid happy creature
Could rouse my whole nature.

Yet I am certain as can be
That every natural victory
Belongs to beast or demon,
That never yet had freeman
Right mastery of natural things,
And that mere growing old, that brings
Chilled blood, this sweetness brought;
Yet have no dearer thought
Than that I may find out a way
To make it linger half a day.

O what a sweetness strayed
Through barren Thebaid,
Or by the Mareotic sea
When that exultant Anthony
And twice a thousand more
Starved upon the shore
And withered to a bag of bones!
What had the Caesars but their thrones?

The Second Coming

Turning and turning in the widening gyre
The falcon cannot hear the falconer;
Things fall apart; the centre cannot hold;
Mere anarchy is loosed upon the world,

The blood-dimmed tide is loosed, and everywhere
The ceremony of innocence is drowned;
The best lack all conviction, while the worst
Are full of passionate intensity.
Surely some revelation is at hand;
Surely the Second Coming is at hand.
The Second Coming! Hardly are those words out
When a vast image out of *Spiritus Mundi*
Troubles my sight: somewhere in sands of the desert
A shape with lion body and the head of a man,
A gaze blank and pitiless as the sun,
Is moving its slow thighs, while all about it
Reel shadows of the indignant desert birds.
The darkness drops again; but now I know
That twenty centuries of stony sleep
Were vexed to nightmare by a rocking cradle,
And what rough beast, its hour come round at last,
Slouches towards Bethlehem to be born?

A Prayer for My Daughter

Once more the storm is howling, and half hid
Under this cradle-hood and coverlid
My child sleeps on. There is no obstacle
But Gregory's wood and one bare hill
Whereby the haystack- and roof-levelling wind,
Bred on the Atlantic, can be stayed;
And for an hour I have walked and prayed
Because of the great gloom that is in my mind.

I have walked and prayed for this young child an hour
And heard the sea-wind scream upon the tower,
And under the arches of the bridge, and scream
In the elms above the flooded stream;
Imagining in excited reverie
That the future years had come,
Dancing to a frenzied drum,
Out of the murderous innocence of the sea.

May she be granted beauty and yet not
Beauty to make a stranger's eye distraught,
Or hers before a looking-glass, for such,
Being made beautiful overmuch,
Consider beauty a sufficient end,
Lose natural kindness and maybe
The heart-revealing intimacy
That chooses right, and never find a friend.

Helen being chosen found life flat and dull
And later had much trouble from a fool,
While that great Queen, that rose out of the spray,
Being fatherless could have her way
Yet chose a bandy-legged smith for man.
It's certain that fine women eat
A crazy salad with their meat
Whereby the Horn of Plenty is undone.

In courtesy I'd have her chiefly learned;
Hearts are not had as a gift but hearts are earned
By those that are not entirely beautiful;
Yet many, that have played the fool
For beauty's very self, has charm made wise,
And many a poor man that has roved,
Loved and thought himself beloved,
From a glad kindness cannot take his eyes.

May she become a flourishing hidden tree
That all her thoughts may like the linnet be,
And have no business but dispensing round
Their magnanimities of sound,
Nor but in merriment begin a chase,
Nor but in merriment a quarrel.
O may she live like some green laurel
Rooted in one dear perpetual place.

My mind, because the minds that I have loved,
The sort of beauty that I have approved,
Prosper but little, has dried up of late,
Yet knows that to be choked with hate

May well be of all evil chances chief.
If there's no hatred in a mind
Assault and battery of the wind
Can never tear the linnet from the leaf.

An intellectual hatred is the worst,
So let her think opinions are accursed.
Have I not seen the loveliest woman born
Out of the mouth of Plenty's horn,
Because of her opinionated mind
Barter that horn and every good
By quiet natures understood
For an old bellows full of angry wind?

Considering that, all hatred driven hence,
The soul recovers radical innocence
And learns at last that it is self-delighting,
Self-appeasing, self-affrighting,
And that its own sweet will is Heaven's will;
She can, though every face should scowl
And every windy quarter howl
Or every bellows burst, be happy still.

And may her bridegroom bring her to a house
Where all's accustomed, ceremonious;
For arrogance and hatred are the wares
Peddled in the thoroughfares.
How but in custom and in ceremony
Are innocence and beauty born?
Ceremony's a name for the rich horn,
And custom for the spreading laurel tree.

A Meditation in Time of War

For one throb of the artery,
While on that old grey stone I sat
Under the old wind-broken tree,
I knew that One is animate,
Mankind inanimate fantasy.

To Be Carved on a Stone at Thoor Ballylee

I, the poet William Yeats,
With old mill boards and sea-green slates,
And smithy work from the Gort forge,
Restored this tower for my wife George;
And may these characters remain
When all is ruin once again.

THE TOWER
1928

Sailing to Byzantium

I
That is no country for old men. The young
In one another's arms, birds in the trees,
— Those dying generations — at their song,
The salmon falls, the mackerel-crowded seas,
Fish, flesh, or fowl, commend all summer long
Whatever is begotten, born, or dies.
Caught in that sensual music, all neglect
Monuments of unaging intellect.

II
An aged man is but a paltry thing,
A tattered coat upon a stick, unless
Soul clap its hands and sing, and louder sing
For every tatter in its mortal dress,
Nor is there singing school but studying
Monuments of its own magnificence;
And therefore I have sailed the seas and come
To the holy city of Byzantium.

III
O sages standing in God's holy fire
As in the gold mosaic of a wall,
Come from the holy fire, perne in a gyre,
And be the singing-masters of my soul.
Consume my heart away; sick with desire
And fastened to a dying animal
It knows not what it is; and gather me
Into the artifice of eternity.

IV
Once out of nature I shall never take
My bodily form from any natural thing,
But such a form as Grecian goldsmiths make
Of hammered gold, and gold enamelling
To keep a drowsy emperor awake;
Or set upon a golden bough to sing
To lords and ladies of Byzantium
Of what is past, or passing, or to come.

The Tower

I
What shall I do with this absurdity —
O heart, O troubled heart — this caricature,
Decrepit age that has been tied to me
As to a dog's tail?
                                        Never had I more
Excited, passionate, fantastical
Imagination, nor an ear and eye
That more expected the impossible -
No, not in boyhood when with rod and fly,
Or the humbler worm, I climbed Ben Bulben's back
And had the livelong summer day to spend.
It seems that I must bid the Muse go pack,
Choose Plato and Plotinus for a friend
Until imagination, ear and eye,
Can be content with argument and deal
In abstract things; or be derided by
A sort of battered kettle at the heel.

II
I pace upon the battlements and stare
On the foundations of a house, or where
Tree, like a sooty finger, starts from the earth;
And send imagination forth
Under the day's declining beam, and call
Images and memories
From ruin or from ancient trees,
For I would ask a question of them all.

Beyond that ridge lived Mrs. French, and once
When every silver candlestick or sconce
Lit up the dark mahogany and the wine,
A serving-man, that could divine
That most respected lady's every wish,
Ran and with the garden shears
Clipped an insolent farmer's ears
And brought them in a little covered dish.

Some few remembered still when I was young
A peasant girl commended by a song,
Who'd lived somewhere upon that rocky place,
And praised the colour of her face,
And had the greater joy in praising her,
Remembering that, if walked she there,
Farmers jostled at the fair
So great a glory did the song confer.

And certain men, being maddened by those rhymes,
Or else by toasting her a score of times,
Rose from the table and declared it right
To test their fancy by their sight;
But they mistook the brightness of the moon
For the prosaic light of day —
Music had driven their wits astray —
And one was drowned in the great bog of Cloone.

Strange, but the man who made the song was blind;
Yet, now I have considered it, I find
That nothing strange; the tragedy began
With Homer that was a blind man,
And Helen has all living hearts betrayed.
O may the moon and sunlight seem
One inextricable beam,
For if I triumph I must make men mad.

And I myself created Hanrahan
And drove him drunk or sober through the dawn
From somewhere in the neighbouring cottages.
Caught by an old man's juggleries

He stumbled, tumbled, fumbled to and fro
And had but broken knees for hire
And horrible splendour of desire;
I thought it all out twenty years ago:

Good fellows shuffled cards in an old bawn;
And when that ancient ruffian's turn was on
He so bewitched the cards under his thumb
That all but the one card became
A pack of hounds and not a pack of cards,
And that he changed into a hare.
Hanrahan rose in frenzy there
And followed up those baying creatures towards —

O towards I have forgotten what — enough!
I must recall a man that neither love
Nor music nor an enemy's clipped ear
Could, he was so harried, cheer;
A figure that has grown so fabulous
There's not a neighbour left to say
When he finished his dog's day:
An ancient bankrupt master of this house.

Before that ruin came, for centuries,
Rough men-at-arms, cross-gartered to the knees
Or shod in iron, climbed the narrow stairs,
And certain men-at-arms there were
Whose images, in the Great Memory stored,
Come with loud cry and panting breast
To break upon a sleeper's rest
While their great wooden dice beat on the board.

As I would question all, come all who can;
Come old, necessitous, half-mounted man;
And bring beauty's blind rambling celebrant;
The red man the juggler sent
Through God-forsaken meadows; Mrs. French,
Gifted with so fine an ear;
The man drowned in a bog's mire,
When mocking Muses chose the country wench.

Did all old men and women, rich and poor,
Who trod upon these rocks or passed this door,
Whether in public or in secret rage
As I do now against old age?
But I have found an answer in those eyes
That are impatient to be gone;
Go therefore; but leave Hanrahan,
For I need all his mighty memories.

Old lecher with a love on every wind,
Bring up out of that deep considering mind
All that you have discovered in the grave,
For it is certain that you have
Reckoned up every unforeknown, unseeing
plunge, lured by a softening eye,
Or by a touch or a sigh,
Into the labyrinth of another's being;

Does the imagination dwell the most
Upon a woman won or woman lost?
If on the lost, admit you turned aside
From a great labyrinth out of pride,
Cowardice, some silly over-subtle thought
Or anything called conscience once;
And that if memory recur, the sun's
Under eclipse and the day blotted out.

III

It is time that I wrote my will;
I choose upstanding men
That climb the streams until
The fountain leap, and at dawn
Drop their cast at the side
Of dripping stone; I declare
They shall inherit my pride,
The pride of people that were
Bound neither to Cause nor to State.
Neither to slaves that were spat on,
Nor to the tyrants that spat,

The people of Burke and of Grattan
That gave, though free to refuse —
Pride, like that of the morn,
When the headlong light is loose,
Or that of the fabulous horn,
Or that of the sudden shower
When all streams are dry,
Or that of the hour
When the swan must fix his eye
Upon a fading gleam,
Float out upon a long
Last reach of glittering stream
And there sing his last song.
And I declare my faith:
I mock Plotinus' thought
And cry in plato's teeth,
Death and life were not
Till man made up the whole,
Made lock, stock and barrel
Out of his bitter soul,
Aye, sun and moon and star, all,
And further add to that
That, being dead, we rise,
Dream and so create
Translunar paradise.
I have prepared my peace
With learned Italian things
And the proud stones of Greece,
Poet's imaginings
And memories of love,
Memories of the words of women,
All those things whereof
Man makes a superhuman,
Mirror-resembling dream.

As at the loophole there
The daws chatter and scream,
And drop twigs layer upon layer.
When they have mounted up,
The mother bird will rest

On their hollow top,
And so warm her wild nest.

I leave both faith and pride
To young upstanding men
Climbing the mountain-side,
That under bursting dawn
They may drop a fly;
Being of that metal made
Till it was broken by
This sedentary trade.

Now shall I make my soul,
Compelling it to study
In a learned school
Till the wreck of body,
Slow decay of blood,
Testy delirium
Or dull decrepitude,
Or what worse evil come —
The death of friends, or death
Of every brilliant eye
That made a catch in the breath — .
Seem but the clouds of the sky
When the horizon fades,
Or a bird's sleepy cry
Among the deepening shades.

Meditations in Time of Civil War

I

Ancestral Houses

Surely among a rich man's flowering lawns,
Amid the rustle of his planted hills,
Life overflows without ambitious pains;
And rains down life until the basin spills,
And mounts more dizzy high the more it rains
As though to choose whatever shape it wills

And never stoop to a mechanical
Or servile shape, at others' beck and call.

Mere dreams, mere dreams! Yet Homer had not sung
Had he not found it certain beyond dreams
That out of life's own self-delight had sprung
The abounding glittering jet; though now it seems
As if some marvellous empty sea-shell flung
Out of the obscure dark of the rich streams,
And not a fountain, were the symbol which
Shadows the inherited glory of the rich.

Some violent bitter man, some powerful man
Called architect and artist in, that they,
Bitter and violent men, might rear in stone
The sweetness that all longed for night and day,
The gentleness none there had ever known;
But when the master's buried mice can play,
And maybe the great-grandson of that house,
For all its bronze and marble, 's but a mouse.

O what if gardens where the peacock strays
With delicate feet upon old terraces,
Or else all Juno from an urn displays
Before the indifferent garden deities;
O what if levelled lawns and gravelled ways
Where slippered Contemplation finds his ease
And Childhood a delight for every sense,
But take our greatness with our violence?

What if the glory of escutcheoned doors,
And buildings that a haughtier age designed,
The pacing to and fro on polished floors
Amid great chambers and long galleries, lined
With famous portraits of our ancestors;
What if those things the greatest of mankind
Consider most to magnify, or to bless,
But take our greatness with our bitterness?

II

My House

An ancient bridge, and a more ancient tower,
A farmhouse that is sheltered by its wall,
An acre of stony ground,
Where the symbolic rose can break in flower,
Old ragged elms, old thorns innumerable,

The sound of the rain or sound
Of every wind that blows;
The stilted water-hen
Crossing stream again
Scared by the splashing of a dozen cows;

A winding stair, a chamber arched with stone,
A grey stone fireplace with an open hearth,
A candle and written page.
Il Penseroso's Platonist toiled on
In some like chamber, shadowing forth
How the daemonic rage
Imagined everything.
Benighted travellers
From markets and from fairs
Have seen his midnight candle glimmering.

Two men have founded here. A man-at-arms
Gathered a score of horse and spent his days
In this tumultuous spot,
Where through long wars and sudden night alarms
His dwindling score and he seemed castaways
Forgetting and forgot;
And I, that after me
My bodily heirs may find,
To exalt a lonely mind,
Befitting emblems of adversity.

III

My Table

Two heavy trestles, and a board
Where Sato's gift, a changeless sword,

By pen and paper lies,
That it may moralise
My days out of their aimlessness.
A bit of an embroidered dress
Covers its wooden sheath.
Chaucer had not drawn breath
When it was forged. In Sato's house,
Curved like new moon, moon-luminous
It lay five hundred years.
Yet if no change appears
No moon; only an aching heart
Conceives a changeless work of art.
Our learned men have urged
That when and where 'twas forged
A marvellous accomplishment,
In painting or in pottery, went
From father unto son
And through the centuries ran
And seemed unchanging like the sword.
Soul's beauty being most adored,
Men and their business took
The soul's unchanging look;
For the most rich inheritor,
Knowing that none could pass Heaven's door,
That loved inferior art,
Had such an aching heart
That he, although a country's talk
For silken clothes and stately walk.
Had waking wits; it seemed
Juno's peacock screamed.

IV

My Descendants

Having inherited a vigorous mind
From my old fathers, I must nourish dreams
And leave a woman and a man behind
As vigorous of mind, and yet it seems
Life scarce can cast a fragrance on the wind,

Scarce spread a glory to the morning beams,
But the torn petals strew the garden plot;
And there's but common greenness after that.

And what if my descendants lose the flower
Through natural declension of the soul,
Through too much business with the passing hour,
Through too much play, or marriage with a fool?
May this laborious stair and this stark tower
Become a roofless ruin that the owl
May build in the cracked masonry and cry
Her desolation to the desolate sky.
The Primum Mobile that fashioned us
Has made the very owls in circles move;
And I, that count myself most prosperous,
Seeing that love and friendship are enough,
For an old neighbour's friendship chose the house
And decked and altered it for a girl's love,
And know whatever flourish and decline
These stones remain their monument and mine.

V

The Road at My Door

An affable Irregular,
A heavily-built Falstaffian man,
Comes cracking jokes of civil war
As though to die by gunshot were
The finest play under the sun.

A brown Lieutenant and his men,
Half dressed in national uniform,
Stand at my door, and I complain
Of the foul weather, hail and rain,
A pear tree broken by the storm.

I count those feathered balls of soot
The moor-hen guides upon the stream.
To silence the envy in my thought;

And turn towards my chamber, caught
In the cold snows of a dream.

VI

The Stare's Nest by My Window

The bees build in the crevices
Of loosening masonry, and there
The mother birds bring grubs and flies.
My wall is loosening; honey-bees,
Come build in the empty house of the stare.

We are closed in, and the key is turned
On our uncertainty; somewhere
A man is killed, or a house burned,
Yet no clear fact to be discerned:
Come build in he empty house of the stare.

A barricade of stone or of wood;
Some fourteen days of civil war;
Last night they trundled down the road
That dead young soldier in his blood:
Come build in the empty house of the stare.

We had fed the heart on fantasies,
The heart's grown brutal from the fare;
More substance in our enmities
Than in our love; O honey-bees,
Come build in the empty house of the stare.

VII

I See Phantoms of Hatred And of the Heart's Fullness And of the Coming Emptiness

I climb to the tower-top and lean upon broken stone,
A mist that is like blown snow is sweeping over all,
Valley, river, and elms, under the light of a moon
That seems unlike itself, that seems unchangeable,
A glittering sword out of the east. A puff of wind
And those white glimmering fragments of the mist sweep by.
Frenzies bewilder, reveries perturb the mind;
Monstrous familiar images swim to the mind's eye.

'Vengeance upon the murderers,' the cry goes up,
'Vengeance for Jacques Molay.' In cloud-pale rags, or in lace,
The rage-driven, rage-tormented, and rage-hungry troop,
Trooper belabouring trooper, biting at arm or at face,
Plunges towards nothing, arms and fingers spreading wide
For the embrace of nothing; and I, my wits astray
Because of all that senseless tumult, all but cried
For vengeance on the murderers of Jacques Molay.

Their legs long, delicate and slender, aquamarine their eyes,
Magical unicorns bear ladies on their backs.
The ladies close their musing eyes. No prophecies,
Remembered out of Babylonian almanacs,
Have closed the ladies' eyes, their minds are but a pool
Where even longing drowns under its own excess;
Nothing but stillness can remain when hearts are full
Of their own sweetness, bodies of their loveliness.

The cloud-pale unicorns, the eyes of aquamarine,
The quivering half-closed eyelids, the rags of cloud or of lace,
Or eyes that rage has brightened, arms it has made lean,
Give place to an indifferent multitude, give place
To brazen hawks. Nor self-delighting reverie,
Nor hate of what's to come, nor pity for what's gone,
Nothing but grip of claw, and the eye's complacency,
The innumerable clanging wings that have put out the moon.

I turn away and shut the door, and on the stair
Wonder how many times I could have proved my worth
In something that all others understand or share;
But O! ambitious heart, had such a proof drawn forth
A company of friends, a conscience set at ease,
It had but made us pine the more. The abstract joy,
The half-read wisdom of daemonic images,
Suffice the ageing man as once the growing boy.

Nineteen Hundred and Nineteen

I

Many ingenious lovely things are gone
That seemed sheer miracle to the multitude,
Protected from the circle of the moon
That pitches common things about. There stood
Amid the ornamental bronze and stone
An ancient image made of olive wood —
And gone are Phidias' famous ivories
And all the golden grasshoppers and bees.

We too had many pretty toys when young:
A law indifferent to blame or praise,
To bribe or threat; habits that made old wrong
Melt down, as it were wax in the sun's rays;
Public opinion ripening for so long
We thought it would outlive all future days.
O what fine thought we had because we thought
That the worst rogues and rascals had died out.

All teeth were drawn, all ancient tricks unlearned,
And a great army but a showy thing;
What matter that no cannon had been turned
Into a ploughshare? Parliament and king
Thought that unless a little powder burned
The trumpeters might burst with trumpeting
And yet it lack all glory; and perchance
The guardsmen's drowsy chargers would not prance.

Now days are dragon-ridden, the nightmare
Rides upon sleep: a drunken soldiery
Can leave the mother, murdered at her door,
To crawl in her own blood, and go scot-free;
The night can sweat with terror as before
We pieced our thoughts into philosophy,
And planned to bring the world under a rule,
Who are but weasels fighting in a hole.

He who can read the signs nor sink unmanned
Into the half-deceit of some intoxicant
From shallow wits; who knows no work can stand,
Whether health, wealth or peace of mind were spent
On master-work of intellect or hand,
No honour leave its mighty monument,
Has but one comfort left: all triumph would
But break upon his ghostly solitude.

But is there any comfort to be found?
Man is in love and loves what vanishes,
What more is there to say? That country round
None dared admit, if Such a thought were his,
Incendiary or bigot could be found
To burn that stump on the Acropolis,
Or break in bits the famous ivories
Or traffic in the grasshoppers or bees.

II
When Loie Fuller's Chinese dancers enwound
A shining web, a floating ribbon of cloth,
It seemed that a dragon of air
Had fallen among dancers, had whirled them round
Or hurried them off on its own furious path;
So the Platonic Year
Whirls out new right and wrong,
Whirls in the old instead;
All men are dancers and their tread
Goes to the barbarous clangour of a gong.

III
Some moralist or mythological poet
Compares the solitary soul to a swan;
I am satisfied with that,
Satisfied if a troubled mirror show it,
Before that brief gleam of its life be gone,
An image of its state;
The wings half spread for flight,
The breast thrust out in pride

Whether to play, or to ride
Those winds that clamour of approaching night.

A man in his own secret meditation
Is lost amid the labyrinth that he has made
In art or politics;
Some Platonist affirms that in the station
Where we should cast off body and trade
The ancient habit sticks,
And that if our works could
But vanish with our breath
That were a lucky death,
For triumph can but mar our solitude.

The swan has leaped into the desolate heaven:
That image can bring wildness, bring a rage
To end all things, to end
What my laborious life imagined, even
The half-imagined, the half-written page;
O but we dreamed to mend
Whatever mischief seemed
To afflict mankind, but now
That winds of winter blow
Learn that we were crack-pated when we dreamed.

IV

We, who seven yeats ago
Talked of honour and of truth,
Shriek with pleasure if we show
The weasel's twist, the weasel's tooth.

V

Come let us mock at the great
That had such burdens on the mind
And toiled so hard and late
To leave some monument behind,
Nor thought of the levelling wind.

Come let us mock at the wise;
With all those calendars whereon

They fixed old aching eyes,
They never saw how seasons run,
And now but gape at the sun.

Come let us mock at the good
That fancied goodness might be gay,
And sick of solitude
Might proclaim a holiday:
Wind shrieked — and where are they?

Mock mockers after that
That would not lift a hand maybe
To help good, wise or great
To bar that foul storm out, for we
Traffic in mockery.

VI

Violence upon the roads: violence of horses;
Some few have handsome riders, are garlanded
On delicate sensitive ear or tossing mane,
But wearied running round and round in their courses
All break and vanish, and evil gathers head:
Herodias' daughters have returned again,
A sudden blast of dusty wind and after
Thunder of feet, tumult of images,
Their purpose in the labyrinth of the wind;
And should some crazy hand dare touch a daughter
All turn with amorous cries, or angry cries,
According to the wind, for all are blind.
But now wind drops, dust settles; thereupon
There lurches past, his great eyes without thought
Under the shadow of stupid straw-pale locks,
That insolent fiend Robert Artisson
To whom the love-lorn Lady Kyteler brought
Bronzed peacock feathers, red combs of her cocks.

The Wheel

Through winter-time we call on spring,
And through the spring on summer call,
And when abounding hedges ring
Declare that winter's best of all;
And after that there's nothing good
Because the spring-time has not come —
Nor know that what disturbs our blood
Is but its longing for the tomb.

Youth And Age

Much did I rage when young,
Being by the world oppressed,
But now with flattering tongue
It speeds the parting guest.

The New Faces

If you, that have grown old, were the first dead,
Neither catalpa tree nor scented lime
Should hear my living feet, nor would I tread
Where we wrought that shall break the teeth of Time.
Let the new faces play what tricks they will
In the old rooms; night can outbalance day,
Our shadows rove the garden gravel still,
The living seem more shadowy than they.

A Prayer for My Son

Bid a strong ghost stand at the head
That my Michael may sleep sound,
Nor cry, nor turn in the bed
Till his morning meal come round;
And may departing twilight keep
All dread afar till morning's back,

That his mother may not lack
Her fill of sleep.

Bid the ghost have sword in fist:
Some there are, for I avow
Such devilish things exist,
Who have planned his murder, for they know
Of some most haughty deed or thought
That waits upon his future days,
And would through hatred of the bays
Bring that to nought.

Though You can fashion everything
From nothing every day, and teach
The morning stars to sing,
You have lacked articulate speech
To tell Your simplest want, and known,
Wailing upon a woman's knee,
All of that worst ignominy
Of flesh and bone;

And when through all the town there ran
The servants of Your enemy,
A woman and a man,
Unless the Holy Writings lie,
Hurried through the smooth and rough
And through the fertile and waste,
protecting, till the danger past,
With human love.

Two Songs from a Play

I

I saw a staring virgin stand
Where holy Dionysus died,
And tear the heart out of his side,
And lay the heart upon her hand
And bear that beating heart away;
And then did all the Muses sing
Of Magnus Annus at the spring,
As though God's death were but a play.

Another Troy must rise and set,
Another lineage feed the crow,
Another Argo's painted prow
Drive to a flashier bauble yet.
The Roman Empire stood appalled:
It dropped the reins of peace and war
When that fierce virgin and her Star
Out of the fabulous darkness called.

II
In pity for man's darkening thought
He walked that room and issued thence
In Galilean turbulence;
The Babylonian starlight brought
A fabulous, formless darkness in;
Odour of blood when Christ was slain
Made all Platonic tolerance vain
And vain all Doric discipline.

Everything that man esteems
Endures a moment or a day.
Love's Pleasure drives his love away,
The painter's brush consumes his dreams;
The herald's cry, the soldier's tread
Exhaust his glory and his might:
Whatever flames upon the night
Man's own resinous heart has fed.

Fragments

I
Locke sank into a swoon;
The Garden died;
God took the spinning-jenny
Out of his side.

II
Where got I that truth?
Out of a medium's mouth.

Out of nothing it came,
Out of the forest loam,
Out of dark night where lay
The crowns of Nineveh.

Leda and the Swan

A sudden blow: the great wings beating still
Above the staggering girl, her thighs caressed
By the dark webs, her nape caught in his bill,
He holds her helpless breast upon his breast.

How can those terrified vague fingers push
The feathered glory from her loosening thighs,
And how can body, laid in that white rush,
But feel the strange heart beating where it lies?

A shudder in the loins engenders there
The broken wall, the burning roof and tower
And Agamemnon dead.

Being so caught up,
So mastered by the brute blood of the air,
Did she put on his knowledge with his power
Before the indifferent beak could let her drop?

On a Picture of a Black Centaur by Edmund Dulac

Your hooves have stamped at the black margin of the wood,
Even where horrible green parrots call and swing.
My works are all stamped down into the sultry mud.
I knew that horse-play, knew it for a murderous thing.
What wholesome sun has ripened is wholesome food to eat,
And that alone; yet I, being driven half insane
Because of some green wing, gathered old mummy wheat
In the mad abstract dark and ground it grain by grain
And after baked it slowly in an oven; but now
I bring full-flavoured wine out of a barrel found
Where seven Ephesian topers slept and never knew
When Alexander's empire passed, they slept so sound.
Stretch out your limbs and sleep a long Saturnian sleep;
I have loved you better than my soul for all my words,
And there is none so fit to keep a watch and keep
Unwearied eyes upon those horrible green birds.

Among School Children

I

I walk through the long schoolroom questioning;
A kind old nun in a white hood replies;
The children learn to cipher and to sing,
To study reading-books and histories,
To cut and sew, be neat in everything
In the best modern way — the children's eyes
In momentary wonder stare upon
A sixty-year-old smiling public man.

II

I dream of a Ledaean body, bent
Above a sinking fire. a tale that she
Told of a harsh reproof, or trivial event
That changed some childish day to tragedy —
Told, and it seemed that our two natures blent
Into a sphere from youthful sympathy,
Or else, to alter Plato's parable,
Into the yolk and white of the one shell.

III
And thinking of that fit of grief or rage
I look upon one child or t'other there
And wonder if she stood so at that age —
For even daughters of the swan can share
Something of every paddler's heritage —
And had that colour upon cheek or hair,
And thereupon my heart is driven wild:
She stands before me as a living child.

IV
Her present image floats into the mind —
Did Quattrocento finger fashion it
Hollow of cheek as though it drank the wind
And took a mess of shadows for its meat?
And I though never of Ledaean kind
Had pretty plumage once — enough of that,
Better to smile on all that smile, and show
There is a comfortable kind of old scarecrow.

V
What youthful mother, a shape upon her lap
Honey of generation had betrayed,
And that must sleep, shriek, struggle to escape
As recollection or the drug decide,
Would think her son, did she but see that shape
With sixty or more winters on its head,
A compensation for the pang of his birth,
Or the uncertainty of his setting forth?

VI
Plato thought nature but a spume that plays
Upon a ghostly paradigm of things;
Solider Aristotle played the taws
Upon the bottom of a king of kings;
World-famous golden-thighed Pythagoras
Fingered upon a fiddle-stick or strings
What a star sang and careless Muses heard:
Old clothes upon old sticks to scare a bird.

VII
Both nuns and mothers worship images,
But those the candles light are not as those
That animate a mother's reveries,
But keep a marble or a bronze repose.
And yet they too break hearts — O presences
That passion, piety or affection knows,
And that all heavenly glory symbolise —
O self-born mockers of man's enterprise;

VIII
Labour is blossoming or dancing where
The body is not bruised to pleasure soul,
Nor beauty born out of its own despair,
Nor blear-eyed wisdom out of midnight oil.
O chestnut tree, great-rooted blossomer,
Are you the leaf, the blossom or the bole?
O body swayed to music, O brightening glance,
How can we know the dancer from the dance?

Colonus' Praise

(From 'Oedipus at Colonus')

Chorus. Come praise Colonus' horses, and come praise
The wine-dark of the wood's intricacies,
The nightingale that deafens daylight there,
If daylight ever visit where,
Unvisited by tempest or by sun,
Immortal ladies tread the ground
Dizzy with harmonious sound,
Semele's lad a gay companion.

And yonder in the gymnasts' garden thrives
The self-sown, self-begotten shape that gives
Athenian intellect its mastery,
Even the grey-leaved olive-tree
Miracle-bred out of the living stone;
Nor accident of peace nor war
Shall wither that old marvel, for
The great grey-eyed Athene stares thereon.

Who comes into this country, and has come
Where golden crocus and narcissus bloom,
Where the Great Mother, mourning for her daughter
And beauty-drunken by the water
Glittering among grey-leaved olive-trees,
Has plucked a flower and sung her loss;
Who finds abounding Cephisus
Has found the loveliest spectacle there is.

because this country has a pious mind
And so remembers that when all mankind
But trod the road, or splashed about the shore,
Poseidon gave it bit and oar,
Every Colonus lad or lass discourses
Of that oar and of that bit;
Summer and winter, day and night,
Of horses and horses of the sea, white horses.

Wisdom

The true faith discovered was
When painted panel, statuary.
Glass-mosaic, window-glass,
Amended what was told awry
By some peasant gospeller;
Swept the sawdust from the floor
Of that working-carpenter.
Miracle had its playtime where
In damask clothed and on a seat
Chryselephantine, cedar-boarded,
His majestic Mother sat
Stitching at a purple hoarded
That He might be nobly breeched
In starry towers of Babylon
Noah's freshet never reached.
King Abundance got Him on
Innocence; and Wisdom He.
That cognomen sounded best

Considering what wild infancy
Drove horror from His Mother's breast.

The Fool by the Roadside

When all works that have
From cradle run to grave
From grave to cradle run instead;
When thoughts that a fool
Has wound upon a spool
Are but loose thread, are but loose thread;

When cradle and spool are past
And I mere shade at last
Coagulate of stuff
Transparent like the wind,
I think that I may find
A faithful love, a faithful love.

Owen Aherne And His Dancers

I

A strange thing surely that my Heart, when love had come unsought
Upon the Norman upland or in that poplar shade,
Should find no burden but itself and yet should be worn out.
It could not bear that burden and therefore it went mad.

The south wind brought it longing, and the east wind despair,
The west wind made it pitiful, and the north wind afraid.
It feared to give its love a hurt with all the tempest there;
It feared the hurt that shc could give and therefore it went mad.

I can exchange opinion with any neighbouring mind,
I have as healthy flesh and blood as any rhymer's had,
But O! my Heart could bear no more when the upland caught the wind;
I ran, I ran, from my love's side because my Heart went mad.

II

The Heart behind its rib laughed out. 'You have called me mad,' it said,
'Because I made you turn away and run from that young child;
How could she mate with fifty years that was so wildly bred?
Let the cage bird and the cage bird mate and the wild bird mate in
the wild.'

'You but imagine lies all day, O murderer,' I replied.
'And all those lies have but one end, poor wretches to betray;
I did not find in any cage the woman at my side.
O but her heart would break to learn my thoughts are far away.'

'Speak all your mind,' my Heart sang out, 'speak all your mind; who cares,
Now that your tongue cannot persuade the child till she mistake
Her childish gratitude for love and match your fifty years?
O let her choose a young man now and all for his wild sake.'

A Man Young And Old

I
First Love

Though nurtured like the sailing moon
In beauty's murderous brood,
She walked awhile and blushed awhile
And on my pathway stood
Until I thought her body bore
A heart of flesh and blood.

But since I laid a hand thereon
And found a heart of stone
I have attempted many things
And not a thing is done,
For every hand is lunatic
That travels on the moon.

She smiled and that transfigured me
And left me but a lout,
Maundering here, and maundering there,
Emptier of thought
Than the heavenly circuit of its stars
When the moon sails out.

II

Human Dignity

Like the moon her kindness is,
If kindness I may call
What has no comprehension in't,
But is the same for all
As though my sorrow were a scene
Upon a painted wall.

So like a bit of stone I lie
Under a broken tree.
I could recover if I shrieked
My heart's agony
To passing bird, but I am dumb
From human dignity.

III

The Mermaid

A mermaid found a swimming lad,
Picked him for her own,
Pressed her body to his body,
Laughed; and plunging down
Forgot in cruel happiness
That even lovers drown.

IV

The Death of the Hare

I have pointed out the yelling pack,
The hare leap to the wood,
And when I pass a compliment
Rejoice as lover should
At the drooping of an eye,
At the mantling of the blood.

Then suddenly my heart is wrung
By her distracted air
And I remember wildness lost
And after, swept from there,
Am set down standing in the wood
At the death of the hare.

V

The Empty Cup

A crazy man that found a cup,
When all but dead of thirst,
Hardly dared to wet his mouth
Imagining, moon-accursed,

That another mouthful
And his beating heart would burst.
October last I found it too
But found it dry as bone,
And for that reason am I crazed
And my sleep is gone.

VI

His Memories

We should be hidden from their eyes,
Being but holy shows
And bodies broken like a thorn
Whereon the bleak north blows,
To think of buried Hector
And that none living knows.

The women take so little stock
In what I do or say
They'd sooner leave their cosseting
To hear a jackass bray;
My arms are like the twisted thorn
And yet there beauty lay;

The first of all the tribe lay there
And did such pleasure take —
She who had brought great Hector down
And put all Troy to wreck —
That she cried into this ear,
'Strike me if I shriek.'

VII

The Friends of His Youth

Laughter not time destroyed my voice
And put that crack in it,
And when the moon's pot-bellied
I get a laughing fit,
For that old Madge comes down the lane,
A stone upon her breast,
And a cloak wrapped about the stone,
And she can get no rest
With singing hush and hush-a-bye;
She that has been wild
And barren as a breaking wave
Thinks that the stone's a child.

And Peter that had great affairs
And was a pushing man
Shrieks, 'I am King of the Peacocks,'
And perches on a stone;
And then I laugh till tears run down
And the heart thumps at my side,
Remembering that her shriek was love
And that he shrieks from pride.

VIII

Summer and Spring

We sat under an old thorn-tree
And talked away the night,
Told all that had been said or done
Since first we saw the light,

And when we talked of growing up
Knew that we'd halved a soul
And fell the one in t'other's arms
That we might make it whole;
Then Peter had a murdering look,
For it seemed that he and she
Had spoken of their childish days
Under that very tree.
O what a bursting out there was,
And what a blossoming,
When we had all the summer-time
And she had all the spring!

IX

The Secrets of the Old

I have old women's secrets now
That had those of the young;
Madge tells me what I dared not think
When my blood was strong,
And what had drowned a lover once
Sounds like an old song.

Though Margery is stricken dumb
If thrown in Madge's way,
We three make up a solitude;
For none alive to-day
Can know the stories that we know
Or say the things we say:

How such a man pleased women most
Of all that are gone,
How such a pair loved many years
And such a pair but one,
Stories of the bed of straw
Or the bed of down.

X

His Wildness

O bid me mount and sail up there
Amid the cloudy wrack,
For peg and Meg and Paris' love
That had so straight a back,
Are gone away, and some that stay
Have changed their silk for sack.

Were I but there and none to hear
I'd have a peacock cry,
For that is natural to a man
That lives in memory,
Being all alone I'd nurse a stone
And sing it lullaby.

XI

From 'Oedipus at Colonus'

Endure what life God gives and ask no longer span;
Cease to remember the delights of youth, travel-wearied aged
man;
Delight becomes death-longing if all longing else be vain.

Even from that delight memory treasures so,
Death, despair, division of families, all entanglements of
mankind grow,
As that old wandering beggar and these God-hated children
know.

In the long echoing street the laughing dancers throng,
The bride is carried to the bridegroom's chamber through
torchlight and tumultuous song;
I celebrate the silent kiss that ends short life or long.

Never to have lived is best, ancient writers say;
Never to have drawn the breath of life, never to have
looked into the eye of day;
The second best's a gay goodnight and quickly turn away.

The Three Monuments

They hold their public meetings where
Our most renowned patriots stand,
One among the birds of the air,
A stumpier on either hand;
And all the popular statesmen say
That purity built up the State
And after kept it from decay;
And let all base ambition be,
For intellect would make us proud
And pride bring in impurity:
The three old rascals laugh aloud.

All Souls' Night

Epilogue to 'A Vision'

Midnight has come, and the great Christ Church Bell
And may a lesser bell sound through the room;
And it is All Souls' Night,
And two long glasses brimmed with muscatel
Bubble upon the table. A ghost may come;
For it is a ghost's right,
His element is so fine
Being sharpened by his death,
To drink from the wine-breath
While our gross palates drink from the whole wine.

I need some mind that, if the cannon sound
From every quarter of the world, can stay
Wound in mind's pondering
As mummies in the mummy-cloth are wound;
Because I have a marvellous thing to say,
A certain marvellous thing
None but the living mock,
Though not for sober ear;
It may be all that hear
Should laugh and weep an hour upon the clock.

Horton's the first I call. He loved strange thought
And knew that sweet extremity of pride
That's called platonic love,
And that to such a pitch of passion wrought
Nothing could bring him, when his lady died,
Anodyne for his love.
Words were but wasted breath;
One dear hope had he:
The inclemency
Of that or the next winter would be death.

Two thoughts were so mixed up I could not tell
Whether of her or God he thought the most,
But think that his mind's eye,
When upward turned, on one sole image fell;
And that a slight companionable ghost,
Wild with divinity,
Had so lit up the whole
Immense miraculous house
The Bible promised us,
It seemed a gold-fish swimming in a bowl.

On Florence Emery I call the next,
Who finding the first wrinkles on a face
Admired and beautiful,
And knowing that the future would be vexed
With 'minished beauty, multiplied commonplace,
preferred to teach a school
Away from neighbour or friend,
Among dark skins, and there
permit foul years to wear
Hidden from eyesight to the unnoticed end.

Before that end much had she ravelled out
From a discourse in figurative speech
By some learned Indian
On the soul's journey. How it is whirled about,
Wherever the orbit of the moon can reach,
Until it plunge into the sun;
And there, free and yet fast,

Being both Chance and Choice,
Forget its broken toys
And sink into its own delight at last.

And I call up MacGregor from the grave,
For in my first hard springtime we were friends.
Although of late estranged.
I thought him half a lunatic, half knave,
And told him so, but friendship never ends;
And what if mind seem changed,
And it seem changed with the mind,
When thoughts rise up unbid
On generous things that he did
And I grow half contented to be blind!

He had much industry at setting out,
Much boisterous courage, before loneliness
Had driven him crazed;
For meditations upon unknown thought
Make human intercourse grow less and less;
They are neither paid nor praised.
but he'd object to the host,
The glass because my glass;
A ghost-lover he was
And may have grown more arrogant being a ghost.

But names are nothing. What matter who it be,
So that his elements have grown so fine
The fume of muscatel
Can give his sharpened palate ecstasy,
No living man can drink from the whole wine.
I have mummy truths to tell
Whereat the living mock,
Though not for sober ear,
For maybe all that hear
Should laugh and weep an hour upon the clock.

Such thought — such thought have I that hold it tight
Till meditation master all its parts,
Nothing can stay my glance

Until that glance run in the world's despite
To where the damned have howled away their hearts,
And where the blessed dance;
Such thought, that in it bound
I need no other thing,
Wound in mind's wandering
As mummies in the mummy-cloth are wound.

THE WINDING STAIR AND OTHER POEMS 1933

To Edmund Dulac

In Memory of Eva Gore-Booth And Con Markiewicz

The light of evening, Lissadell,
Great windows open to the south,
Two girls in silk kimonos, both
Beautiful, one a gazelle.
But a raving autumn shears
Blossom from the summer's wreath;
The older is condemned to death,
Pardoned, drags out lonely years
Conspiring among the ignorant.
I know not what the younger dreams —
Some vague Utopia — and she seems,
When withered old and skeleton-gaunt,
An image of such politics.
Many a time I think to seek
One or the other out and speak
Of that old Georgian mansion, mix
Pictures of the mind, recall
That table and the talk of youth,
Two girls in silk kimonos, both
Beautiful, one a gazelle.

Dear shadows, now you know it all,
All the folly of a fight
With a common wrong or right.
The innocent and the beautiful.
Have no enemy but time;
Arise and bid me strike a match
And strike another till time catch;

Should the conflagration climb,
Run till all the sages know.
We the great gazebo built,
They convicted us of guilt;
Bid me strike a match and blow.

Death

Nor dread nor hope attend
A dying animal;
A man awaits his end
Dreading and hoping all;
Many times he died,
Many times rose again.
A great man in his pride
Confronting murderous men
Casts derision upon
Supersession of breath;
He knows death to the bone —
Man has created death.

A Dialogue of Self And Soul

I

My Soul. I summon to the winding ancient stair;
Set all your mind upon the steep ascent,
Upon the broken, crumbling battlement,
Upon the breathless starlit air,
Upon the star that marks the hidden pole;
Fix every wandering thought upon
That quarter where all thought is done:
Who can distinguish darkness from the soul?

My Self. The consecrated blade upon my knees
Is Sato's ancient blade, still as it was,
Still razor-keen, still like a looking-glass
Unspotted by the centuries;
That flowering, silken, old embroidery, torn

From some court-lady's dress and round
The wodden scabbard bound and wound
Can, tattered, still protect, faded adorn.

My Soul. Why should the imagination of a man
Long past his prime remember things that are
Emblematical of love and war?
Think of ancestral night that can,
If but imagination scorn the earth
And intellect is wandering
To this and that and t'other thing,
Deliver from the crime of death and birth.

My self. Montashigi, third of his family, fashioned it
Five hundred years ago, about it lie
Flowers from I know not what embroidery —
Heart's purple — and all these I set
For emblems of the day against the tower
Emblematical of the night,
And claim as by a soldier's right
A charter to commit the crime once more.

My Soul. Such fullness in that quarter overflows
And falls into the basin of the mind
That man is stricken deaf and dumb and blind,
For intellect no longer knows
Is from the *Ought,* or *knower* from the *Known* —
That is to say, ascends to Heaven;
Only the dead can be forgiven;
But when I think of that my tongue's a stone.

II

My Self. A living man is blind and drinks his drop.
What matter if the ditches are impure?
What matter if I live it all once more?
Endure that toil of growing up;
The ignominy of boyhood; the distress
Of boyhood changing into man;
The unfinished man and his pain
Brought face to face with his own clumsiness;

The finished man among his enemies? —
How in the name of Heaven can he escape
That defiling and disfigured shape
The mirror of malicious eyes
Casts upon his eyes until at last
He thinks that shape must be his shape?
And what's the good of an escape
If honour find him in the wintry blast?

I am content to live it all again
And yet again, if it be life to pitch
Into the frog-spawn of a blind man's ditch,
A blind man battering blind men;
Or into that most fecund ditch of all,
The folly that man does
Or must suffer, if he woos
A proud woman not kindred of his soul.

I am content to follow to its source
Every event in action or in thought;
Measure the lot; forgive myself the lot!
When such as I cast out remorse
So great a sweetness flows into the breast
We must laugh and we must sing,
We are blest by everything,
Everything we look upon is blest.

Blood And the Moon

I

Blessed be this place,
More blessed still this tower;
A bloody, arrogant power
Rose out of the race
Uttering, mastering it,
Rose like these walls from these
Storm-beaten cottages —
In mockery I have set
A powerful emblem up,
And sing it rhyme upon rhyme

In mockery of a time
Half dead at the top.

II
Alexandria's was a beacon tower, and Babylon's
An image of the moving heavens, a log-book of the
sun's journey and the moon's;
And Shelley had his towers, thought's crowned powers
he called them once.

I declare this tower is my symbol; I declare
This winding, gyring, spiring treadmill of a stair is my
ancestral stair;
That Goldsmith and the Dean, Berkeley and Burke
have travelled there.

Swift beating on his breast in sibylline frenzy blind
Because the heart in his blood-sodden breast had dragged him
down into mankind,
Goldsmith deliberately sipping at the honey-pot of his mind,

And haughtier-headed Burke that proved the State a tree,
That this unconquerable labyrinth of the birds, century after
century,
Cast but dead leaves to mathematical equality;

And God-appointed Berkeley that proved all things a dream,
That this pragmatical, preposterous pig of a world, its farrow
that so solid seem,
Must vanish on the instant if the mind but change its theme;

Saeva Indignatio and the labourer's hire,
The strength that gives our blood and state magnanimity of its
own desire;
Everything that is not God consumed with intellectual fire.

III
The purity of the unclouded moon
Has flung its arrowy shaft upon the floor.
Seven centuries have passed and it is pure,

The blood of innocence has left no stain.
There, on blood-saturated ground, have stood
Soldier, assassin, executioner,
Whether for daily pittance or in blind fear
Or out of abstract hatred, and shed blood,
But could not cast a single jet thereon.
Odour of blood on the ancestral stair!
And we that have shed none must gather there
And clamour in drunken frenzy for the moon.

IV
Upon the dusty, glittering windows cling,
And seem to cling upon the moonlit skies,
Tortoiseshell butterflies, peacock butterflies,
A couple of night-moths are on the wing.
Is every modern nation like the tower,
Half dead at the top? No matter what I said,
For wisdom is the property of the dead,
A something incompatible with life; and power,
Like everything that has the stain of blood,
A property of the living; but no stain
Can come upon the visage of the moon
When it has looked in glory from a cloud.

Oil And Blood

In tombs of gold and lapis lazuli
Bodies of holy men and women exude
Miraculous oil, odour of violet.

But under heavy loads of trampled clay
Lie bodies of the vampires full of blood;
Their shrouds are bloody and their lips are wet.

Veronica's Napkin

The Heavenly Circuit; Berenice's Hair;
Tent-pole of Eden; the tent's drapery;
Symbolical glory of the earth and air!

The Father and His angelic hierarchy
That made the magnitude and glory there
Stood in the circuit of a needle's eye.

Some found a different pole, and where it stood
A pattern on a napkin dipped in blood.

Symbols

A storm-beaten old watch-tower,
A blind hermit rings the hour.

All-destroying sword-blade still
Carried by the wandering fool.

Gold-sewn silk on the sword-blade,
Beauty and fool together laid.

Spilt Milk

We that have done and thought,
That have thought and done,
Must ramble, and thin out
Like milk spilt on a stone.

The Nineteenth Century And After

Though the great song return no more
There's keen delight in what we have:
The rattle of pebbles on the shore
Under the receding wave.

Statistics

'Those Platonists are a curse,' he said,
'God's fire upon the wane,

A diagram hung there instead,
More women born than men.'

Three Movements

Shakespearean fish swam the sea, far away from land;
Romantic fish swam in nets coming to the hand;
What are all those fish that lie gasping on the strand?

The Seven Sages

The First. My great-grandfather spoke to Edmund Burke
In Grattan's house.

The Second. My great-grandfather shared
A pot-house bench with Oliver Goldsmith once.

The Third. My great-grandfather's father talked of music,
Drank tar-water with the Bishop of Cloyne.

The Fourth. But mine saw Stella once.

The Fifth. Whence came our thought?

The Sixth. From four great minds that hated Whiggery.

The Fifth. Burke was a Whig.

The Sixth. Whether they knew or not,
Goldsmith and Burke, Swift and the Bishop of Cloyne
All hated Whiggery; but what is Whiggery?
A levelling, rancorous, rational sort of mind
That never looked out of the eye of a saint
Or out of drunkard's eye.

The Seventh. All's Whiggery now,
But we old men are massed against the world.

The First. American colonies, Ireland, France and India
Harried, and Burke's great melody against it.

The Second. Oliver Goldsmith sang what he had seen,
Roads full of beggars, cattle in the fields,
But never saw the trefoil stained with blood,
The avenging leaf those fields raised up against it.

The Fourth. The tomb of Swift wears it away.

The Third. A voice
Soft as the rustle of a reed from Cloyne
That gathers volume; now a thunder-clap.

The Sixth. What schooling had these four?

The Seventh. They walked the roads
Mimicking what they heard, as children mimic;
They understood that wisdom comes of beggary.

The Crazed Moon

Crazed through much child-bearing
The moon is staggering in the sky;
Moon-struck by the despairing
Glances of her wandering eye
We grope, and grope in vain,
For children born of her pain.

Children dazed or dead!
When she in all her virginal pride
First trod on the mountain's head
What stir ran through the countryside
Where every foot obeyed her glance!
What manhood led the dance!

Fly-catchers of the moon,
Our hands are blenched, our fingers seem
But slender needles of bone;

Blenched by that malicious dream
They are spread wide that each
May rend what comes in reach.

Coole Park, 1929

I meditate upon a swallow's flight,
Upon an aged woman and her house,
A sycamore and lime-tree lost in night
Although that western cloud is luminous,
Great works constructed there in nature's spite
For scholars and for poets after us,
Thoughts long knitted into a single thought,
A dance-like glory that those walls begot.

There Hyde before he had beaten into prose
That noble blade the Muses buckled on,
There one that ruffled in a manly pose
For all his timid heart, there that slow man,
That meditative man, John Synge, and those
Impetuous men, Shawe Taylor and Hugh Lane,
Found pride established in humility,
A scene well set and excellent company.

They came like swallows and like swallows went,
And yet a woman's powerful character
Could keep a swallow to its first intent;
And half a dozen in formation there,
That seemed to whirl upon a compass-point,
Found certainty upon the dreaming air,
The intellectual sweetness of those lines
That cut through time or cross it withershins.

Here, traveller, scholar, poet, take your stand
When all those rooms and passages are gone,
When nettles wave upon a shapeless mound
And saplings root among the broken stone,
And dedicate — eyes bent upon the ground,

Back turned upon the brightness of the sun
And all the sensuality of the shade —
A moment's memory to that laurelled head.

Coole And Ballylee, 1931

Under my window-ledge the waters race,
Otters below and moor-hens on the top,
Run for a mile undimmed in Heaven's face
Then darkening through 'dark' Raftery's 'cellar' drop,
Run underground, rise in a rocky place
In Coole demesne, and there to finish up
Spread to a lake and drop into a hole.
What's water but the generated soul?

Upon the border of that lake's a wood
Now all dry sticks under a wintry sun,
And in a copse of beeches there I stood,
For Nature's pulled her tragic buskin on
And all the rant's a mirror of my mood:
At sudden thunder of the mounting swan
I turned about and looked where branches break
The glittering reaches of the flooded lake.

Another emblem there! That stormy white
But seems a concentration of the sky;
And, like the soul, it sails into the sight
And in the morning's gone, no man knows why;
And is so lovely that it sets to right
What knowledge or its lack had set awry,
So arrogantly pure, a child might think
It can be murdered with a spot of ink.

Sound of a stick upon the floor, a sound
From somebody that toils from chair to chair;
Beloved books that famous hands have bound,

Old marble heads, old pictures everywhere;
Great rooms where travelled men and children found
Content or joy; a last inheritor
Where none has reigned that lacked a name and fame
Or out of folly into folly came.

A spot whereon the founders lived and died
Seemed once more dear than life; ancestral trees,
Or gardens rich in memory glorified
Marriages, alliances and families,
And every bride's ambition satisfied.
Where fashion or mere fantasy decrees
We shift about — all that great glory spent —
Like some poor Arab tribesman and his tent.

We were the last romantics — chose for theme
Traditional sanctity and loveliness;
Whatever's written in what poets name
The book of the people; whatever most can bless
The mind of man or elevate a rhyme;
But all is changed, that high horse riderless,
Though mounted in that saddle Homer rode
Where the swan drifts upon a darkening flood.

For Anne Gregory

'Never shall a young man,
Thrown into despair
By those great honey-coloured
Ramparts at your ear,
Love you for yourself alone
And not your yellow hair.'

'But I can get a hair-dye
And set such colour there,
Brown, or black, or carrot,
That young men in despair

May love me for myself alone
And not my yellow hair.'

'I heard an old religious man
But yesternight declare
That he had found a text to prove
That only God, my dear,
Could love you for yourself alone
And not your yellow hair.'

Swift's Epitaph

Swift has sailed into his rest;
Savage indignation there
Cannot lacerate his breast.
Imitate him if you dare,
World-besotted traveller; he
Served human liberty.

At Algeciras — A Meditaton upon Death

The heron-billed pale cattle-birds
That feed on some foul parasite
Of the Moroccan flocks and herds
Cross the narrow Straits to light
In the rich midnight of the garden trees
Till the dawn break upon those mingled seas.

Often at evening when a boy
Would I carry to a friend —
Hoping more substantial joy
Did an older mind commend —
Not such as are in Newton's metaphor,
But actual shells of Rosses' level shore.

Greater glory in the sun,
An evening chill upon the air,
Bid imagination run
Much on the Great Questioner;
What He can question, what if questioned I
Can with a fitting confidence reply.

The Choice

The intellect of man is forced to choose
perfection of the life, or of the work,
And if it take the second must refuse
A heavenly mansion, raging in the dark.
When all that story's finished, what's the news?
In luck or out the toil has left its mark:
That old perplexity an empty purse,
Or the day's vanity, the night's remorse.

Mohini Chatterjee

I asked if I should pray.
But the Brahmin said,
'Pray for nothing, say
Every night in bed,
"I have been a king,
I have been a slave,
Nor is there anything.
Fool, rascal, knave,
That I have not been,
And yet upon my breast
A myriad heads have lain."'

That he might Set at rest
A boy's turbulent days
Mohini Chatterjee
Spoke these, or words like these,

I add in commentary,
'Old lovers yet may have
All that time denied —
Grave is heaped on grave
That they be satisfied —
Over the blackened earth
The old troops parade,
Birth is heaped on birth
That such cannonade
May thunder time away,
Birth-hour and death-hour meet,
Or, as great sages say,
Men dance on deathless feet.'

Byzantium

The unpurged images of day recede;
The Emperor's drunken soldiery are abed;
Night resonance recedes, night-walkers' song
After great cathedral gong;
A starlit or a moonlit dome disdains
All that man is,
All mere complexities,
The fury and the mire of human veins.

Before me floats an image, man or shade,
Shade more than man, more image than a shade;
For Hades' bobbin bound in mummy-cloth
May unwind the winding path;
A mouth that has no moisture and no breath
Breathless mouths may summon;
I hail the superhuman;
I call it death-in-life and life-in-death.

Miracle, bird or golden handiwork,
More miracle than bird or handiwork,
Planted on the star-lit golden bough,
Can like the cocks of Hades crow,

Or, by the moon embittered, scorn aloud
In glory of changeless metal
Common bird or petal
And all complexities of mire or blood.

At midnight on the Emperor's pavement flit
Flames that no faggot feeds, nor steel has lit,
Nor storm disturbs, flames begotten of flame,
Where blood-begotten spirits come
And all complexities of fury leave,
Dying into a dance,
An agony of trance,
An agony of flame that cannot singe a sleeve.

Astraddle on the dolphin's mire and blood,
Spirit after Spirit! The smithies break the flood.
The golden smithies of the Emperor!
Marbles of the dancing floor
Break bitter furies of complexity,
Those images that yet
Fresh images beget,
That dolphin-torn, that gong-tormented sea.

The Mother of God

The threefold terror of love; a fallen flare
Through the hollow of an ear;
Wings beating about the room;
The terror of all terrors that I bore
The Heavens in my womb.
Had I not found content among the shows
Every common woman knows,
Chimney corner, garden walk,
Or rocky cistern where we tread the clothes
And gather all the talk?

What is this flesh I purchased with my pains,
This fallen star my milk sustains,
This love that makes my heart's blood stop
Or strikes a sudden chill into my bones
And bids my hair stand up?

Vacillation

I

Between extremities
Man runs his course;
A brand, or flaming breath.
Comes to destroy
All those antinomies
Of day and night;
The body calls it death,
The heart remorse.
But if these be right
What is joy?

II

A tree there is that from its topmost bough
Is half all glittering flame and half all green
Abounding foliage moistened with the dew;
And half is half and yet is all the scene;
And half and half consume what they renew,
And he that Attis' image hangs between
That staring fury and the blind lush leaf
May know not what he knows, but knows not grief

III

Get all the gold and silver that you can,
Satisfy ambition, animate
The trivial days and ram them with the sun,
And yet upon these maxims meditate:
All women dote upon an idle man
Although their children need a rich estate;

No man has ever lived that had enough
Of children's gratitude or woman's love.

No longer in Lethean foliage caught
Begin the preparation for your death
And from the fortieth winter by that thought
Test every work of intellect or faith,
And everything that your own hands have wrought
And call those works extravagance of breath
That are not suited for such men as come
Proud, open-eyed and laughing to the tomb.

IV
My fiftieth year had come and gone,
I sat, a solitary man,
In a crowded London shop,
An open book and empty cup
On the marble table-top.

While on the shop and street I gazed
My body of a sudden blazed;
And twenty minutes more or less
It seemed, so great my happiness,
That I was blessed and could bless.

V
Although the summer sunlight gild
Cloudy leafage of the sky,
Or wintry moonlight sink the field
In storm-scattered intricacy,
I cannot look thereon,
Responsibility so weighs me down.

Things said or done long years ago,
Or things I did not do or say
But thought that I might say or do,
Weigh me down, and not a day
But something is recalled,
My conscience or my vanity appalled.

VI

A rivery field spread out below,
An odour of the new-mown hay
In his nostrils, the great lord of Chou
Cried, casting off the mountain snow,
'Let all things pass away.'

Wheels by milk-white asses drawn
Where Babylon or Nineveh
Rose; some conquer drew rein
And cried to battle-weary men,
'Let all things pass away.'

From man's blood-sodden heart are sprung
Those branches of the night and day
Where the gaudy moon is hung.
What's the meaning of all song?
'Let all things pass away.'

VII

The Soul. Seek out reality, leave things that seem.

The Heart. What, be a singer born and lack a theme?

The Soul. Isaiah's coal, what more can man desire?

The Heart. Struck dumb in the simplicity of fire!

The Soul. Look on that fire, salvation walks within.

The Heart. What theme had Homer but original sin?

VIII

Must we part, Von Hügel, though much alike, for we
Accept the miracles of the saints and honour sanctity?
The body of Saint Teresa lies undecayed in tomb,
Bathed in miraculous oil, sweet odours from it come,
Healing from its lettered slab. Those self-same hands perchance
Eternalised the body of a modern saint that once
Had scooped out pharaoh's mummy. I — though heart might
find relief

Did I become a Christian man and choose for my belief
What seems most welcome in the tomb — play a predestined
    part.
Homer is my example and his unchristened heart.
The lion and the honeycomb, what has Scripture said?
So get you gone, Von Hügel, though with blessings on your head.

Quarrel in Old Age

Where had her sweetness gone?
What fanatics invent
In this blind bitter town,
Fantasy or incident
Not worth thinking of,
Put her in a rage.
I had forgiven enough
That had forgiven old age.

All lives that has lived;
So much is certain;
Old sages were not deceived:
Somewhere beyond the curtain
Of distorting days
Lives that lonely thing
That shone before these eyes
Targeted, trod like Spring.

The Results of Thought

Acquaintance; companion;
One dear brilliant woman;
The best-endowed, the elect,
All by their youth undone,
All, all, by that inhuman
Bitter glory wrecked.

But I have straightened out
Ruin, wreck and wrack;

I toiled long years and at length
Came to so deep a thought
I can summon back
All their wholesome strength.

What images are these
That turn dull-eyed away,
Or shift Time's filthy load,
Straighten aged knees,
Hesitate or stay?
What heads shake or nod?

Gratitude to the Unknown Instructors

What they undertook to do
They brought to pass;
All things hang like a drop of dew
Upon a blade of grass.

Remorse for Intemperate Speech

I ranted to the knave and fool,
But outgrew that school,
Would transform the part,
Fit audience found, but cannot rule
My fanatic heart.

I sought my betters: though in each
Fine manners, liberal speech,
Turn hatred into sport,
Nothing said or done can reach
My fanatic heart.

Out of Ireland have we come.
Great hatred, little room,
Maimed us at the start.
I carry from my mother's womb
A fanatic heart.

Stream and Sun at Glendalough

Through intricate motions ran
Stream and gliding sun
And all my heart seemed gay:
Some stupid thing that I had done
Made my attention stray.

Repentance keeps my heart impure;
But what am I that dare
Fancy that I can
Better conduct myself or have more
Sense than a common man?

What motion of the sun or stream
Or eyelid shot the gleam
That pierced my body through?
What made me live like these that seem
Self-born, born anew?

Words for Music Perhaps

I
Crazy Jane And the Bishop
Bring me to the blasted oak
That I, midnight upon the stroke,
(*All find safety in the tomb.*)
May call down curses on his head
Because of my dear Jack that's dead.
Coxcomb was the least he said:
The solid man and the coxcomb.

Nor was he Bishop when his ban
Banished Jack the Journeyman,
(*All find safety in the tomb.*)
Nor so much as parish priest,
Yet he, an old book in his fist,
Cried that we lived like beast and beast:
The solid man and the coxcomb.

The Bishop has a skin, God knows,
Wrinkled like the foot of a goose,
(*All find safety in the tomb.*)
Nor can he hide in holy black
The heron's hunch upon his back,
But a birch-tree stood my Jack:
The solid man and the coxcomb.

Jack had my virginity,
And bids me to the oak, for he
(*All find safety in the tomb.*)
Wanders out into the night
And there is shelter under it,
But should that other come, I spit:
The solid man and the coxcomb.

II
Crazy Jane Reproved
I care not what the sailors say:
All those dreadful thunder-stones,
All that storm that blots the day
Can but show that Heaven yawns;
Great Europa played the fool
That changed a lover for a bull.
Fol de rol, fol de rol.

To round that shell's elaborate whorl,
Adorning every secret track
With the delicate mother-of-pearl,
Made the joints of Heaven crack:
So never hang your heart upon
A roaring, ranting journeyman.
Fol de rol, fol de rol.

III
Crazy Jane on The Day of Judgment
'Love is all
Unsatisfied
That cannot take the whole

Body and soul';
And that is what Jane said.
'Take the sour
If you take me
I can scoff and lour
And scold for an hour.'
'That's certainly the case,' said he.

'Naked I lay,
The grass my bed;
Naked and hidden away,
That black day';
And that is what Jane said.

'What can be shown?
What true love be?
All could be known or shown
If Time were but gone.'
'That's certainly the case,' said he.

IV

Crazy Jane And Jack the Journeyman

I know, although when looks meet
I tremble to the bone,
The more I leave the door unlatched
The sooner love is gone,
For love is but a skein unwound
Between the dark and dawn.

A lonely ghost the ghost is
That to God shall come;
I — love's skein upon the ground,
My body in the tomb —
Shall leap into the light lost
In my mother's womb.

But were I left to lie alone
In an empty bed,
The skein so bound us ghost to ghost
When he turned his head

passing on the road that night,
Mine must walk when dead.

V

Crazy Jane on God

That lover of a night
Came when he would,
Went in the dawning light
Whether I would or no;
Men come, men go;
All things remain in God.

Banners choke the sky;
Men-at-arms tread;
Armoured horses neigh
In the narrow pass:
All things remain in God.

Before their eyes a house
That from childhood stood
Uninhabited, ruinous,
Suddenly lit up
From door to top:
All things remain in God.

I had wild Jack for a lover;
Though like a road
That men pass over
My body makes no moan
But sings on:
All things remain in God.

VI

Crazy Jane Talks with the Bishop

I met the Bishop on the road
And much said he and I.
'Those breasts are flat and fallen now,
Those veins must soon be dry;
Live in a heavenly mansion,

Not in some foul sty.'
'Fair and foul are near of kin,
And fair needs foul,' I cried.
'My friends are gone, but that's a truth
Nor grave nor bed denied,
Learned in bodily lowliness
And in the heart's pride.

'A woman can be proud and stiff
When on love intent;
But Love has pitched his mansion in
The place of excrement;
For nothing can be sole or whole
That has not been rent.'

VII

Crazy Jane Grown Old Looks at the Dancers

I found that ivory image there
Dancing with her chosen youth,
But when he wound her coal-black hair
As though to strangle her, no scream
Or bodily movement did I dare,
Eyes under eyelids did so gleam;
Love is like the lion's tooth.

When she, and though some said she played
I said that she had danced heart's truth,
Drew a knife to strike him dead,
I could but leave him to his fate;
For no matter what is said
They had all that had their hate;
Love is like the lion's tooth.

Did he die or did she die?
Seemed to die or died they both?
God be with the times when I
Cared not a thraneen for what chanced
So that I had the limbs to try
Such a dance as there was danced —
Love is like the lion's tooth.

VIII

Girl's Song

I went out alone
To sing a song or two,
My fancy on a man,
And you know who.

Another came in sight
That on a stick relied
To hold himself upright;
I sat and cried.

And that was all my song —
When everything is told,
Saw I an old man young
Or young man old?

IX

Young Man's Song

'She will change,' I cried.
'Into a withered crone.'
The heart in my side,
That so still had lain,
In noble rage replied
And beat upon the bone:

'Uplift those eyes and throw
Those glances unafraid:
She would as bravely show
Did all the fabric fade;
No withered crone I saw
Before the world was made.'

Abashed by that report,
For the heart cannot lie,
I knelt in the dirt.
And all shall bend the knee
To my offended heart
Until it pardon me.

X

Her Anxiety

Earth in beauty dressed
Awaits returning spring.
All true love must die,
Alter at the best
Into some lesser thing.
Prove that I lie.

Such body lovers have,
Such exacting breath,
That they touch or sigh.
Every touch they give,
Love is nearer death.
Prove that I lie.

XI

His Confidence

Undying love to buy
I wrote upon
The corners of this eye
All wrongs done.
What payment were enough
For undying love?

I broke my heart in two
So hard I struck.
What matter? for I know
That out of rock,
Out of a desolate source,
Love leaps upon its course.

XII

Love's Loneliness

Old fathers, great-grandfathers,
Rise as kindred should.
If ever lover's loneliness
Came where you stood,
Pray that Heaven protect us
That protect your blood.

The mountain throws a shadow,
Thin is the moon's horn;
What did we remember
Under the ragged thorn?
Dread has followed longing,
And our hearts are torn.

XIII

Her Dream

I dreamed as in my bed I lay,
All night's fathomless wisdom come,
That I had shorn my locks away
And laid them on Love's lettered tomb:
But something bore them out of sight
In a great tumult of the air,
And after nailed upon the night
Berenice's burning hair.

XIV

His Bargain

Who talks of Plato's spindle;
What set it whirling round?
Eternity may dwindle,
Time is unwound,
Dan and Jerry Lout
Change their loves about.

However they may take it,
Before the thread began

I made, and may not break it
When the last thread has run,
A bargain with that hair
And all the windings there.

XV

Three Things

'O cruel Death, give three things back,'
Sang a bone upon the shore;
'A child found all a child can lack,
Whether of pleasure or of rest,
Upon the abundance of my breast':
A bone wave-whitened and dried in the wind.

'Three dear things that women know,'
Sang a bone upon the shore;
'A man if I but held him so
When my body was alive
Found all the pleasure that life gave':
A bone wave-whitened and dried in the wind.

'The third thing that I think of yet,'
Sang a bone upon the shore,
'Is that morning when I met
Face to face my rightful man
And did after stretch and yawn':
A bone wave-whitened and dried in the wind.

XVI

Lullaby

Beloved, may your sleep be sound
That have found it where you fed.
What were all the world's alarms
To mighty paris when he found
Sleep upon a golden bed
That first dawn in Helen's arms?

Sleep, beloved, such a sleep
As did that wild Tristram know
When, the potion's work being done,

Roe could run or doe could leap
Under oak and beechen bough,
Roe could leap or doe could run;

Such a sleep and sound as fell
Upon Eurotas' grassy bank
When the holy bird, that there
Accomplished his predestined will,
From the limbs of Leda sank
But not from her protecting care.

XVII
After Long Silence
Speech after long silence; it is right,
All other lovers being estranged or dead,
Unfriendly lamplight hid under its shade,
The curtains drawn upon unfriendly night,
That we descant and yet again descant
Upon the supreme theme of Art and Song:
Bodily decrepitude is wisdom; young
We loved each other and were ignorant.

XVIII
Mad As the Mist And Snow
Bolt and bar the shutter,
For the foul winds blow:
Our minds are at their best this night,
And I seem to know
That everything outside us is
Mad as the mist and snow.

Horace there by Homer stands,
Plato stands below,
And here is Tully's open page.
How many years ago
Were you and I unlettered lads
Mad as the mist and snow?

You ask what makes me sigh, old friend,
What makes me shudder so?

I shudder and I sigh to think
That even Cicero
And many-minded Homer were
Mad as the mist and snow.

XIX

Those Dancing Days Are Gone

Come, let me sing into your ear;
Those dancing days are gone,
All that silk and satin gear;
Crouch upon a stone,
Wrapping that foul body up
In as foul a rag:
I carry the sun in a golden cup.
The moon in a silver bag.

Curse as you may I sing it through;
What matter if the knave
That the most could pleasure you,
The children that he gave,
Are somewhere sleeping like a top
Under a marble flag?
I carry the sun in a golden cup.
The moon in a silver bag.

I thought it out this very day.
Noon upon the clock,
A man may put pretence away
Who leans upon a stick,
May sing, and sing until he drop,
Whether to maid or hag:
I carry the sun in a golden cup,
The moon in a silver bag.

XX

'I Am of Ireland'

'I am of Ireland,
And the Holy Land of Ireland,
And time runs on,' cried she.
'Come out of charity,
Come dance with me in Ireland.'

One man, one man alone
In that outlandish gear,
One solitary man
Of all that rambled there
Had turned his stately head.
'That is a long way off,
And time runs on,' he said,
'And the night grows rough.'

'I am of Ireland,
And the Holy Land of Ireland,
And time runs on,' cried she.
'Come out of charity
And dance with me in Ireland.'

'The fiddlers are all thumbs,
Or the fiddle-string accursed,
The drums and the kettledrums
And the trumpets all are burst,
And the trombone,' cried he,
'The trumpet and trombone,'
And cocked a malicious eye,
'But time runs on, runs on.'

'I am of Ireland,
And the Holy Land of Ireland,
And time runs on,' cried she.
"Come out of charity
And dance with me in Ireland.'

XXI

The Dancer at Cruachan And Cro-Patrick

I, proclaiming that there is
Among birds or beasts or men
One that is perfect or at peace.
Danced on Cruachan's windy plain,
Upon Cro-patrick sang aloud;
All that could run or leap or swim
Whether in wood, water or cloud,
Acclaiming, proclaiming, declaiming Him.

XXII

Tom the Lunatic

Sang old Tom the lunatic
That sleeps under the canopy:
'What change has put my thoughts astray
And eyes that had so keen a sight?
What has turned to smoking wick
Nature's pure unchanging light?

'Huddon and Duddon and Daniel O'Leary.
Holy Joe, the beggar-man,
Wenching, drinking, still remain
Or sing a penance on the road;
Something made these eyeballs weary
That blinked and saw them in a shroud.

'Whatever stands in field or flood,
Bird, beast, fish or man,
Mare or stallion, cock or hen,
Stands in God's unchanging eye
In all the vigour of its blood;
In that faith I live or die.'

XXIII

Tom at Cruachan

On Cruachan's plain slept he
That must sing in a rhyme
What most could shake his soul:
'The stallion Eternity

Mounted the mare of Time,
'Gat the foal of the world.'

XXIV
Old Tom Again
Things out of perfection sail,
And all their swelling canvas wear,
Nor shall the self-begotten fail
Though fantastic men suppose
Building-yard and stormy shore,
Winding-sheet and swaddling-clothes.

XXV
The Delphic Oracle upon Plotinus
Behold that great Plotinus swim,
Buffeted by such seas;
Bland Rhadamanthus beckons him,
But the Golden Race looks dim,
Salt blood blocks his eyes.

Scattered on the level grass
Or winding through the grove
Plato there and Minos pass,
There stately Pythagoras
And all the choir of Love.

A Woman Young And Old

I
Father And Child
She hears me strike the board and say
That she is under ban
Of all good men and women,
Being mentioned with a man
That has the worst of all bad names;
And thereupon replies
That his hair is beautiful,
Cold as the March wind his eyes.

II

Before The World Was Made

If I make the lashes dark
And the eyes more bright
And the lips more scarlet,
Or ask if all be right
From mirror after mirror,
No vanity's displayed:
I'm looking for the face I had
Before the world was made.
What if I look upon a man
As though on my beloved,
And my blood be cold the while
And my heart unmoved?
Why should he think me cruel
Or that he is betrayed?
I'd have him love the thing that was
Before the world was made.

III

A First Confession

I admit the briar
Entangled in my hair
Did not injure me;
My blenching and trembling,
Nothing but dissembling,
Nothing but coquetry.

I long for truth, and yet
I cannot stay from that
My better self disowns,
For a man's attention
Brings such satisfaction
To the craving in my bones.
Brightness that I pull back
From the Zodiac,
Why those questioning eyes
That are fixed upon me?
What can they do but shun me
If empty night replies?

IV

Her Triumph

I did the dragon's will until you came
Because I had fancied love a casual
Improvisation, or a settled game
That followed if I let the kerchief fall:
Those deeds were best that gave the minute wings
And heavenly music if they gave it wit;
And then you stood among the dragon-rings.
I mocked, being crazy, but you mastered it
And broke the chain and set my ankles free,
Saint George or else a pagan Perseus;
And now we stare astonished at the sea,
And a miraculous strange bird shrieks at us.

V

Consolation

O but there is wisdom
In what the sages said;
But stretch that body for a while
And lay down that head
Till I have told the sages
Where man is comforted.

How could passion run so deep
Had I never thought
That the crime of being born
Blackens all our lot?
But where the crime's committed
The crime can be forgot.

VI

Chosen

The lot of love is chosen. I learnt that much
Struggling for an image on the track
Of the whirling Zodiac.
Scarce did he my body touch,
Scarce sank he from the west
Or found a subtetranean rest

On the maternal midnight of my breast
Before I had marked him on his northern way,
And seemed to stand although in bed I lay.

I struggled with the horror of daybreak,
I chose it for my lot! If questioned on
My utmost pleasure with a man
By some new-married bride, I take
That stillness for a theme
Where his heart my heart did seem
And both adrift on the miraculous stream
Where — wrote a learned astrologer —
The Zodiac is changed into a sphere.

VII

Parting

He. Dear, I must be gone
While night shuts the eyes
Of the household spies;
That song announces dawn.

She. No, night's bird and love's
Bids all true lovers rest,
While his loud song reproves
The murderous stealth of day.

He. Daylight already flies
From mountain crest to crest

She. That light is from the moon.

He. That bird ...

She. Let him sing on,
I offer to love's play
My dark declivities.

VIII

Her Vision in the Wood

Dry timber under that rich foliage,
At wine-dark midnight in the sacred wood,
Too old for a man's love I stood in rage
Imagining men. Imagining that I could
A greater with a lesser pang assuage
Or but to find if withered vein ran blood,
I tore my body that its wine might cover
Whatever could recall the lip of lover.

And after that I held my fingers up,
Stared at the wine-dark nail, or dark that ran
Down every withered finger from the top;
But the dark changed to red, and torches shone,
And deafening music shook the leaves; a troop
Shouldered a litter with a wounded man,
Or smote upon the string and to the sound
Sang of the beast that gave the fatal wound.

All stately women moving to a song
With loosened hair or foreheads grief-distraught,
It seemed a Quattrocento painter's throng,
A thoughtless image of Mantegna's thought —
Why should they think that are for ever young?
Till suddenly in grief's contagion caught,
I stared upon his blood-bedabbled breast
And sang my malediction with the rest.

That thing all blood and mire, that beast-torn wreck,
Half turned and fixed a glazing eye on mine,
And, though love's bitter-sweet had all come back,
Those bodies from a picture or a coin
Nor saw my body fall nor heard it shriek,
Nor knew, drunken with singing as with wine,
That they had brought no fabulous symbol there
But my heart's victim and its torturer.

IX

A Last Confession

What lively lad most pleasured me
Of all that with me lay?
I answer that I gave my soul
And loved in misery,
But had great pleasure with a lad
That I loved bodily.

Flinging from his arms I laughed
To think his passion such
He fancied that I gave a soul
Did but our bodies touch,
And laughed upon his breast to think
Beast gave beast as much.

I gave what other women gave
That stepped out of their clothes.
But when this soul, its body off,
Naked to naked goes,
He it has found shall find therein
What none other knows,

And give his own and take his own
And rule in his own right;
And though it loved in misery
Close and cling so tight,
There's not a bird of day that dare
Extinguish that delight.

X

Meeting

Hidden by old age awhile
In masker's cloak and hood,
Each hating what the other loved,
Face to face we stood:
'That I have met with such,' said he,
'Bodes me little good.'

'Let others boast their fill,' said I,
'But never dare to boast
That such as I had such a man
For lover in the past;
Say that of living men I hate
Such a man the most.'

'A loony'd boast of such a love,'
He in his rage declared:
But such as he for such as me —
Could we both discard
This beggarly habiliment —
Had found a sweeter word.

XI

From the 'Antigone'

Overcome — O bitter sweetness,
Inhabitant of the soft cheek of a girl —
The rich man and his affairs,
The fat flocks and the fields' fatness,
Mariners, rough harvesters;
Overcome Gods upon Parnassus;

Overcome the Empyrean; hurl
Heaven and Earth out of their places,
That in the same calamity
Brother and brother, friend and friend,
Family and family,
City and city may contend,
By that great glory driven wild.

Pray I will and sing I must,
And yet I weep — Oedipus' child
Descends into the loveless dust.

FROM A FULL MOON IN MARCH
1933

Parnell's Funeral

I
Under the Great Comedian's tomb the crowd.
A bundle of tempestuous cloud is blown
About the sky; where that is clear of cloud
Brightness remains; a brighter star shoots down;
What shudders run through all that animal blood?
What is this sacrifice? Can someone there
Recall the Cretan barb that pierced a star?

Rich foliage that the starlight glittered through,
A frenzied crowd, and where the branches sprang
A beautiful seated boy; a sacred bow;
A woman, and an arrow on a string;
A pierced boy, image of a star laid low.
That woman, the Great Mother imaging,
Cut out his heart. Some master of design
Stamped boy and tree upon Sicilian coin.

An age is the reversal of an age:
When strangers murdered Emmet, Fitzgerald, Tone,
We lived like men that watch a painted stage.
What matter for the scene, the scene once gone:
It had not touched our lives. But popular rage,
Hysterica passio dragged this quarry down.
None shared our guilt; nor did we play a part
Upon a painted stage when we devoured his heart.

Come, fix upon me that accusing eye.
I thirst for accusation. All that was sung.
All that was said in Ireland is a lie
Bred out of the contagion of the throng,
Saving the rhyme rats hear before they die.
Leave nothing but the nothings that belong
To this bare soul, let all men judge that can
Whether it be an animal or a man.

II

The rest I pass, one sentence I unsay.
Had de Valera eaten Parnell's heart
No loose-lipped demagogue had won the day.
No civil rancour torn the land apart.

Had Cosgrave eaten Parnell's heart, the land's
Imagination had been satisfied,
Or lacking that, government in such hands,
O'Higgins its sole statesman had not died.

Had even O'Duffy – but I name no more -
Their school a crowd, his master solitude;
Through Jonathan Swift's dark grove he passed, and there
Plucked bitter wisdom that enriched his blood.

Three Songs to the Same Tune

I

Grandfather sang it under the gallows:
'Hear, gentlemen, ladies, and all mankind:
Money is good and a girl might be better.
But good strong blows are delights to the mind.'
There, standing on the cart,
He sang it from his heart.

Those fanatics all that we do would undo;
Down the fanatic, down the clown;

Down, down, hammer them down,
Down to the tune of O'Donnell Abu.

'A girl I had, but she followed another,
Money I had, and it went in the night,
Strong drink I had, and it brought me to sorrow,
But a good strong cause and blows are delight.'
All there caught up the tune:
'On, on, my darling man'.

Those fanatics all that we do would undo;
Down the fanatic, down the clown;
Down, down, hammer them down,
Down to the tune of O'Donnell Abu.

'Money is good and a girl might be better,
No matter what happens and who takes the fall,
But a good strong cause' — the rope gave a jerk there,
No more sang he, for his throat was too small;
But he kicked before he died,
He did it out of pride.

Those fanatics all that we do would undo;
Down the fanatic, down the clown;
Down, down, hammer them down,
Down to the tune of O'Donnell Abu.

II

Justify all those renowned generations;
They left their bodies to fatten the wolves,
They left their homesteads to fatten the foxes,
Fled to far countries, or sheltered themselves
In cavem, crevice, hole,
Defending Ireland's soul.

'Drown all the dogs,' said the fierce young woman,
'They killed my goose and a cat.
Drown, drown in the water-but,
Drown all the dogs,' said the fierce young woman.

Justify all those renowned generations,
Justify all that have sunk in their blood,
Justify all that have died on the scaffold,
Justify all that have fled, that have stood,
Stood or have marched the night long
Singing, singing a song.

'Drown all the dogs,' said the fierce young woman.
'They killed my goose and a cat.
Drown, drown in the water-butt,
Drown all the dogs,' said the fierce young woman.

Fail, and that history turns into rubbish,
All that great past to a trouble of fools;
Those that come after shall mock at O'Donnell,
Mock at the memory of both O'Neills,
Mock Emmet, mock Parnell:
All the renown that fell.

'Drown all the dogs,' said the fierce young woman,
'They killed my goose and a cat.
Drown, drown in the water-butt,
Drown all the dogs,' said the fierce young woman.

III

The soldier takes pride in saluting his Captain,
The devotee proffers a knee to his Lord,
Some back a mare thrown from a thoroughbred,
Troy backed its Helen; Troy died and adored;
Great nations blossom above;
A slave bows down to a slave.

'Who'd care to dig em,' said the old, old man,
'Those six feet marked in chalk?
Much I talk, more I walk;
Time I were buried,' said the old, old man.

When nations are empty up there at the top,
When order has weakened or faction is strong,

Time for us all to pick out a good tune,
Take to the roads and go marching along.
March, march — How does it run? —
O any old words to a tune.

Who'd care to dig 'em,' said the old, old man,
'Those six feet marked in chalk?
Much I talk, more I walk;}
Time I were buried,' said the old, old man.

Soldiers take pride in saluting their Captain,
Where are the captains that govern mankind?
What happens a tree that has nothing within it?
O marching wind, O a blast of the wind,
Marching, marching along.
March, march, lift up the song:

'Who'd care to dig 'em,' said the old, old man.
'Those six feet marked in chalk?
Much I talk, more I walk;
Time I were buried,' said the old, old man.

Alternative Song for the Severed Head in 'The King of the Great Clock Tower'

Saddle and ride, I heard a man say,
Out of Ben Bulben and Knocknarea,
What says the Clock in the Great Clock Tower?
All those tragic characters ride
But turn from Rosses' crawling tide,
The meet's upon the mountain-side.
A slow low note and an iron bell.

What brought them there so far from their home.
Cuchulain that fought night long with the foam,
What says the Clock in the Great Clock Tower?
Niamh that rode on it; lad and lass
That sat so still and played at the chess?
What but heroic wantonness?
A slow low note and an iron bell.

Aleel, his Countess; Hanrahan
That seemed but a wild wenching man;
What says the Clock in the Great Clock Tower?
And all alone comes riding there
The King that could make his people stare,
Because he had feathers instead of hair.
A slow low note and an iron bell.

Two Songs Rewritten for the Tune's Sake

I
My Paistin Finn is my sole desire,
And I am shrunken to skin and bone,
For all my heart has had for its hire
Is what I can whistle alone and alone.
Oro, oro!
Tomorrow night I will break down the door.

What is the good of a man and he
Alone and alone, with a speckled shin?
I would that I drank with my love on my knee,
Between two barrels at the inn.
Oro, oro!
Tomorrow night I will break down the door.

Alone and alone nine nights I lay
Between two bushes under the rain;
I thought to have whistled her down that way,
I whistled and whistled and whistled in vain.
Oro, oro!
Tomorrow night I will break down the door.

from The Pot of Broth
Tune: Paistin Firm

II
I would that I were an old beggar
Rolling a blind pearl eye,
For he cannot see my lady
Go gallivanting by;

A dreary, dreepy beggar
Without a friend on the earth
But a thieving rascally cur —
O a beggar blind from his birth;

Or anything else but a rhymer
Without a thing in his head
But rhymes for a beautiful lady,
He rhyming alone in his bed.

from The Player Queen

A Prayer for Old Age

God guard me from those thoughts men think
In the mind alone;
He that sings a lasting song
Thinks in a marrow-bone;

From all that makes a wise old man
That can be praised of all;
O what am I that I should not seem
For the song's sake a fool?

I pray — for word is out
And prayer comes round again —
That I may seem, though I die old,
A foolish, passionate man

Church And State

Here is fresh matter, poet,
Matter for old age meet;
Might of the Church and the State,
Their mobs put under their feet.
O but heart's wine shall run pure,
Mind's bread grow sweet.

That were a cowardly song,
Wander in dreams no more;
What if the Church and the State
Are the mob that howls at the door!
Wine shall run thick to the end,
Bread taste sour.

Supernatural Songs

I

Ribh at the Tomb of Baile And Aillinn
Because you have found me in the pitch-dark night
With open book you ask me what I do.
Mark and digest my tale, carry it afar
To those that never saw this tonsured head
Nor heard this voice that ninety years have cracked.
Of Baile and Aillinn you need not speak,
All know their tale, all know what leaf and twig,
What juncture of the apple and the yew,
Surmount their bones; but speak what none have heard.
The miracle that gave them such a death
Transfigured to pure substance what had once
Been bone and sinew; when such bodies join
There is no touching here, nor touching there,
Nor straining joy, but whole is joined to whole;
For the intercourse of angels is a light
Where for its moment both seem lost, consumed.

Here in the pitch-dark atmosphere above
The trembling of the apple and the yew,
Here on the anniversary of their death,
The anniversary of their first embrace,
Those lovers, purified by tragedy,
Hurry into each other's arms; these eyes,
By water, herb and solitary prayer
Made aquiline, are open to that light.
Though somewhat broken by the leaves, that light
Lies in a circle on the grass; therein
I turn the pages of my holy book.

II
Ribh Denounces Patrick
An abstract Greek absurdity has crazed the man —
Recall that masculine Trinity. Man, woman, child
(a daughter or a son)
That's how all natural or supernatural stories run.
Natural and supernatural with the self-same ring are wed.
As man, as beast, as an ephemeral fly begets,
Godhead begets Godhead,
For things below are copies, the Great Smaragdine Tablet said.

Yet all must copy copies, all increase their kind;
When the conflagration of their passion sinks,
damped by the body or the mind,
That juggling nature mounts, her coil in their embraces twined.

The mirror-scaled serpent is multiplicity,
But all that run in couples, on earth, in flood or air,
share God that is but three,
And could beget or bear themselves could they but love as He.

III
Ribh in Ecstasy
What matter that you understood no word!
Doubtless I spoke or sang what I had heard
In broken sentences. My soul had found
All happiness in its own cause or ground.
Godhead on Godhead in sexual spasm begot

Godhead. Some shadow fell. My soul forgot
Those amorous cries that out of quiet come
And must the common round of day resume.

IV

There

There all the barrel-hoops are knit,
There all the serpent-tails are bit,
There all the gyres converge in one,
There all the planets drop in the Sun.

V

Ribh Considers Christian Love Insufficient

Why should I seek for love or study it?
It is of God and passes human wit.
I study hatred with great diligence,
For that's a passion in my own control,
A sort of besom that can clear the soul
Of everything that is not mind or sense.

Why do I hate man, woman or event?
That is a light my jealous soul has sent.
From terror and deception freed it can
Discover impurities, can show at last
How soul may walk when all such things are past,
How soul could walk before such things began.

Then my delivered soul herself shall learn
A darker knowledge and in hatred turn
From every thought of God mankind has had.
Thought is a garment and the soul's a bride
That cannot in that trash and tinsel hide:
Hatred of God may bring the soul to God.

At stroke of midnight soul cannot endure
A bodily or mental furniture.
What can she take until her Master give!
Where can she look until He make the show!
What can she know until He bid her know!
How can she live till in her blood He live!

VI

He And She

As the moon sidles up
Must she sidle up,
As trips the scared moon
Away must she trip:
'His light had struck me blind
Dared I stop.'

She sings as the moon sings:
'I am I, am I;
The greater grows my light
The further that I fly'.
All creation shivers
With that sweet cry

VII

What Magic Drum?

He holds him from desire, all but stops his breathing lest
Primordial Motherhood forsake his limbs, the child no longer rest,
Drinking joy as it were milk upon his breast.

Through light-obliterating garden foliage what magic drum?
Down limb and breast or down that glimmering belly move his
mouth and sinewy tongue.
What from the forest came? What beast has licked its young?

VIII

Whence Had They Come?

Eternity is passion, girl or boy
Cry at the onset of their sexual joy
'For ever and for ever'; then awake
Ignorant what Dramatis Personae spake;
A passion-driven exultant man sings out
Sentences that he has never thought;
The Flagellant lashes those submissive loins
Ignorant what that dramatist enjoins,
What master made the lash. Whence had they come,
The hand and lash that beat down frigid Rome?

What sacred drama through her body heaved
When world-transforming Charlemagne was conceived?

IX

The Four Ages of Man

He with body waged a fight,
But body won; it walks upright.

Then he struggled with the heart;
Innocence and peace depart.

Then he struggled with the mind;
His proud heart he left behind.

Now his wars on God begin;
At stroke of midnight God shall win.

X

Conjunctions

If Jupiter and Saturn meet,
What a crop of mummy wheat!

The sword's a cross; thereon He died:
On breast of Mars the goddess sighed.

XI

A Needle's Eye

All the stream that's roaring by
Came out of a needle's eye;
Things unborn, things that are gone,
From needle's eye still goad it on.

XII

Meru

Civilisation is hooped together, brought
Under a rule, under the semblance of peace
By manifold illusion; but man's life is thought,
And he, despite his terror, cannot cease
Ravening through century after century,
Ravening, raging and uprooting that he may come

Into the desolation of reality:
Egypt and Greece, goodbye, and goodbye, Rome!

Hermits upon Mount Meru or Everest,
Caverned in night under the drifted snow,
Or where that snow and winter's dreadful blast
Beat down upon their naked bodies, know
That day brings round the night, that before dawn
His glory and his monuments are gone.

LAST POEMS
1936–1939

The Gyres

The gyres! the gyres! Old Rocky Face, look forth;
Things thought too long can be no longer thought,
For beauty dies of beauty, worth of worth,
And ancient lineaments are blotted out.
Irrational streams of blood are staining earth;
Empedocles has thrown all things about;
Hector is dead and there's a light in Troy;
We that look on but laugh in tragic joy.

What matter though numb nightmare ride on top,
And blood and mire the sensitive body stain?
What matter? Heave no sigh, let no tear drop,
A greater, a more gracious time has gone;
For painted forms or boxes of make-up
In ancient tombs I sighed, but not again;
What matter? Out of cavern comes a voice,
And all it knows is that one word 'Rejoice!'

Conduct and work grow coarse, and coarse the soul,
What matter? Those that Rocky Face holds dear,
Lovers of horses and of women, shall,
From marble of a broken sepulchre,
Or dark betwixt the polecat and the owl,
Or any rich, dark nothing disinter
The workman, noble and saint, and all things run
On that unfashionable gyre again.

Lapis Lazuli

(For Harry Clifton)

I have heard that hysterical women say
They are sick of the palette and fiddle-bow.
Of poets that are always gay,
For everybody knows or else should know
That if nothing drastic is done
Aeroplane and Zeppelin will come out.
Pitch like King Billy bomb-balls in
Until the town lie beaten flat.

All perform their tragic play,
There struts Hamlet, there is Lear,
That's Ophelia, that Cordelia;
Yet they, should the last scene be there,
The great stage curtain about to drop,
If worthy their prominent part in the play,
Do not break up their lines to weep.
They know that Hamlet and Lear are gay;
Gaiety transfiguring all that dread.
All men have aimed at, found and lost;
Black out; Heaven blazing into the head:
Tragedy wrought to its uttermost.
Though Hamlet rambles and Lear rages,
And all the drop-scenes drop at once
Upon a hundred thousand stages,
It cannot grow by an inch or an ounce.

On their own feet they came, or on shipboard,'
Camel-back; horse-back, ass-back, mule-back,
Old civilisations put to the sword.
Then they and their wisdom went to rack:
No handiwork of Callimachus,
Who handled marble as if it were bronze,
Made draperies that seemed to rise
When sea-wind swept the corner, stands;
His long lamp-chimney shaped like the stem
Of a slender palm, stood but a day;
All things fall and are built again,
And those that build them again are gay.

Two Chinamen, behind them a third,
Are carved in lapis lazuli,
Over them flies a long-legged bird,
A symbol of longevity;
The third, doubtless a serving-man,
Carries a musical instrument.

Every discoloration of the stone,
Every accidental crack or dent,
Seems a watercourse or an avalanche,
Or lofty slope where it still snows
Though doubtless plum or cherry-branch
Sweetens the little halfway house
Those Chinamen climb towards, and I
Delight to imagine them seated there;
There, on the mountain and the sky,
On all the tragic scene they stare.
One asks for mournful melodies;
Accomplished fingers begin to play.
Their eyes mid many wrinkles, their eyes,
Their ancient, glittering eyes, are gay.

Imitated from the Japanese

A most astonishing thing —
Seventy years have I lived;

(Hurrah for the flowers of Spring,
For Spring is here again.)

Seventy years have I lived
No ragged beggar-man,
Seventy years have I lived,
Seventy years man and boy,
And never have I danced for joy.

Sweet Dancer

The girl goes dancing there
On the leaf-sown, new-mown, smooth
Grass plot of the garden;
Escaped from bitter youth,
Escaped out of her crowd,
Or out of her black cloud.
Ah, dancer, ah, sweet dancer!

If strange men come from the house
To lead her away, do not say
That she is happy being crazy;
Lead them gently astray;
Let her finish her dance,
Let her finish her dance.
Ah, dancer, ah, sweet dancer!

The Three Bushes

(*An incident from the 'Historia mei Temporis' of the Abbe Michel de Bourdeille*)

Said lady once to lover,
'None can rely upon
A love that lacks its proper food;
And if your love were gone
How could you sing those songs of love?
I should be blamed, young man.
O my dear, O my dear.

Have no lit candles in your room,'
That lovely lady said,
'That I at midnight by the clock
May creep into your bed,
For if I saw myself creep in
I think I should drop dead.'
O my dear, O my dear.

'I love a man in secret,
Dear chambermaid,' said she.

'I know that I must drop down dead
If he stop loving me,
Yet what could I but drop down dead
If I lost my chastity?
O my dear, O my dear.

'So you must lie beside him
And let him think me there.
And maybe we are all the same
Where no candles are,
And maybe we are all the same
That strip the body bare.'
O my dear, O my dear.

But no dogs barked, and midnights chimed,
And through the chime she'd say,
'That was a lucky thought of mine,
My lover looked so gay';
But heaved a sigh if the chambermaid
Looked half asleep all day.
O my dear, O my dear.

'No, not another song,' said he,
'Because my lady came
A year ago for the first time
At midnight to my room,
And I must lie between the sheets
When the clock begins to chime.'
O my dear, O my dear.

'A laughing, crying, sacred song,
A leching song,' they said.
Did ever men hear such a song?
No, but that day they did.
Did ever man ride such a race?
No, not until he rode.
O my dear, O my dear.

But when his horse had put its hoof
Into a rabbit-hole
He dropped upon his head and died.

His lady saw it all
And dropped and died thereon, for she
Loved him with her soul.
O my dear, O my dear.

The chambermaid lived long, and took
Their graves into her charge,
And there two bushes planted
That when they had grown large
Seemed sprung from but a single root
So did their roses merge.
O my dear, O my dear.

When she was old and dying,
The priest came where she was;
She made a full confession.
Long looked he in her face,
And O he was a good man
And understood her case.
O my dear, O my dear.

He bade them take and bury her
Beside her lady's man,
And set a rose-tree on her grave,
And now none living can,
When they have plucked a rose there,
Know where its roots began.
O my dear, O my dear.

The Lady's First Song

I turn round
Like a dumb beast in a show.
Neither know what I am
Nor where I go,
My language beaten
Into one name;

I am in love
And that is my shame.

What hurts the soul
My soul adores,
No better than a beast
Upon all fours.

The Lady's Second Song

What sort of man is coming
To lie between your feet?
What matter, we are but women.
Wash; make your body sweet;
I have cupboards of dried fragrance.
I can strew the sheet.
The Lord have mercy upon us.

He shall love my soul as though
Body were not at all,
He shall love your body
Untroubled by the soul,
Love cram love's two divisions
Yet keep his substance whole.
The Lord have mercy upon us.

Soul must learn a love that is
Proper to my breast,
Limbs a love in common
With every noble beast.
If soul may look and body touch,
Which is the more blest?
The Lord have mercy upon us.

The Lady's Third Song

When you and my true lover meet
And he plays tunes between your feet,
Speak no evil of the soul,
Nor think that body is the whole,
For I that am his daylight lady

Know worse evil of the body;
But in honour split his love
Till either neither have enough,
That I may hear if we should kiss
A contrapuntal serpent hiss,
You, should hand explore a thigh,
All the labouring heavens sigh.

The Lover's Song

Bird sighs for the air,
Thought for I know not where,
For the womb the seed sighs.
Now sinks the same rest
On mind, on nest,
On straining thighs.

The Chambermaid's First Song

How came this ranger
Now sunk in rest,
Stranger with stranger.
On my cold breast?

What's left to sigh for?
Strange night has come;
God's love has hidden him
Out of all harm,
Pleasure has made him
Weak as a worm.

The Chambermaid's Second Song

From pleasure of the bed,
Dull as a worm,
His rod and its butting head
Limp as a worm,
His spirit that has fled
Blind as a worm.

An Acre of Grass

Picture and book remain,
An acre of green grass
For air and exercise,
Now strength of body goes;
Midnight, an old house
Where nothing stirs but a mouse.

My temptation is quiet.
Here at life's end
Neither loose imagination,
Nor the mill of the mind
Consuming its rag and bone,
Can make the truth known.

Grant me an old man's frenzy,
Myself must I remake
Till I am Timon and Lear
Or that William Blake
Who beat upon the wall
Till Truth obeyed his call;

A mind Michael Angelo knew
That can pierce the clouds,
Or inspired by frenzy
Shake the dead in their shrouds;
Forgotten else by mankind,
An old man's eagle mind.

What Then?

His chosen comrades thought at school
He must grow a famous man;
He thought the same and lived by rule,
All his twenties crammed with toil;
'What then?' sang Plato's ghost. 'What then?'

Everything he wrote was read,
After certain years he won
Sufficient money for his need,
Friends that have been friends indeed;
'What then?' sang Plato's ghost. 'What then?'

All his happier dreams came true —
A small old house, wife, daughter, son,
Grounds where plum and cabbage grew,
Poets and Wits about him drew;
'What then?' sang Plato's ghost. 'What then?'

'The work is done,' grown old he thought,
'According to my boyish plan;
Let the fools rage, I swerved in naught,
Something to perfection brought';
But louder sang that ghost, 'What then?'

Beautiful Lofty Things

Beautiful lofty things: O'Leary's noble head;
My father upon the Abbey stage, before him a raging crowd:
'This Land of Saints,' and then as the applause died out,
'Of plaster Saints'; his beautiful mischievous head thrown back.
Standish O'Grady supporting himself between the tables
Speaking to a drunken audience high nonsensical words;
Augusta Gregory seated at her great ormolu table,
Her eightieth winter approaching: 'Yesterday he threatened my life.
I told him that nightly from six to seven I sat at this table,
The blinds drawn up'; Maud Gonne at Howth station waiting a train,
Pallas Athene in that straight back and arrogant head:
All the Olympians; a thing never known again.

A Crazed Girl

That crazed girl improvising her music,
Her poetry, dancing upon the shore,
Her soul in division from itself
Climbing, falling she knew not where,
Hiding amid the cargo of a steamship,
Her knee-cap broken, that girl I declare
A beautiful lofty thing, or a thing
Heroically lost, heroically found.

No matter what disaster occurred
She stood in desperate music wound,
Wound, wound, and she made in her triumph
Where the bales and the baskets lay
No common intelligible sound
But sang, 'O sea-starved, hungry sea.'

To Dorothy Wellesley

Stretch towards the moonless midnight of the trees,
As though that hand could reach to where they stand,
And they but famous old upholsteries
Delightful to the touch; tighten that hand
As though to draw them closer yet.

Rammed full
Of that most sensuous silence of the night
(For since the horizon's bought strange dogs are still)
Climb to your chamber full of books and wait,
No books upon the knee, and no one there
But a Great Dane that cannot bay the moon
And now lies sunk in sleep.

What climbs the stair?
Nothing that common women ponder on
If you are worth my hope! Neither Content
Nor satisfied Conscience, but that great family
Some ancient famous authors misrepresent,
The Proud Furies each with her torch on high.

The Curse of Cromwell

You ask what — I have found, and far and wide I go,
Nothing but Cromwell's house and Cromwell's murderous crew,
The lovers and the dancers are beaten into the clay,
And the tall men and the swordsmen and the horsemen, where
are they?
And there is an old beggar wandering in his pride —
His fathers served their fathers before Christ was crucified.
O what of that, O what of that,
What is there left to say?

All neighbourly content and easy talk are gone,
But there's no good complaining, for money's rant is on.
He that's mounting up must on his neighbour mount,
And we and all the Muses are things of no account.
They have schooling of their own, but I pass their schooling by,
What can they know that we know that know the time to die?
O what of that, O what of that,
What is there left to say?

But there's another knowledge that my heart destroys,
As the fox in the old fable destroyed the Spartan boy's
Because it proves that things both can and cannot be;
That the swordsmen and the ladies can still keep company,
Can pay the poet for a verse and hear the fiddle sound,
That I am still their servant though all are underground.
O what of that, O what of that,
What is there left to say?

I came on a great house in the middle of the night,
Its open lighted doorway and its windows all alight,
And all my friends were there and made me welcome too;
But I woke in an old ruin that the winds howled through;
And when I pay attention I must out and walk
Among the dogs and horses that understand my talk.
O what of that, O what of that,
What is there left to say?

Roger Casement

(*After reading 'The Forged Casement Diaries' by Dr Maloney*)

I say that Roger Casement
Did what he had to do.
He died upon the gallows,
But that is nothing new.

Afraid they might be beaten
Before the bench of Time,
They turned a trick by forgery
And blackened his good name.

A perjurer stood ready
To prove their forgery true;
They gave it out to all the world,
And that is something new;

For Spring Rice had to whisper it,
Being their Ambassador,
And then the speakers got it
And writers by the score.

Come Tom and Dick, come all the troop
That cried it far and wide,
Come from the forger and his desk,
Desert the perjurer's side;

Come speak your bit in public
That some amends be made
To this most gallant gentleman
That is in quicklime laid.

The Ghost of Roger Casement

O what has made that sudden noise?
What on the threshold stands?
It never crossed the sea because
John Bull and the sea are friends;
But this is not the old sea
Nor this the old seashore.
What gave that roar of mockery,
That roar in the sea's roar?
The ghost of Roger Casement
Is beating on the door.

John Bull has stood for Parliament,
A dog must have his day,
The country thinks no end of him,
For he knows how to say,
At a beanfeast or a banquet,
That all must hang their trust
Upon the British Empire,
Upon the Church of Christ.
The ghost of Roger Casement
Is beating on the door.

John Bull has gone to India
And all must pay him heed,
For histories are there to prove
That none of another breed
Has had a like inheritance,
Or sucked such milk as he,
And there's no luck about a house
If it lack honesty.
The ghost of Roger Casement
Is beating on the door.

I poked about a village church
And found his family tomb
And copied out what I could read
In that religious gloom;
Found many a famous man there;

But fame and virtue rot.
Draw round, beloved and bitter men,
Draw round and raise a shout;
The ghost of Roger Casement
Is beating on the door.

The O'Rahilly

Sing of the O'Rahilly,
Do not deny his right;
Sing a 'the' before his name
Allow that he, despite
All those learned historians,
Established it for good;
He wrote out that word himself,
He christened himself with blood.
How goes the weather?

Sing of the O'Rahilly
That had such little sense
He told Pearse and Connolly
He'd gone to great expense
Keeping all the Kerry men
Out of that crazy fight;
That he might be there himself
Had travelled half the night.
How goes the weather?

'Am I such a craven that
I should not get the word
But for what some travelling man
Had heard I had not heard?'
Then on Pearse and Connolly
He fixed a bitter look:
'Because I helped to wind the clock
I come to hear it strike.'
How goes the weather?

What remains to sing about
But of the death he met
Stretched under a doorway
Somewhere off Henry Street;
They that found him found upon
The door above his head
'Here died the O'Rahilly.
R.I.P.' writ in blood.
How goes the weather.?

Come Gather round Me, Parnellites

Come gather round me, Parnellites,
And praise our chosen man;
Stand upright on your legs awhile,
Stand upright while you can,
For soon we lie where he is laid,
And he is underground;
Come fill up all those glasses
And pass the bottle round.

And here's a cogent reason,
And I have many more,
He fought the might of England
And saved the Irish poor,
Whatever good a farmer's got
He brought it all to pass;
And here's another reason,
That Parnell loved a lass.

And here's a final reason,
He was of such a kind
Every man that sings a song
Keeps Parnell in his mind.
For Parnell was a proud man,
No prouder trod the ground,
And a proud man's a lovely man,
So pass the bottle round.

The Bishops and the party
That tragic story made,
A husband that had sold his wife
And after that betrayed;
But stories that live longest
Are sung above the glass,
And Parnell loved his country
And Parnell loved his lass.

The Wild Old Wicked Man

'Because I am mad about women
I am mad about the hills,'
Said that wild old wicked man
Who travels where God wills.
'Not to die on the straw at home.
Those hands to close these eyes,
That is all I ask, my dear,
From the old man in the skies.
Daybreak and a candle-end.

'Kind are all your words, my dear,
Do not the rest withhold.
Who can know the year, my dear,
When an old man's blood grows cold?
I have what no young man can have
Because he loves too much.
Words I have that can pierce the heart,
But what can he do but touch?'
Daybreak and a candle-end.

Then said she to that wild old man,
His stout stick under his hand,
'Love to give or to withhold
Is not at my command.
I gave it all to an older man:
That old man in the skies.
Hands that are busy with His beads
Can never close those eyes.'
Daybreak and a candle-end.

'Go your ways, O go your ways,
I choose another mark,
Girls down on the seashore
Who understand the dark;
Bawdy talk for the fishermen;
A dance for the fisher-lads;
When dark hangs upon the water
They turn down their beds.
Daybreak and a candle-end.

'A young man in the dark am I,
But a wild old man in the light,
That can make a cat laugh, or
Can touch by mother wit
Things hid in their marrowbones
From time long passed away,
Hid from all those warty lads
That by their bodies lay.
Daybreak and a candle-end.

'All men live in suffering,
I know as few can know,
Whether they take the upper road
Or stay content on the low,
Rower bent in his row-boat
Or weaver bent at his loom,
Horseman erect upon horseback
Or child hid in the womb.
Daybreak and a candle-end.

'That some stream of lightning
From the old man in the skies
Can burn out that suffering
No right-taught man denies.
But a coarse old man am I,
I choose the second-best,
I forget it all awhile
Upon a woman's breast.'
Daybreak and a candle-end.

The Great Day

Hurrah for revolution and more cannon-shot!
A beggar upon horseback lashes a beggar on foot.
Hurrah for revolution and cannon come again!
The beggars have changed places, but the lash goes on.

Parnell

Parnell came down the road, he said to a cheering man:
'Ireland shall get her freedom and you still break stone.'

What Was Lost

I sing what was lost and dread what was won,
I walk in a battle fought over again,
My king a lost king, and lost soldiers my men;
Feet to the Rising and Setting may run,
They always beat on the same small stone.

The Spur

You think it horrible that lust and rage
Should dance attention upon my old age;
They were not such a plague when I was young;
What else have I to spur me into song?

A Drunken Man's Praise of Sobriety

Come swish around, my pretty punk,
And keep me dancing still
That I may stay a sober man
Although I drink my fill.
Sobriety is a jewel
That I do much adore;
And therefore keep me dancing

Though drunkards lie and snore.
O mind your feet, O mind your feet,
Keep dancing like a wave,
And under every dancer
A dead man in his grave.
No ups and downs, my pretty,
A mermaid, not a punk;
A drunkard is a dead man,
And all dead men are drunk.

The Pilgrim

I fasted for some forty days on bread and buttermilk,
For passing round the bottle with girls in rags or silk,
In country shawl or Paris cloak, had put my wits astray,
And what's the good of women, for all that they can say
Is fol de rol de rolly O.

Round Lough Derg's holy island I went upon the stones,
I prayed at all the Stations upon my matrowbones,
And there I found an old man, and though, I prayed all day
And that old man beside me, nothing would he say
But fol de rol de rolly O.

All know that all the dead in the world about that place are stuck,
And that should mother seek her son she'd have but little luck
Because the fires of purgatory have ate their shapes away;
I swear to God I questioned them, and all they had to say
Was fol de rol de rolly O.

A great black ragged bird appeared when I was in the boat;
Some twenty feet from tip to tip had it stretched rightly out,
With flopping and with flapping it made a great display,
But I never stopped to question, what could the boatman say
But fol de rol de rolly O.

Now I am in the public-house and lean upon the wall,
So come in rags or come in silk, in cloak or country shawl,
And come with learned lovers or with what men you may,

For I can put the whole lot down, and all I have to say
Is fol de rol de rolly O.

Colonel Martin

I
The Colonel went out sailing,
He spoke with Turk and Jew,
With Christian and with Infidel,
For all tongues he knew.
'O what's a wifeless man?' said he,
And he came sailing home.
He rose the latch and went upstairs
And found an empty room.
The Colonel went out sailing.

II
'I kept her much in the country
And she was much alone,
And though she may be there,' he said,
'She may be in the town.
She may be all alone there,
For who can say?' he said.
'I think that I shall find her
In a young man's bed.'
The Colonel went out sailing.

III
The Colonel met a pedlar,
Agreed their clothes to swop,
And bought the grandest jewelry
In a Galway shop,
Instead of thread and needle
Put jewelry in the pack,
Bound a thong about his hand,
Hitched it on his back.
The Colonel went out sailing.

IV
The Colonel knocked on the rich man's door,
'I am sorry,' said the maid,
'My mistress cannot see these things,
But she is still abed,
And never have I looked upon
Jewelry so grand.'
'Take all to your mistress,'
And he laid them on her hand.
The Colonel went out sailing.

V
And he went in and she went on
And both climbed up the stair,
And O he was a clever man,
For he his slippers wore.
And when they came to the top stair
He ran on ahead,
His wife he found and the rich man
In the comfort of a bed.
The Colonel went out sailing.

VI
The Judge at the Assize Court,
When he heard that story told,
Awarded him for damages
Three kegs of gold.
The Colonel said to Tom his man,
'Harness an ass and cart,
Carry the gold about the town,
Throw it in every part.'
The Colonel went out sailing.

VII
And there at all street-corners
A man with a pistol stood,
And the rich man had paid them well
To shoot the Colonel dead;
But they threw down their pistols
And all men heard them swear

That they could never shoot a man
Did all that for the poor.
The Colonel went out sailing.

VIII
'And did you keep no gold, Tom?
You had three kegs,' said he.
'I never thought of that, sir.'
'Then want before you die.'
And want he did; for my own grand-dad
Saw the story's end,
And Tom make out a living
From the seaweed on the strand.
The Colonel went out sailing.

A Model for the Laureate

On thrones from China to Peru
All sorts of kings have sat
That men and women of all sorts
Proclaimed both good and great;
And what's the odds if such as these
For reason of the State
Should keep their lovers waiting,
        Keep their lovers waiting?

Some boast of beggar-kings and kings
Of rascals black and white
That rule because a strong right arm
Puts all men in a fright,
And drunk or sober live at ease
Where none gainsay their right,
And keep their lovers waiting,
        Keep their lovers waiting.

The Muse is mute when public men
Applaud a modern throne:
Those cheers that can be bought or sold,
That office fools have run,

That waxen seal, that signature.
For things like these what decent man
Would keep his lover waiting,
    Keep his lover waiting?

The Old Stone Cross

A statesman is an easy man,
He tells his lies by rote;
A journalist makes up his lies
And takes you by the throat;
So stay at home and drink your beer
And let the neighbours' vote,
        Said the man in the golden breastplate
        Under the old stone Cross.

Because this age and the next age
Engender in the ditch,
No man can know a happy man
From any passing wretch;
If Folly link with Elegance
No man knows which is which,
        Said the man in the golden breastplate
        Under the old stone Cross.

But actors lacking music
Do most excite my spleen,
They say it is more human
To shuffle, grunt and groan,
Not knowing what unearthly stuff
Rounds a mighty scene,
        Said the man in the golden breastplate
        Under the old stone Cross.

The Spirit Medium

Poetry, music, I have loved, and yet
Because of those new dead
That come into my soul and escape
Confusion of the bed,
Or those begotten or unbegotten
Perning in a band,
I bend my body to the spade
Or grope with a dirty hand.

Or those begotten or unbegotten,
For I would not recall
Some that being unbegotten
Are not individual,
But copy some one action,
Moulding it of dust or sand,
I bend my body to the spade
Or grope with a dirty hand.

An old ghost's thoughts are lightning,
To follow is to die;
Poetry and music I have banished,
But the stupidity
Of root, shoot, blossom or clay
Makes no demand.
I bend my body to the spade
Or grope with a dirty hand.

Those Images

What if I bade you leave
The cavern of the mind?
There's better exercise
In the sunlight and wind.

I never bade you go
To Moscow or to Rome.
Renounce that drudgery,
Call the Muses home.

Seek those images
That constitute the wild,
The lion and the virgin,
The harlot and the child.

Find in middle air
An eagle on the wing,
Recognise the five
That make the Muses sing.

The Municipal Gallery Revisited

I
Around me the images of thirty years:
An ambush; pilgrims at the waterside;
Casement upon trial, half hidden by the bars,
Guarded; Griffith staring in hysterical pride;
Kevin O'Higgins' countenance that wears
A gentle questioning look that cannot hide
A soul incapable of remorse or rest;
A revolutionary soldier kneeling to be blessed;

II
An Abbot or Archbishop with an upraised hand
Blessing the Tricolour. 'This is not,' I say,
'The dead Ireland of my youth, but an Ireland
The poets have imagined, terrible and gay.'
Before a woman's portrait suddenly I stand,
Beautiful and gentle in her Venetian way.
I met her all but fifty years ago
For twenty minutes in some studio.

III
Heart-smitten with emotion I sink down,
My heart recovering with covered eyes;
Wherever I had looked I had looked upon
My permanent or impermanent images:
Augusta Gregory's son; her sister's son,

Hugh Lane, 'onlie begetter' of all these;
Hazel Lavery living and dying, that tale
As though some ballad-singer had sung it all;

Mancini's portrait of Augusta Gregory,
'Greatest since Rembrandt,' according to John Synge;
A great ebullient portrait certainly;
But where is the brush that could show anything
Of all that pride and that humility?
And I am in despair that time may bring
Approved patterns of women or of men
But not that selfsame excellence again.

My mediaeval knees lack health until they bend,
But in that woman, in that household where
Honour had lived so long, all lacking found.
Childless I thought, 'My children may find here
Deep-rooted things,' but never foresaw its end,
And now that end has come I have not wept;
No fox can foul the lair the badger swept —

VI
(An image out of Spenser and the common tongue).
John Synge, I and Augusta Gregory, thought
All that we did, all that we said or sang
Must come from contact with the soil, from that
Contact everything Antaeus-like grew strong.
We three alone in modern times had brought
Everything down to that sole test again,
Dream of the noble and the beggar-man.

VII
And here's John Synge himself, that rooted man,
'Forgetting human words,' a grave deep face.
You that would judge me, do not judge alone
This book or that, come to this hallowed place
Where my friends' portraits hang and look thereon;
Ireland's history in their lineaments trace;
Think where man's glory most begins and ends,
And say my glory was I had such friends.

Are You Content?

I call on those that call me son,
Grandson, or great-grandson,
On uncles, aunts, great-uncles or great-aunts,
To judge what I have done.
Have I, that put it into words,
Spoilt what old loins have sent?
Eyes spiritualised by death can judge,
I cannot, but I am not content.

He that in Sligo at Drumcliff
Set up the old stone Cross,
That red-headed rector in County Down,
A good man on a horse,
Sandymount Corbets, that notable man
Old William pollexfen,
The smuggler Middleton, Butlers far back,
Half legendary men.

Infirm and aged I might stay
In some good company,
I who have always hated work,
Smiling at the sea,
Or demonstrate in my own life
What Robert Browning meant
By an old hunter talking with Gods;
But I am not content.

Three Songs to the One Burden

I
The Roaring Tinker if you like,
But Mannion is my name,
And I beat up the common sort
And think it is no shame.
The common breeds the common,
A lout begets a lout,
So when I take on half a score

I knock their heads about.
From mountain to mountain ride the fierce horsemen.

All Mannions come from Manannan,
Though rich on every shore
He never lay behind four walls
He had such character,
Nor ever made an iron red
Nor soldered pot or pan;
His roaring and his ranting
Best please a wandering man.
From mountain to mountain ride the fierce horsemen.

Could Crazy Jane put off old age
And ranting time renew,
Could that old god rise up again
We'd drink a can or two,
And out and lay our leadership
On country and on town,
Throw likely couples into bed
And knock the others down.
From mountain to mountain ride the fierce horsemen.

II

My name is Henry Middleton,
I have a small demesne,
A small forgotten house that's set
On a storm-bitten green.
I scrub its floors and make my bed,
I cook and change my plate,
The post and garden-boy alone
Have keys to my old gate.
From mountain to mountain ride the fierce horsemen.

Though I have locked my gate on them,
I pity all the young,
I know what devil's trade they learn
From those they live among,
Their drink, their pitch-and-toss by day,
Their robbery by night;

The wisdom of the people's gone,
How can the young go straight?
From mountain to mountain ride the fierce horsemen.

When every Sunday afternoon
On the Green Lands I walk
And wear a coat in fashion,
Memories of the talk
Of henwives and of queer old men
Brace me and make me strong;
There's not a pilot on the perch
Knows I have lived so long.
From mountain to mountain ride the fierce horsemen.

III

Come gather round me, players all:
Come praise Nineteen-Sixteen,
Those from the pit and gallery
Or from the painted scene
That fought in the Post Office
Or round the City Hall,
Praise every man that came again,
Praise every man that fell.
From mountain to mountain ride the fierce horsemen.

Who was the first man shot that day?
The player Connolly,
Close to the City Hall he died;
Catriage and voice had he;
He lacked those years that go with skill,
But later might have been
A famous, a brilliant figure
Before the painted scene.
From mountain to mountain ride the fierce horsemen.

Some had no thought of victory
But had gone out to die
That Ireland's mind be greater,
Her heart mount up on high;
And yet who knows what's yet to come?

For Patrick Pearse had said
That in every generation
Must Ireland's blood be shed.
From mountain to mountain ride the fierce horsemen.

In Tara's Halls

A man I praise that once in Tara's Halls
Said to the woman on his knees, 'Lie still.
My hundredth year is at an end. I think
That something is about to happen, I think
That the adventure of old age begins.
To many women I have said, "Lie still,"
And given everything a woman needs,
A roof, good clothes, passion, love perhaps,
But never asked for love; should I ask that,
I shall be old indeed.'
Thereon the man
Went to the Sacred House and stood between
The golden plough and harrow and spoke aloud
That all attendants and the casual crowd might hear.
'God I have loved, but should I ask return
Of God or woman, the time were come to die.'
He bade, his hundred and first year at end,
Diggers and carpenters make grave and coffin;
Saw that the grave was deep, the coffin sound,
Summoned the generations of his house,
Lay in the coffin, stopped his breath and died.

The Statues

Pythagoras planned it. Why did the people stare?
His numbers, though they moved or seemed to move
In marble or in bronze, lacked character.
But boys and girls, pale from the imagined love
Of solitary beds, knew what they were,
That passion could bring character enough,
And pressed at midnight in some public place
Live lips upon a plummet-measured face.

No! Greater than Pythagoras, for the men
That with a mallet or a chisel modelled these
Calculations that look but casual flesh, put down
All Asiatic vague immensities,
And not the banks of oars that swam upon
The many-headed foam at Salamis.
Europe put off that foam when Phidias
Gave women dreams and dreams their looking-glass.

One image crossed the many-headed, sat
Under the tropic shade, grew round and slow,
No Hamlet thin from eating flies, a fat
Dreamer of the Middle Ages. Empty eyeballs knew
That knowledge increases unreality, that
Mirror on mirror mirrored is all the show.
When gong and conch declare the hour to bless
Grimalkin crawls to Buddha's emptiness.

When Pearse summoned Cuchulain to his side.
What stalked through the Post Office? What intellect,
What calculation, number, measurement, replied?
We Irish, born into that ancient sect
But thrown upon this filthy modern tide
And by its formless spawning fury wrecked,
Climb to our proper dark, that we may trace
The lineaments of a plummet-measured face.

News for the Delphic Oracle

I
There all the golden codgers lay,
There the silver dew,
And the great water sighed for love,
And the wind sighed too.
Man-picker Niamh leant and sighed
By Oisin on the grass;
There sighed amid his choir of love
Tall Pythagoras.
Plotinus came and looked about,
The salt-flakes on his breast,

And having stretched and yawned awhile
Lay sighing like the rest.

II

Straddling each a dolphin's back
And steadied by a fin,
Those Innocents relive their death,
Their wounds open again.
The ecstatic waters laugh because
Their cries are sweet and strange,
Through their ancestral patterns dance,
And the brute dolphins plunge
Until, in some cliff-sheltered bay
Where wades the choir of love
Proffering its sacred laurel crowns,
They pitch their burdens off.

III

Slim adolescence that a nymph has stripped,
Peleus on Thetis stares.
Her limbs are delicate as an eyelid,
Love has blinded him with tears;
But Thetis' belly listens.
Down the mountain walls
From where pan's cavern is
Intolerable music falls.
Foul goat-head, brutal arm appear,
Belly, shoulder, bum,
Flash fishlike; nymphs and satyrs
Copulate in the foam.

Three Marching Songs[1]

Remember all those renowned generations,
They left their bodies to fatten the wolves,

[1] Later versions on page 238–41.

They left their homesteads to fatten the foxes,
Fled to far countries, or sheltered themselves
In cavern, crevice, or hole,
Defending Ireland's soul.

Be still, be still, what can be said?
My father sang that song,
But time amends old wrong,
All that is finished, let it fade.

Remember all those renowned generations,
Remember all that have sunk in their blood,
Remember all that have died on the scaffold,
Remember all that have fled, that have stood,
Stood, took death like a tune
On an old,tambourine.

Be still, be still, what can be said?
My father sang that song,
But time amends old wrong,
And all that's finished, let it fade.

Fail, and that history turns into rubbish,
All that great past to a trouble of fools;
Those that come after shall mock at O'Donnell,
Mock at the memory of both O'Neills,
Mock Emmet, mock Parnell,
All the renown that fell.

Be still, be still, what can be said?
My father sang that song,
But time amends old wrong,
And all that's finished, let it fade.

II

The soldier takes pride in saluting his Captain,
The devotee proffers a knee to his Lord,
Some back a mare thrown from a thoroughbred,
Troy backed its Helen; Troy died and adored;
Great nations blossom above;
A slave bows down to a slave.

What marches through the mountain pass?
No, no, my son, not yet;
That is an airy spot,
And no man knows what treads the grass.

We know what rascal might has defiled,
The lofty innocence that it has slain,
Were we not born in the peasant's cot
Where men forgive if the belly gain?
More dread the life that we live,
How can the mind forgive?

What marches down the mountain pass?
No, no, my son, not yet;
That is an airy spot,
And no man knows what treads the grass.

What if there's nothing up there at the top?
Where are the captains that govern mankind?
What tears down a tree that has nothing within it?
A blast of the wind, O a marching wind,
March wind, and any old tune,
March, march, and how does it run?

What marches down the mountain pass?
No, no, my son, not yet;
That is an airy spot,
And no man knows what treads the grass.

III

Grandfather sang it under the gallows:
'Hear, gentlemen, ladies, and all mankind:
Money is good and a girl might be better,
But good strong blows are delights to the mind.'
There, standing on the cart,
He sang it from his heart.

Robbers had taken his old tambourine,
But he took down the moon

And rattled out a tunc;
Robbers had taken his old tambourinc.

'A girl I had, but she followed another,
Money I had, and it went in the night,
Strong drink I had, and it brought me to sorrow,
But a good strong cause and blows are delight.'
All there caught up the tune:
'Oh, on, my darling man.'

Robbers had taken his old tambourine,
But he took down the moon
And rattled out a tune;
Robbers had taken his old tambourine.

'Money is good and a girl might be better,
No matter what happens and who takes the fall,
But a good strong cause' the rope gave a jerk there,
No more sang he, for his throat was too small;
But he kicked before he died,
He did it out of pride.

Robbers had taken his old tambourine,
But he took down the moon
And rattled out a tune;
Robbers had taken his old tambourine.

Long-legged Fly

That civilisation may not sink,
Its great battle lost,
Quiet the dog, tether the pony
To a distant post;
Our master Caesar is in the tent
Where the maps are spread,
His eyes fixed upon nothing,
A hand under his head.
Like a long-legged fly upon the stream
His mind moves upon silence.

That the topless towers be burnt
And men recall that face,
Move most gently if move you must
In this lonely place.
She thinks, part woman, three parts a child,
That nobody looks; her feet
Practise a tinker shuffle
Picked up on a street.
Like a long-legged fly upon the stream
His mind moves upon silence.

That girls at puberty may find
The first Adam in their thought,
Shut the door of the Pope's chapel,
Keep those children out.
There on that scaffolding reclines
Michael Angelo.
With no more sound than the mice make
His hand moves to and fro.
Like a long-legged fly upon the stream
His mind moves upon silence.

A Bronze Head

Here at right of the entrance this bronze head,
Human, superhuman, a bird's round eye,
Everything else withered and mummy-dead.
What great tomb-haunter sweeps the distant sky
(Something may linger there though all else die);
And finds there nothing to make its terror less
Hysterica passio of its own emptiness?

No dark tomb-haunter once; her form all full
As though with magnanimity of light,
Yet a most gentle woman; who can tell
Which of her forms has shown her substance right?
Or maybe substance can be composite,
profound McTaggart thought so, and in a breath
A mouthful held the extreme of life and death.

But even at the starting-post, all sleek and new,
I saw the wildness in her and I thought
A vision of terror that it must live through
Had shattered her soul. Propinquity had brought
Imagination to that pitch where it casts out
All that is not itself: I had grown wild
And wandered murmuring everywhere, 'My child, my child!'

Or else I thought her supernatural;
As though a sterner eye looked through her eye
On this foul world in its decline and fall;
On gangling stocks grown great, great stocks run dry,
Ancestral pearls all pitched into a sty,
Heroic reverie mocked by clown and knave,
And wondered what was left for massacre to save.

A Stick of Incense

Whence did all that fury come?
From empty tomb or Virgin womb?
Saint Joseph thought the world would melt
But liked the way his finger smelt.

John Kinsella's Lament for Mrs Mary Moore

A bloody and a sudden end,
Gunshot or a noose,
For Death who takes what man would keep,
Leaves what man would lose.
He might have had my sister,
My cousins by the score,
But nothing satisfied the fool
But my dear Mary Moore,
None other knows what pleasures man
At table or in bed.
What shall I do for pretty girls
Now my old bawd is dead?

Though stiff to strike a bargain,
Like an old Jew man,
Her bargain struck we laughed and talked
And emptied many a can;
And O! but she had stories,
Though not for the priest's ear,
To keep the soul of man alive,
Banish age and care,
And being old she put a skin
On everything she said.
What shall I do for pretty girls
Now my old bawd is dead?

The priests have got a book that says
But for Adam's sin
Eden's Garden would be there
And I there within.
No expectation fails there,
No pleasing habit ends,
No man grows old, no girl grows cold
But friends walk by friends.
Who quarrels over halfpennies
That plucks the trees for bread?
What shall I do for pretty girls
Now my old bawd is dead?

Hound Voice

Because we love bare hills and stunted trees
And were the last to choose the settled ground,
Its boredom of the desk or of the spade, because
So many years companioned by a hound,
Our voices carry; and though slumber-bound,
Some few half wake and half renew their choice,
Give tongue, proclaim their hidden name — 'Hound Voice.'

The women that I picked spoke sweet and low
And yet gave tongue. 'Hound Voices' were they all.

We picked each other from afar and knew
What hour of terror comes to test the soul,
And in that terror's name obeyed the call,
And understood, what none have understood,
Those images that waken in the blood.

Some day we shall get up before the dawn
And find our ancient hounds before the door,
And wide awake know that the hunt is on;
Stumbling upon the blood-dark track once more,
Then stumbling to the kill beside the shore;
Then cleaning out and bandaging of wounds,
And chants of victory amid the encircling hounds.

High Talk

Processions that lack high stilts have nothing that catches the eye.
What if my great-granddad had a pair that were twenty foot high,
And mine were but fifteen foot, no modern stalks upon higher,
Some rogue of the world stole them to patch up a fence or a fire.
Because piebald ponies, led bears, caged lions, make but poor
 shows,
Because children demand Daddy-long-legs upon his timber toes,
Because women in the upper storeys demand a face at the pane,
That patching old heels they may shriek, I take to chisel and
 plane.

Malachi Stilt-Jack am I, whatever I learned has run wild,
From collar to collar, from stilt to stilt, from father to child.
All metaphor, Malachi, stilts and all. A barnacle goose
Far up in the stretches of night; night splits and the dawn
 breaks loose;
I, through the terrible novelty of light, stalk on, stalk on;
Those great sea-horses bare their teeth and laugh at the dawn.

The Apparitions

Because there is safety in derision
I talked about an apparition,
I took no trouble to convince,
Or seem plausible to a man of sense.
Distrustful of thar popular eye
Whether it be bold or sly.
Fifteen apparitions have I seen;
The worst a coat upon a coat-hanger.

I have found nothing half so good
As my long-planned half solitude,
Where I can sit up half the night
With some friend that has the wit
Not to allow his looks to tell
When I am unintelligible.
Fifteen apparitions have I seen;
The worst a coat upon a coat-hanger.

When a man grows old his joy
Grows more deep day after day,
His empty heart is full at length,
But he has need of all that strength
Because of the increasing Night
That opens her mystery and fright.
Fifteen apparitions have I seen;
The worst a coat upon a coat-hanger.

A Nativity

What woman hugs her infant there?
Another star has shot an ear.

What made the drapery glisten so?
Not a man but Delacroix.

What made the ceiling waterproof?
Landor's tarpaulin on the roof

What brushes fly and moth aside?
Irving and his plume of pride.

What hurries out the knave and dolt?
Talma and his thunderbolt.

Why is the woman terror-struck?
Can there be mercy in that look?

Why Should Not Old Men Be Mad?

Why should not old men be mad?
Some have known a likely lad
That had a sound fly-fisher's wrist
Turn to a drunken journalist;
A girl that knew all Dante once
Live to bear children to a dunce;
A Helen of social welfare dream,
Climb on a wagonette to scream.
Some think it a matter of course that chance
Should starve good men and bad advance,
That if their neighbours figured plain,
As though upon a lighted screen,
No single story would they find
Of an unbroken happy mind,
A finish worthy of the start.
Young men know nothing of this sort,
Observant old men know it well;
And when they know what old books tell
And that no better can be had,
Know why an old man should be mad.

The Statesman's Holiday

I lived among great houses,
Riches drove out rank,
Base drove out the better blood,
And mind and body shrank.
No Oscar ruled the table,
But I'd a troop of friends
That knowing better talk had gone
Talked of odds and ends.
Some knew what ailed the world
But never said a thing,
So I have picked a better trade
And night and morning sing:
Tall dames go walking in grass-green Avalon.

Am I a great Lord Chancellor
That slept upon the Sack?
Commanding officer that tore
The khaki from his back?
Or am I de Valera,
Or the King of Greece,
Or the man that made the motors?
Ach, call me what you please!
Here's a Montenegrin lute,
And its old sole string
Makes me sweet music
And I delight to sing:
Tall dames go walking in grass-green Avalon.

With boys and girls about him.
With any sort of clothes,
With a hat out of fashion,
With old patched shoes,
With a ragged bandit cloak,
With an eye like a hawk,
With a stiff straight back,
With a strutting turkey walk.
With a bag full of pennies,
With a monkey on a chain,

With a great cock's feather,
With an old foul tune.
Tall dames go walking in grass-green Avalon.

Crazy Jane on the Mountain

I am tired of cursing the Bishop,
(Said Crazy Jane),
Nine books or nine hats
Would not make him a man.
I have found something worse
To meditate on.
A King had some beautiful cousins.
But where are they gone?
Battered to death in a cellar,
And he stuck to his throne.
Last night I lay on the mountain
(Said Crazy Jane)
There in a two-horsed carriage
That on two wheels ran
Great-bladdered Emer sat.
Her violent man
Cuchulain sat at her side;
Thereupon
Propped upon my two knees,
I kissed a stone;
I lay stretched out in the dirt
And I cried tears down.

The Circus Animals' Desertion

I

I sought a theme and sought for it in vain,
I sought it daily for six weeks or so.
Maybe at last, being but a broken man,
I must be satisfied with my heart, although
Winter and summer till old age began

My circus animals were all on show,
Those stilted boys, that burnished chariot,
Lion and woman and the Lord knows what.

II

What can I but enumerate old themes?
First that sea-rider Oisin led by the nose
Through three enchanted islands, allegorical dreams,
Vain gaiety, vain battle, vain repose,
Themes of the embittered heart, or so it seems,
That might adorn old songs or courtly shows;
But what cared I that set him on to ride,
I, starved for the bosom of his faery bride?

And then a counter-truth filled out its play,
The Countess Cathleen was the name I gave it;
She, pity-crazed, had given her soul away,
But masterful Heaven had intervened to save it.
I thought my dear must her own soul destroy,
So did fanaticism and hate enslave it,
And this brought forth a dream and soon enough
This dream itself had all my thought and love.

And when the Fool and Blind Man stole the bread
Cuchulain fought the ungovernable sea;
Heart-mysteries there, and yet when all is said
It was the dream itself enchanted me:
Character isolated by a deed
To engross the present and dominate memory.
Players and painted stage took all my love,
And not those things that they were emblems of.

III

Those masterful images because complete
Grew in pure mind, but out of what began?
A mound of refuse or the sweepings of a street,
Old kettles, old bottles, and a broken can,
Old iron, old bones, old rags, that raving slut
Who keeps the till. Now that my ladder's gone,

I must lie down where all the ladders start
In the foul rag-and-bone shop of the heart.

Politics

'In our time the destiny of man presents its meaning in political terms.'
THOMAS MANN

How can I, that girl standing there,
My attention fix
On Roman or on Russian
Or on Spanish politics?
Yet here's a travelled man that knows
What he talks about,
And there's a politician
That has read and thought,
And maybe what they say is true
Of war and war's alarms,
But O that I were young again
And held her in my arms!

The Man And the Echo

Man
In a cleft that's christened Alt
Under broken stone I halt
At the bottom of a pit
That broad noon has never lit,
And shout a secret to the stone.
All that I have said and done,
Now that I am old and ill,
Turns into a question till
I lie awake night after night
And never get the answers right.
Did that play of mine send out
Certain men the English shot?
Did words of mine put too great strain
On that woman's reeling brain?
Could my spoken words have checked

That whereby a house lay wrecked?
And all seems evil until I
Sleepless would lie down and die.

Echo
Lie down and die.

Man

That were to shirk
The spiritual intellect's great work,
And shirk it in vain. There is no release
In a bodkin or disease,
Nor can there be work so great
As that which cleans man's dirty slate.
While man can still his body keep
Wine or love drug him to sleep,
Waking he thanks the Lord that he
Has body and its stupidity,
But body gone he sleeps no more,
And till his intellect grows sure
That all's arranged in one clear view,
Pursues the thoughts that I pursue,
Then stands in judgment on his soul,
And, all work done, dismisses all
Out of intellect and sight
And sinks at last into the night.

Echo
Into the night.

Man

O Rocky Voice,
Shall we in that great night rejoice?
What do we know but that we face
One another in this place?
But hush, for I have lost the theme,
Its joy or night seem but a dream;
Up there some hawk or owl has struck,

Dropping out of sky or rock,
A stricken rabbit is crying out,
And its cry distracts my thought.

Cuchulain Comforted

A man that had six mortal wounds, a man
Violent and famous, strode among the dead;
Eyes stared out of the branches and were gone.

Then certain Shrouds that muttered head to head
Came and were gone. He leant upon a tree
As though to meditate on wounds and blood.

A Shroud that seemed to have authority
Among those bird-like things came, and let fall
A bundle of linen. Shrouds by two and three

Came creeping up because the man was still.
And thereupon that linen-carrier said:
'Your life can grow much sweeter if you will

'Obey our ancient rule and make a shroud;
Mainly because of what we only know
The rattle of those arms makes us afraid.

'We thread the needles' eyes, and all we do
All must together do.' That done, the man
Took up the nearest and began to sew.

'Now must we sing and sing the best we can,
But first you must be told our character:
Convicted cowards all, by kindred slain

'Or driven from home and left to die in fear.'
They sang, but had nor human tunes nor words,
Though all was done in common as before;

They had changed their throats and had the throats of birds.

The Black Tower

Say that the men of the old black tower,
Though they but feed as the goatherd feeds,
Their money spent, their wine gone sour,
Lack nothing that a soldier needs,
That all are oath-bound men:
Those banners come not in.

There in the tomb stand the dead upright,
But winds come up from the shore:
They shake when the winds roar,
Old bones upon the mountain shake.

Those banners come to bribe or threaten,
Or whisper that a man's a fool
Who, when his own right king's forgotten,
Cares what king sets up his rule.
If he died long ago
Why do you dread us so?

There in the tomb drops the faint moonlight,
But wind comes up from the shore:
They shake when the winds roar,
Old bones upon the mountain shake.

The tower's old cook that must climb and clamber
Catching small birds in the dew of the morn
When we hale men lie stretched in slumber
Swears that he hears the king's great horn.
But he's a lying hound:
Stand we on guard oath-bound!

There in the tomb the dark grows blacker,
But wind comes up from the shore:
They shake when the winds roar,
Old bones upon the mountain shake.

Under Ben Bulben

I
Swear by what the sages spoke
Round the Mareotic Lake
That the Witch of Atlas knew,
Spoke and set the cocks a-crow.

Swear by those horsemen, by those women
Complexion and form prove superhuman,
That pale, long-visaged company
That air in immortality
Completeness of their passions won;
Now they ride the wintry dawn
Where Ben Bulben sets the scene.

Here s the gist of what they mean.

II
Many times man lives and dies
Between his two eternities,
That of race and that of soul,
And ancient Ireland knew it all.
Whether man die in his bed
Or the rifle knocks him dead,
A brief parting from those dear
Is the worst man has to fear.
Though grave-diggers' toil is long,
Sharp their spades, their muscles strong.
They but thrust their buried men
Back in the human mind again.

III
You that Mitchel's prayer have heard,
'Send war in our time, O Lord!'
Know that when all words are said
And a man is fighting mad,
Something drops from eyes long blind,
He completes his partial mind,
For an instant stands at ease,

Laughs aloud, his heart at peace.
Even the wisest man grows tense
With some sort of violence
Before he can accomplish fate,
Know his work or choose his mate.

IV
Poet and sculptor, do the work,
Nor let the modish painter shirk
What his great forefathers did.
Bring the soul of man to God,
Make him fill the cradles right.

Measurement began our might:
Forms a stark Egyptian thought,
Forms that gentler Phidias wrought.
Michael Angelo left a Proof
On the Sistine Chapel roof,
Where but half-awakened Adam
Can disturb globe-trotting Madam
Till her bowels are in heat,
Proof that there's a purpose set
Before the secret working mind:
Profane perfection of mankind.

Quattrocento put in paint
On backgrounds for a God or Saint
Gardens where a soul's at ease;
Where everything that meets the eye,
Flowers and grass and cloudless sky,
Resemble forms that are or seem
When sleepers wake and yet still dream,
And when it's vanished still declare,
With only bed and bedstead there,
That heavens had opened.
Gyres run on;
When that greater dream had gone
Calvert and Wilson, Blake and Claude,
Prepared a rest for the people of God,

Palmer's phrase, but after that
Confusion fell upon our thought.

V

Irish poets, earn your trade,
Sing whatever is well made,
Scorn the sort now growing up
All out of shape from toe to top,
Their unremembering hearts and heads
Base-born products of base beds.
Sing the peasantry, and then
Hard-riding country gentlemen,
The holiness of monks, and after
Porter-drinkers' randy laughter;
Sing the lords and ladies gay
That were beaten into the clay
Through seven heroic centuries;
Cast your mind on other days
That we in coming days may be
Still the indomitable Irishry.

VI

Under bare Ben Bulben's head
In Drumcliff churchyard Yeats is laid.
An ancestor was rector there
Long years ago, a church stands near,
By the road an ancient cross.

No marble, no conventional phrase;
On limestone quarried near the spot
By his command these words are cut:

Cast a cold eye
On life, on death.
Horseman, pass by!

NARRATIVE AND DRAMATIC

THE WANDERINGS OF OISIN
1889

'Give me tha world if thou wilt, but grant me an asylum for my affection.' Tulka

TO EDWIN J. ELLIS

The Wanderings of Oisin

Book I

S. Patrick. You who are bent, and bald, and blind,
With a heavy heart and a wandering mind,
Have known three centuries, poets sing,
Of dalliance with a demon thing.

Oisin. Sad to remember, sick with years,
The swift innumerable spears,
The horsemen with their floating hair,
And bowls of barley, honey and wine,
Those merry couples dancing in tune,
And the white body that lay by mine;
But the tale, though words be lighter than air,
Must live to be old like the wandering moon.

Caoilte, and Conan, and Finn were there,
When we followed a deer with our baying hounds,
With Bran, Sceolan and Lomair,
And passing the Firbolgs' burial-moteds,
Came to the cairn-heaped grassy hill
Where passionate Maeve is stony-still;
And found on the dove-grey edge of the sea
A pearl-pale, high-born lady, who rode
On a horse with bridle of findrinny;
And like a sunset were her lips,

A stormy sunset on doomed ships;
A citron colour gloomed in her hair,

But down to her feet white vesture flowed,
And with the glimmering crimson glowed
Of many a figured embroidery;
And it was bound with a pearl-pale shell
That wavered like the summer streams,
As her soft bosom rose and fell.

S. Patrick. You are still wrecked among heathen dreams.

Oisin. 'Why do you wind no horn?' she said,
'And every hero droop his head?
The hornless deer is not more sad
That many a peaceful moment had,
More sleek than any granary mouse,
In his own leafy forest house
Among the waving fields of fern:
The hunting of heroes should be glad.'

'O pleasant woman,' answered Finn,
'We think on Oscar's pencilled urn,
And on the heroes lying slain
On Gabhra's raven-covered plain;
But where are your noble kith and kin,
And from what country do you ride?'

'My father and my mother are
Aengus and Edain, my own name
Niamh, and my country far
Beyond the tumbling of this tide.'

'What dream came with you that you came
Through bitter tide on foam-wet feet?
Did your companion wander away
From where the birds of Aengus wing?'

Thereon did she look haughty and sweet:
'I have not yet, war-weary king,
Been spoken of with any man;
Yet now I choose, for these four feet

Ran through the foam and ran to this
That I might have your son to kiss.'

'Were there no better than my son
That you through all that foam should run?'

'I loved no man, though kings besought,
Until the Danaan poets brought
Rhyme that rhymed upon Oisin's name,
And now I am dizzy with the thought
Of all that wisdom and the fame
Of battles broken by his hands,
Of stories builded by his words
That are like coloured Asian birds
At evening in their rainless lands.'

O Patrick, by your brazen bell,
There was no limb of mine but fell
Into a desperate gulph of love!
'You only will I wed,' I cried,
'And I will make a thousand songs,
And set your name all names above,
And captives bound with leathern thongs
Shall kneel and praise you, one by one,
At evening in my western dun.'

'O Oisin, mount by me and ride
To shores by the wash of the tremulous tide,
Where men have heaped no burial-mounds,
And the days pass by like a wayward tune,
Where broken faith has never been known
And the blushes of first love never have flown;
And there I will give you a hundred hounds;
No mightier creatures bay at the moon;
And a hundred robes of murmuring silk,
And a hundred calves and a hundred sheep
Whose long wool whiter than sea-froth flows,
And a hundred spears and a hundred bows,
And oil and wine and honey and milk,
And always never-anxious sleep;

While a hundred youths, mighty of limb,
But knowing nor tumult nor hate nor strife,
And a hundred ladies, merry as birds,
Who when they dance to a fitful measure
Have a speed like the speed of the salmon herds,
Shall follow your horn and obey your whim,
And you shall know the Danaan leisure;
And Niamh be with you for a wife.'
Then she sighed gently, 'It grows late.
Music and love and sleep await,
Where I would be when the white moon climbs,
The red sun falls and the world grows dim.'

And then I mounted and she bound me
With her triumphing arms around me,
And whispering to herself enwound me;
He shook himself and neighed three times:
Caoilte, Conan, and Finn came near,
And wept, and raised their lamenting hands,
And bid me stay, with many a tear;
But we rode out from the human lands.

In what far kingdom do you go
Ah Fenians, with the shield and bow?
Or are you phantoms white as snow,
Whose lips had life's most prosperous glow?
O you, with whom in sloping valleys,
Or down the dewy forest alleys,
I chased at morn the flying deer,
With whom I hurled the hurrying spear,
And heard the foemen's bucklers rattle,
And broke the heaving ranks of battle!
And Bran, Sceolan, and Lomair,
Where are you with your long rough hair?
You go not where the red deer feeds,
Nor tear the foemen from their steeds.

S. Patrick. Boast not, nor mourn with drooping head
Companions long accurst and dead,
And hounds for centuries dust and air.

Oisin. We galloped over the glossy sea:
I know not if days passed or hours,
And Niamh sang continually
Danaan songs, and their dewy showers
Of pensive laughter, unhuman sound,
Lulled weariness, and softly round
My human sorrow her white arms wound.
We galloped; now a hornless deer
Passed by us, chased by a phantom hound
All pearly white, save one red ear;
And now a lady rode like the wind
With an apple of gold in her tossing hand;
And a beautiful young man followed behind
With quenchless gaze and fluttering hair.

'Were these two born in the Danaan land,
Or have they breathed the mortal air?'

'Vex them no longer,' Niamh said,
And sighing bowed her gentle head,
And sighing laid the pearly tip
Of one long finger on my lip.

But now the moon like a white rose shone
In the pale west, and the sun's rim sank,
And clouds atrayed their rank on rank
About his fading crimson ball:
The floor of Almhuin's hosting hall
Was not more level than the sea,
As, full of loving fantasy,
And with low murmurs, we rode on,
Where many a trumpet-twisted shell
That in immortal silence sleeps
Dreaming of her own melting hues,
Her golds, her ambers, and her blues,
Pierced with soft light the shallowing deeps.
But now a wandering land breeze came
And a far sound of feathery quires;
It seemed to blow from the dying flame,
They seemed to sing in the smouldering fires.

The horse towards the music raced,
Neighing along the lifeless waste;
Like sooty fingers, many a tree
Rose ever out of the warm sea;
And they were trembling ceaselessly,
As though they all were beating time,
Upon the centre of the sun,
To that low laughing woodland rhyme.
And, now our wandering hours were done,
We cantered to the shore, and knew
The reason of the trembling trees:
Round every branch the song-birds flew,
Or clung thereon like swarming bees;
While round the shore a million stood
Like drops of frozen rainbow light,
And pondered in a soft vain mood
Upon their shadows in the tide,
And told the purple deeps their pride,
And murmured snatches of delight;
And on the shores were many boats
With bending sterns and bending bows,
And carven figures on their prows
Of bitterns, and fish-eating stoats,
And swans with their exultant throats:
And where the wood and waters meet
We tied the horse in a leafy clump,
And Niamh blew three merry notes
Out of a little silver trump;
And then an answering whispering flew
Over the bare and woody land,
A whisper of impetuous feet,
And ever nearer, nearer grew;
And from the woods rushed out a band
Of men and ladies, hand in hand,
And singing, singing all together;
Their brows were white as fragrant milk,
Their cloaks made out of yellow silk,
And trimmed with many a crimson feather;
And when they saw the cloak I wore
Was dim with mire of a mortal shore,

They fingered it and gazed on me
And laughed like murmurs of the sea;
But Niamh with a swift distress
Bid them away and hold their peace;
And when they heard her voice they ran
And knelt there, every girl and man,
And kissed, as they would never cease,
Her pearl-pale hand and the hem of her dress.
She bade them bring us to the hall
Where Aengus dreams, from sun to sun,
A Druid dream of the end of days
When the stars are to wane and the world be done.

They led us by long and shadowy ways
Where drops of dew in myriads fall,
And tangled creepers every hour
Blossom in some new crimson flower,
And once a sudden laughter sprang
From all their lips, and once they sang
Together, while the dark woods rang,
And made in all their distant parts,
With boom of bees in honey-marts,
A rumour of delighted hearts.
And once a lady by my side
Gave me a harp, and bid me sing,
And touch the laughing silver string;
But when I sang of human joy
A sorrow wrapped each merry face,
And, Patrick! by your beard, they wept,
Until one came, a tearful boy;
'A sadder creature never stept
Than this strange human bard,' he cried;
And caught the silver harp away,
And, weeping over the white strings, hurled
It down in a leaf-hid, hollow place
That kept dim waters from the sky;
And each one said, with a long, long sigh,
'O saddest harp in all the world,
Sleep there till the moon and the stars die!'

And now, still sad, we came to where
A beautiful young man dreamed within
A house of wattles, clay, and skin;
One hand upheld his beardless chin,
And one a sceptre flashing out
Wild flames of red and gold and blue,
Like to a merry wandering rout
Of dancers leaping in the air;
And men and ladies knelt them there
And showed their eyes with teardrops dim,
And with low murmurs prayed to him,
And kissed the sceptre with red lips,
And touched it with their finger-tips.

He held that flashing sceptre up.
'Joy drowns the twilight in the dew,
And fills with stars night's purple cup,
And wakes the sluggard seeds of corn,
And stirs the young kid's budding horn,
And makes the infant ferns unwrap,
And for the peewit paints his cap,
And rolls along the unwieldy sun,
And makes the little planets run:
And if joy were not on the earth,
There were an end of change and birth,
And Earth and Heaven and Hell would die,
And in some gloomy barrow lie
Folded like a frozen fly;
Then mock at Death and Time with glances
And wavering arms and wandering dances.

'Men's hearts of old were drops of flame
That from the saffron morning came,
Or drops of silver joy that fell
Out of the moon's pale twisted shell;
But now hearts cry that hearts are slaves,
And toss and turn in narrow caves;
But here there is nor law nor rule,
Nor have hands held a weary tool;

And here there is nor Change nor Death,
But only kind and merry breath,
For joy is God and God is joy.'
With one long glance for girl and boy
And the pale blossom of the moon,
He fell into a Druid swoon.

And in a wild and sudden dance
We mocked at Time and Fate and Chance
And swept out of the wattled hall
And came to where the dewdrops fall
Among the foamdrops of the sea,
And there we hushed the revelry;
And, gathering on our brows a frown,
Bent all our swaying bodies down,
And to the waves that glimmer by
That sloping green De Danaan sod
Sang, 'God is joy and joy is God,
And things that have grown sad are wicked,
And things that fear the dawn of the morrow
Or the grey wandering osprey Sorrow.'

We danced to where in the winding thicket
The damask roses, bloom on bloom,
Like crimson meteors hang in the gloom.
And bending over them softly said,
Bending over them in the dance,
With a swift and friendly glance
From dewy eyes: 'Upon the dead
Fall the leaves of other roses,
On the dead dim earth encloses:
But never, never on our graves,
Heaped beside the glimmering waves,
Shall fall the leaves of damask roses.
For neither Death nor Change comes near us,
And all listless hours fear us,
And we fear no dawning morrow,
Nor the grey wandering osprey Sorrow.'

The dance wound through the windless woods;
The ever-summered solitudes;
Until the tossing arms grew still
Upon the woody central hill;
And, gathered in a panting band,
We flung on high each waving hand,
And sang unto the starry broods.
In our raised eyes there flashed a glow
Of milky brightness to and fro
As thus our song arose: 'You stars,
Across your wandering ruby cars
Shake the loose reins: you slaves of God,
He rules you with an iron rod,
He holds you with an iron bond,
Each one woven to the other,
Each one woven to his brother
Like bubbles in a frozen pond;
But we in a lonely land abide
Unchainable as the dim tide,
With hearts that know nor law nor rule,
And hands that hold no wearisome tool,
Folded in love that fears no morrow,
Nor the grey wandering osprey Sorrow.'

O Patrick! for a hundred years
I chased upon that woody shore
The deer, the badger, and the boar.
O patrick! for a hundred years
At evening on the glimmering sands,
Beside the piled-up hunting spears,
These now outworn and withered hands
Wrestled among the island bands.
O patrick! for a hundred years
We went a-fishing in long boats
With bending sterns and bending bows,
And carven figures on their prows
Of bitterns and fish-eating stoats.
O patrick! for a hundred years

The gentle Niamh was my wife;
But now two things devour my life;
The things that most of all I hate:
Fasting and prayers.

S. Patrick. Tell on.

Oisin. Yes, yes,
For these were ancient Oisin's fate
Loosed long ago from Heaven's gate,
For his last days to lie in wait.

When one day by the tide I stood,
I found in that forgetfulness
Of dreamy foam a staff of wood
From some dead warrior's broken lance:
I turned it in my hands; the stains
Of war were on it, and I wept,
Remembering how the Fenians stept
Along the blood-bedabbled plains,
Equal to good or grievous chance:
Thereon young Niamh softly came
And caught my hands, but spake no word
Save only many times my name,
In murmurs, like a frighted bird.
We passed by woods, and lawns of clover,
And found the horse and bridled him,
For we knew well the old was over.
I heard one say, 'His eyes grow dim
With all the ancient sorrow of men';
And wrapped in dreams rode out again
With hoofs of the pale findrinny
Over the glimmering purple sea.
Under the golden evening light,
The Immortals moved among the fountains
By rivers and the woods' old night;
Some danced like shadows on the mountains,
Some wandered ever hand in hand;
Or sat in dreams on the pale strand,
Each forehead like an obscure star

Bent down above each hooked knee,
And sang, and with a dreamy gaze
Watched where the sun in a saffron blaze
Was slumbering half in the sea-ways;
And, as they sang, the painted birds
Kept time with their bright wings and feet;
Like drops of honey came their words,
But fainter than a young lamb's bleat.

'An old man stirs the fire to a blaze,
In the house of a child, of a friend, of a brother.
He has over-lingered his welcome; the days,
Grown desolate, whisper and sigh to each other;
He hears the storm in the chimney above,
And bends to the fire and shakes with the cold,
While his heart still dreams of battle and love,
And the cry of the hounds on the hills of old.

'But we are apart in the grassy places,
Where care cannot trouble the least of our days,
Or the softness of youth be gone from our faces,
Or love's first tenderness die in our gaze.
The hare grows old as she plays in the sun
And gazes around her with eyes of brightness;
Before the swift things that she dreamed of were done
She limps along in an aged whiteness;
A storm of birds in the Asian trees
Like tulips in the air a-winging,
And the gentle waves of the summer seas,
That raise their heads and wander singing,
Must murmur at last, "Unjust, unjust";
And "My speed is a weariness," falters the mouse,
And the kingfisher turns to a ball of dust,
And the roof falls in of his tunnelled house.
But the love-dew dims our eyes till the day
When God shall come from the sea with a sigh
And bid the stars drop down from the sky,
And the moon like a pale rose wither away.'

Book II

Now, man of croziers, shadows called our names
And then away, away, like whirling flames;
And now fled by, mist-covered, without sound,
The youth and lady and the deer and hound;
'Gaze no more on the phantoms,' Niamh said,
And kissed my eyes, and, swaying her bright head
And her bright body, sang of faery and man
Before God was or my old line began;
Wars shadowy, vast, exultant; faeries of old
Who wedded men with rings of Druid gold;
And how those lovers never turn their eyes
Upon the life that fades and flickers and dies,
Yet love and kiss on dim shores far away
Rolled round with music of the sighing spray:
Yet sang no more as when, like a brown bee
That has drunk full, she crossed the misty sea
With me in her white arms a hundred years
Before this day; for now the fall of tears
Troubled her song.
I do not know if days
Or hours passed by, yet hold the morning rays
Shone many times among the glimmering flowers
Woven into her hair, before dark towers
Rose in the darkness, and the white surf gleamed
About them; and the horse of Faery screamed
And shivered, knowing the Isle of Many Fears,
Nor ceased until white Niamh stroked his ears
And named him by sweet names.
A foaming tide
Whitened afar with surge, fan-formed and wide,
Burst from a great door marred by many a blow
From mace and sword and pole-axe, long ago
When gods and giants warred. We rode between
The seaweed-covered pillars; and the green
And surging phosphorus alone gave light
On our dark pathway, till a countless flight
Of moonlit steps glimmered; and left and right

Dark statues glimmered over the pale tide
Upon dark thrones. Between the lids of one
The imaged meteors had flashed and run
And had disported in the stilly jet,
And the fixed stars had dawned and shone and set,
Since God made Time and Death and Sleep: the other
Stretched his long arm to where, a misty smother,
The stream churned, churned, and churned — his lips apart,
As though he told his never-slumbering heart
Of every foamdrop on its misty way.
Tying the horse to his vast foot that lay
Half in the unvesselled sea, we climbed the stair
And climbed so long, I thought the last steps were
Hung from the morning star; when these mild words
Fanned the delighted air like wings of birds:
'My brothers spring out of their beds at morn,
A-murmur like young partridge: with loud horn
They chase the noontide deer;
And when the dew-drowned stars hang in the air
Look to long fishing-lines, or point and pare
An ashen hunting spear.
O sigh, O fluttering sigh, be kind to me;
Flutter along the froth lips of the sea,
And shores the froth lips wet:
And stay a little while, and bid them weep:
Ah, touch their blue-veined eyelids if they sleep,
And shake their coverlet.
When you have told how I weep endlessly,
Flutter along the froth lips of the sea
And home to me again,
And in the shadow of my hair lie hid,
And tell me that you found a man unbid,
The saddest of all men.'

A lady with soft eyes like funeral tapers,
And face that seemed wrought out of moonlit vapours,
And a sad mouth, that fear made tremulous
As any ruddy moth, looked down on us;
And she with a wave-rusted chain was tied
To two old eagles, full of ancient pride,

That with dim eyeballs stood on either side.
Few feathers were on their dishevelled wings,
For their dim minds were with the ancient things.

'I bring deliverance,' pearl-pale Niamh said.

'Neither the living, nor the unlabouring dead,
Nor the high gods who never lived, may fight
My enemy and hope; demons for fright
Jabber and scream about him in the night;
For he is strong and crafty as the seas
That sprang under the Seven Hazel Trees,
And I must needs endure and hate and weep,
Until the gods and demons drop asleep,
Hearing Aed touch the mournful strings of gold.'

'Is he so dreadful?'
'Be not over-bold,
But fly while still you may.'
And thereon I:
'This demon shall be battered till he die,
And his loose bulk be thrown in the loud tide.'

'Flee from him,' pearl-pale Niamh weeping cried,
'For all men flee the demons'; but moved not
My angry king-remembering soul one jot.
There was no mightier soul of Heber's line;
Now it is old and mouse-like. For a sign
I burst the chain: still earless, nerveless, blind,
Wrapped in the things of the unhuman mind,
In some dim memory or ancient mood,
Still earless, nerveless, blind, the eagles stood.

And then we climbed the stair to a high door;
A hundred horsemen on the basalt floor
Beneath had paced content: we held our way
And stood within: clothed in a misty ray
I saw a foam-white seagull drift and float
Under the roof, and with a straining throat
Shouted, and hailed him: he hung there a star,

For no man's cry shall ever mount so far;
Not even your God could have thrown down that hall;
Stabling His unloosed lightnings in their stall,
He had sat down and sighed with cumbered heart,
As though His hour were come.

We sought the part
That was most distant from the door; green slime
Made the way slippery, and time on time
Showed prints of sea-born scales, while down through it
The captive's journeys to and fro were writ
Like a small river, and where feet touched came
A momentary gleam of phosphorus flame.
Under the deepest shadows of the hall
That woman found a ring hung on the wall,
And in the ring a torch, and with its flare
Making a world about her in the air,
Passed under the dim doorway, out of sight,
And came again, holding a second light
Burning between her fingers, and in mine
Laid it and sighed: I held a sword whose shine
No centuries could dim, and a word ran
Thereon in Ogham letters, 'Manannan';
That sea-god's name, who in a deep content
Sprang dripping, and, with captive demons sent
Out of the sevenfold seas, built the dark hall
Rooted in foam and clouds, and cried to all
The mightier masters of a mightier race;
And at his cry there came no milk-pale face
Under a crown of thorns and dark with blood,
But only exultant faces.

Niamh stood
With bowed head, trembling when the white blade shone,
But she whose hours of tenderness were gone
Had neither hope nor fear. I bade them hide
Under the shadows till the tumults died
Of the loud-crashing and earth-shaking fight,
Lest they should look upon some dreadful sight;
And thrust the torch between the slimy flags.

A dome made out of endless carven jags,
Where shadowy face flowed into shadowy face,
Looked down on me; and in the self-same place
I waited hour by hour, and the high dome,
Windowless, pillarless, multitudinous home
Of faces, waited; and the leisured gaze
Was loaded with the memory of days
Buried and mighty. When through the great door
The dawn came in, and glimmered on the floor
With a pale light, I journeyed round the hall
And found a door deep sunken in the wall,
The least of doors; beyond on a dim plain
A little runnel made a bubbling strain,
And on the runnel's stony and bare edge
A dusky demon dry as a withered sedge
Swayed, crooning to himself an unknown tongue:
In a sad revelry he sang and swung
Bacchant and mournful, passing to and fro
His hand along the runnel's side, as though
The flowers still grew there: far on the sea's waste
Shaking and waving, vapour vapour chased,
While high frail cloudlets, fed with a green light,
Like drifts of leaves, immovable and bright,
Hung in the passionate dawn. He slowly turned:
A demon's leisure: eyes, first white, now burned
Like wings of kingfishers; and he arose
Barking. We trampled up and down with blows
Of sword and brazen battle-axe, while day
Gave to high noon and noon to night gave way;
And when he knew the sword of Manannan
Amid the shades of night, he changed and ran
Through many shapes; I lunged at the smooth throat
Of a great eel; it changed, and I but smote
A fir-tree roaring in its leafless top;
And thereupon I drew the livid chop
Of a drowned dripping body to my breast;
Horror from horror grew; but when the west
Had surged up in a plumy fire, I drave
Through heart and spine; and cast him in the wave
Lest Niamh shudder.

Full of hope and dread
Those two came carrying wine and meat and bread,
And healed my wounds with unguents out of flowers
That feed white moths by some De Danaan shrine;
Then in that hall, lit by the dim sea-shine,
We lay on skins of otters, and drank wine,
Brewed by the sea-gods, from huge cups that lay
Upon the lips of sea-gods in their day;
And then on heaped-up skins of otters slept.
And when the sun once more in saffron stept,
Rolling his flagrant wheel out of the deep,
We sang the loves and angers without sleep,
And all the exultant labours of the strong.
But now the lying clerics murder song
With barren words and flatteries of the weak.
In what land do the powerless turn the beak
Of ravening Sorrow, or the hand of Wrath?
For all your croziers, they have left the path
And wander in the storms and clinging snows,
Hopeless for ever: ancient Oisin knows,
For he is weak and poor and blind, and lies
On the anvil of the world.

S. Patrick. Be still: the skies
Are choked with thunder, lightning, and fierce wind,
For God has heard, and speaks His angry mind;
Go cast your body on the stones and pray,
For He has wrought midnight and dawn and day.

Oisin. Saint, do you weep? I hear amid the thunder
The Fenian horses; atmour torn asunder;
Laughter and cries. The armies clash and shock,
And now the daylight-darkening ravens flock.
Cease, cease, O mournful, laughing Fenian horn!

We feasted for three days. On the fourth morn
I found, dropping sea-foam on the wide stair,
And hung with slime, and whispering in his hair,
That demon dull and unsubduable;
And once more to a day-long battle fell,
And at the sundown threw him in the surge,

To lie until the fourth morn saw emerge
His new-healed shape; and for a hundred years
So warred, so feasted, with nor dreams nor fears,
Nor languor nor fatigue: an endless feast,
An endless war.

The hundred years had ceased;
I stood upon the stair: the surges bore
A beech-bough to me, and my heart grew sore,
Remembering how I had stood by white-haired Finn
Under a beech at Almhuin and heard the thin
Outcry of bats.

And then young Niamh came
Holding that horse, and sadly called my name;
I mounted, and we passed over the lone
And drifting greyness, while this monotone,
Surly and distant, mixed inseparably
Into the clangour of the wind and sea.

'I hear my soul drop down into decay,
And Mananna's dark tower, stone after stone,
Gather sea-slime and fall the seaward way,
And the moon goad the waters night and day,
That all be overthrown.

'But till the moon has taken all, I wage
War on the mightiest men under the skies,
And they have fallen or fled, age after age.
Light is man's love, and lighter is man's rage;
His purpose drifts and dies.'

And then lost Niamh murmured, 'Love, we go
To the Island of Forgetfulness, for lo!
The Islands of Dancing and of Victories
Are empty of all power.'

'And which of these
Is the Island of Content?'

'None know,' she said;
And on my bosom laid her weeping head.

Book III

Fled foam underneath us, and round us, a wandering and
milky smoke,
High as the saddle-girth, covering away from our glances the
tide;
And those that fled, and that followed, from the foam-pale
distance broke;
The immortal desire of Immortals we saw in their faces, and
sighed.

I mused on the chase with the Fenians, and Bran, Sceolan,
Lomair,
And never a song sang Niamh, and over my finger-tips
Came now the sliding of tears and sweeping of mist-cold hair,
And now the warmth of sighs, and after the quiver of lips.

Were we days long or hours long in riding, when, rolled in a
grisly peace,
An isle lay level before us, with dripping hazel and oak?
And we stood on a sea's edge we saw not; for whiter than new-
washed fleece
Fled foam underneath us, and round us, a wandering and
milky smoke.

And we rode on the plains of the sea's edge; the sea's edge
barren and grey,
Grey sand on the green of the grasses and over the dripping trees,
Dripping and doubling landward, as though they would hasten
away,
Like an army of old men longing for rest from the moan of the
seas.

But the trees grew taller and closer, immense in their wrinkling
bark;
Dropping; a murmurous dropping; old silence and that one
sound;
For no live creatures lived there, no weasels moved in the dark:
Long sighs arose in our spirits, beneath us bubbled the ground.

And the ears of the horse went sinking away in the hollow
night,
For, as drift from a sailor slow drowning the gleams of the
world and the sun,
Ceased on our hands and our faces, on hazel and oak leaf, the
light,
And the stars were blotted above us, and the whole of the
world was one.

Till the horse gave a whinny; for, cumbrous with stems of the
hazel and oak,
A valley flowed down from his hoofs, and there in the long
grass lay,
Under the starlight and shadow, a monstrous slumbering folk,
Their naked and gleaming bodies poured out and heaped in the
way.

And by them were arrow and war-axe, arrow and shield and
blade;
And dew-blanched horns, in whose hollow a child of three
years old
Could sleep on a couch of rushes, and all inwrought and inlaid,
And more comely than man can make them with bronze and
silver and gold.

And each of the huge white creatures was huger than fourscore
men;
The tops of their ears were feathered, their hands were the
claws of birds,
And, shaking the plumes of the grasses and the leaves of the
mural glen,
The breathing came from those bodies, long warless, grown
whiter than curds.

The wood was so spacious above them, that He who has stars
for His flocks
Could fondle the leaves with His fingers, nor go from His dew-
cumbered skies;
So long were they sleeping, the owls had builded their nests in
their locks,
Filling the fibrous dimness with long generations of eyes.

And over the limbs and the valley the slow owls wandered and
came,
Now in a place of star-fire, and now in a shadow-place wide;
And the chief of the huge white creatures, his knees in the soft
star-flame,
Lay loose in a place of shadow: we drew the reins by his side.

Golden the nails of his bird-claws, flung loosely along the dim
ground;
In one was a branch soft-shining with bells more many than
sighs
In midst of an old man's bosom; owls ruffling and pacing
around
Sidled their bodies against him, filling the shade with their
eyes.

And my gaze was thronged with the sleepers; no, not since the
world began,
In realms where the handsome were many, nor in glamours by
demons flung,
Have faces alive with such beauty been known to the salt eye of
man,
Yet weary with passions that faded when the sevenfold seas
were young.

And I gazed on the bell-branch, sleep's forebear, far sung by
the Sennachies.
I saw how those slumberers, grown weary, there camping in
grasses deep,
Of wars with the wide world and pacing the shores of the
wandering seas,
Laid hands on the bell-branch and swayed it, and fed of
unhuman sleep.

Snatching the horn of Niamh, I blew a long lingering note.
Came sound from those monstrous sleepers, a sound like the
stirring of flies.
He, shaking the fold of his lips, and heaving the pillar of his
throat,
Watched me with mournful wonder out of the wells of his eyes.

I cried, 'Come out of the shadow, king of the nails of gold!
And tell of your goodly household and the goodly works of
your hands,
That we may muse in the starlight and talk of the battles of old;
Your questioner, Oisin, is worthy, he comes from the Fenian
lands.'

Half open his eyes were, and held me, dull with the smoke of
their dreams;
His lips moved slowly in answer, no answer out of them came;
Then he swayed in his fingers the bell-branch, slow dropping a
sound in faint streams
Softer than snow-flakes in April and piercing the marrow like
flame.

Wrapt in the wave of that music, with weariness more than of
earth,
The moil of my centuries filled me; and gone like a sea-covered
stone
Were the memories of the whole of my sorrow and the
memories of the whole of my mirth,
And a softness came from the starlight and filled me full to the
bone.

In the roots of the grasses, the sorrels, I laid my body as low;
And the pearl-pale Niamh lay by me, her brow on the midst of
my breast;
And the horse was gone in the distance, and years after years
'gan flow;
Square leaves of the ivy moved over us, binding us down to our
rest.

And, man of the many white croziers, a century there I forgot
How the fetlocks drip blood in the battle, when the fallen on
fallen lie rolled;
How the falconer follows the falcon in the weeds of the heron's
plot,
And the name of the demon whose hammer made Conchubar's
sword-blade of old.

And, man of the many white croziers, a century there I forgot
That the spear-shaft is made out of ashwood, the shield out of osier and hide;
How the hammers spring on the anvil, on the spearhead's burning spot;
How the slow, blue-eyed oxen of Finn low sadly at evening tide.

But in dreams, mild man of the croziers, driving the dust with their throngs,
Moved round me, of seamen or landsmen, all who are winter tales;
Came by me the kings of the Red Branch, with roaring of laughter and songs,
Or moved as they moved once, love-making or piercing the tempest with sails.

Came Blanid, Mac Nessa, tall Fergus who feastward of old time slunk,
Cook Barach, the traitor; and warward, the spittle on his beard never dry,
Dark Balor, as old as a forest, car-borne, his mighty head sunk
Helpless, men lifting the lids of his weary and death making eye.

And by me, in soft red raiment, the Fenians moved in loud streams,
And Grania, walking and smiling, sewed with her needle of bone.
So lived I and lived not, so wrought I and wrought not, with creatures of dreams,
In a long iron sleep, as a fish in the water goes dumb as a stone.

At times our slumber was lightened. When the sun was on silver or gold;
When brushed with the wings of the owls, in the dimness they love going by;
When a glow-worm was green on a grass-leaf, lured from his lair in the mould;
Half wakening, we lifted our eyelids, and gazed on the grass with a sigh.

So watched I when, man of the croziers, at the heel of a century
fell,
Weak, in the midst of the meadow, from his miles in the midst
of the air,
A starling like them that forgathered 'neath a moon waking
white as a shell
When the Fenians made foray at morning with Bran, Sceolan,
Lomair.

I awoke: the strange horse without summons out of the
distance ran,
Thrusting his nose to my shoulder; he knew in his bosom deep
That once more moved in my bosom the ancient sadness of man,
And that I would leave the Immortals, their dimness, their
dews dropping sleep.

O had you seen beautiful Niamh grow white as the waters are
white,
Lord of the croziers, you even had lifted your hands and wept:
But, the bird in my fingers, I mounted, remembering alone
that delight
Of twilight and slumber were gone, and that hoofs impatiently
stept.

I died, 'O Niamh! O white one! if only a twelve-houred day,
I must gaze on the beard of Finn, and move where the old men
and young
In the Fenians' dwellings of wattle lean on the chessboards and
play,
Ah, sweet to me now were even bald Conan's slanderous tongue!

'Like me were some galley forsaken far off in Meridian isle,
Remembering its long-oared companions, sails turning to
threadbare rags;
No more to crawl on the seas with long oars mile after mile,
But to be amid shooting of flies and flowering of rushes and flags.'

Their motionless eyeballs of spirits grown mild with
mysterious thought,
Watched her those seamless faces from the valley's glimmering
girth;

As she murmured, 'O wandering Oisin, the strength of the bell-branch is naught,
For there moves alive in your fingers the fluttering sadness of earth.

'Then go through the lands in the saddle and see what the mortals do,
And softly come to your Niamh over the tops of the tide;
But weep for your Niamh, O Oisin, weep; for if only your shoe
Brush lightly as haymouse earth's pebbles, you will come no more to my side.

'O flaming lion of the world, O when will you turn to your rest?'
I saw from a distant saddle; from the earth she made her moan:
'I would die like a small withered leaf in the autumn, for breast unto breast
We shall mingle no more, nor our gazes empty their sweetness lone

'In the isles of the farthest seas where only the spirits come.
Were the winds less soft than the breath of a pigeon who sleeps on her nest,
Nor lost in the star-fires and odours the sound of the sea's vague drum?
O flaming lion of the world, O when will you turn to your rest?'

The wailing grew distant; I rode by the woods of the wrinkling bark,
Where ever is murmurous dropping, old silence and that one sound;
For no live creatures live there, no weasels move in the dark:
In a reverie forgetful of all things, over the bubbling ground.

And I rode by the plains of the sea's edge, where all is barren and grey,
Grey sand on the green of the grasses and over the dripping trees,
Dripping and doubling landward, as though they would hasten away,
Like an army of old men longing for rest from the moan of the seas.

And the winds made the sands on the sea's edge turning and
turning go,
As my mind made the names of the Fenians. Far from the hazel
and oak,
I rode away on the surges, where, high as the saddle-bow,
Fled foam underneath me, and round me, a wandering and
milky smoke.

Long fled the foam-flakes around me, the winds fled out of the
vast,
Snatching the bird in secret; nor knew I, embosomed apart,
When they froze the cloth on my body like armour riveted fast,
For Remembrance, lifting her leanness, keened in the gates of
my heart.

Till, fattening the winds of the morning, an odour of new-
mown hay
Came, and my forehead fell low, and my tears like berries fell
down;
Later a sound came, half lost in the sound of a shore far away,
From the great grass-barnacle calling, and later the shore-
weeds brown.

If I were as I once was, the strong hoofs crushing the sand and
the shells,
Coming out of the sea as the dawn comes, a chaunt of love on
my lips,
Not coughing, my head on my knees, and praying, and wroth
with the bells,
I would leave no saint's head on his body from Rachlin to Bera
of ships.

Making way from the kindling surges, I rode on a bridle-path
Much wondering to see upon all hands, of wattles and
woodwork made,
Your bell-mounted churches, and guardless the sacred cairn
and the rath,
And a small and a feeble populace stooping with mattock and
spade,

Or weeding or ploughing with faces a-shining with much-toil wet;
While in this place and that place, with bodies unglorious,
their chieftains stood,
Awaiting in patience the straw-death, croziered one, caught in
your net:
Went the laughter of scorn from my mouth like the roaring of
wind in a wood.

And before I went by them so huge and so speedy with eyes so
bright,
Came after the hard gaze of youth, or an old man lifted his head:
And I rode and I rode, and I cried out, 'The Fenians hunt
wolves in the night,
So sleep thee by daytime.' A voice cried, 'The Fenians a long
time are dead.'

A whitebeard stood hushed on the pathway, the flesh of his
face as dried grass,
And in folds round his eyes and his mouth, he sad as a child
without milk;
And the dreams of the islands were gone, and I knew how men
sorrow and pass,
And their hound, and their horse, and their love, and their eyes
that glimmer like silk.

And wrapping my face in my hair, I murmured, 'In old age
they ceased';
And my tears were larger than berries, and I murmured,
'Where white clouds lie spread
On Crevroe or broad Knockfefin, with many of old they feast
On the floors of the gods.' He cried, 'No, the gods a long time
are dead.'

And lonely and longing for Niamh, I shivered and turned me
about,
The heart in me longing to leap like a grasshopper into her heart;
I turned and rode to the westward, and followed the sea's old
shout
Till I saw where Maeve lies sleeping till starlight and midnight
part.

And there at the foot of the mountain, two carried a sack full of sand,
They bore it with staggering and sweating, but fell with their burden at length.
Leaning down from the gem-studded saddle, I flung it five yards with my hand,
With a sob for men waxing so weakly, a sob for the Fenians' old strength.

The rest you have heard of, O croziered man; how, when divided the girth,
I fell on the path, and the horse went away like a summer fly;
And my years three hundred fell on me, and I rose, and walked on the earth,
A creeping old man, full of sleep, with the spittle on his beard never dry.

How the men of the sand-sack showed me a church with its belfry in air;
Sorry place, where for swing of the war-axe in my dim eyes the crozier gleams;
What place have Caoilte and Conan, and Bran, Sceolan, Lomair?
Speak, you too are old with your memories, an old man surrounded with dreams.

S. Patrick. Where the flesh of the footsole clingeth on the burning stones is their place;
Where the demons whip them with wires on the burning stones of wide Hell,
Watching the blessed ones move far off, and the smile on God's face,
Between them a gateway of brass, and the howl of the angels who fell.

Oisin. Put the staff in my hands; for I go to the Fenians, O cleric, to chaunt
The war-songs that roused them of old; they will rise, making clouds with their breath,

Innumerable, singing, exultant; the clay underneath them shall pant,
And demons be broken in pieces, and trampled beneath them in death.

And demons afraid in their darkness; deep horror of eyes and of wings,
Afraid, their ears on the earth laid, shall listen and rise up and weep;
Hearing the shaking of shields and the quiver of stretched bowstrings,
Hearing Hell loud with a murmur, as shouting and mocking we sweep.

We will tear out the flaming stones, and batter the gateway of brass
And enter, and none sayeth 'No' when there enters the strongly armed guest;
Make clean as a broom cleans, and march on as oxen move over young grass;
Then feast, making converse of wars, and of old wounds, and turn to our rest.

S. *Patrick.* On the flaming stones, without refuge, the limbs of the Fenians are lost;
None war on the masters of Hell, who could break up the world in their rage;
But kneel and wear out the flags and pray for your soul that is lost
Through the demon love of its youth and its godless and passionate age.

Oisin. Ah me! to be shaken with coughing and broken
with old age and pain,
Without laughter, a show unto children, alone with remembrance and fear;
All emptied of purple hours as a beggar's cloak in the rain,
As a hay-cock out on the flood, or a wolf sucked under a weir.

It were sad to gaze on the blessed and no man I loved of old
there;
I throw down the chain of small stones! when life in my body
has ceased,
I will go to Caoilte, and Conan, and Bran, Sceolan, Lomair,
And dwell in the house of the Fenians, be they in flames or at
feast.

THE OLD AGE OF QUEEN MAEVE
1903

The Old Age of Queen Maeve

A certain poet in outlandish clothes
Gathered a crowd in some Byzantine lane,
Talked of his country and its people, sang
To some stringed instrument none there had seen,
A wall behind his back, over his head
A latticed window. His glance went up at time
As though one listened there, and his voice sank
Or let its meaning mix into the strings.

Maeve the great queen was pacing to and fro,
Between the walls covered with beaten bronze,
In her high house at Cruachan; the long hearth,
Flickering with ash and hazel, but half showed
Where the tired horse-boys lay upon the rushes,
Or on the benches underneath the walls,
In comfortable sleep; all living slept
But that great queen, who more than half the night
Had paced from door to fire and fire to door.
Though now in her old age, in her young age
She had been beautiful in that old way
That's all but gone; for the proud heart is gone,
And the fool heart of the counting-house fears all
But soft beauty and indolent desire.
She could have called over the rim of the world
Whatever woman's lover had hit her fancy,
And yet had been great-bodied and great-limbed,
Fashioned to be the mother of strong children;
And she'd had lucky eyes and high heart,

And wisdom that caught fire like the dried flax,
At need, and made her beautiful and fierce,
Sudden and laughing.
                O unquiet heart,
Why do you praise another, praising her,
As if there were no tale but your own tale
Worth knitting to a measure of sweet sound?
Have I not bid you tell of that great queen
Who has been buried some two thousand years?

When night was at its deepest, a wild goose
Cried from the porter's lodge, and with long clamour
Shook the ale-horns and shields upon their hooks;
But the horse-boys slept on, as though some power
Had filled the house with Druid heaviness;
And wondering who of the many-changing Sidhe
Had come as in the old times to counsel her,
Maeve walked, yet with slow footfall, being old,
To that small chamber by the outer gate.
The porter slept, although he sat upright
With still and stony limbs and open eyes.
Maeve waited, and when that ear-piercing noise
Broke from his parted lips and broke again,
She laid a hand on either of his shoulders,
And shook him wide awake, and bid him say
Who of the wandering many-changing ones
Had troubled his sleep. But all he had to say
Was that, the air being heavy and the dogs
More still than they had been for a good month,
He had fallen asleep, and, though he had dreamed nothing,
He could remember when he had had fine dreams.
It was before the time of the great war
Over the White-Horned Bull and the Brown Bull.

She turned away; he turned again to sleep
That no god troubled now, and, wondering
What matters were afoot among the Sidhe,
Maeve walked through that great hall, and with a sigh
Lifted the curtain of her sleeping-room,
Remembering that she too had seemed divine

To many thousand eyes, and to her own
One that the generations had long waited
That work too difficult for mortal hands
Might be accomplished. Bunching the curtain up
She saw her husband Ailell sleeping there,
And thought of days when he'd had a straight body,
And of that famous Fergus, Nessa's husband,
Who had been the lover of her middle life.

Suddenly Ailell spoke out of his sleep,
And not with his own voice or a man's voice,
But with the burning, live, unshaken voice
Of those that, it may be, can never age.
He said, 'High Queen of Cruachan and Magh Ai,
A king of the Great Plain would speak with you.'
And with glad voice Maeve answered him, 'What king
Of the far-wandering shadows has come to me,
As in the old days when they would come and go
About my threshold to counsel and to help?'
The parted lips replied, 'I seek your help,
For I am Aengus, and I am crossed in love.'
'How may a mortal whose life gutters out
Help them that wander with hand clasping hand,
Their haughty images that cannot wither,
For all their beauty's like a hollow dream,
Mirrored in streams that neither hail nor rain
Nor the cold North has troubled?'
He replied,
'I am from those rivers and I bid you call
The children of the Maines out of sleep,
And set them digging under Bual's hill.
We shadows, while they uproot his earthy house,
Will overthrow his shadows and carry off
Caer, his blue-eyed daughter that I love.
I helped your fathers when they built these walls,
And I would have your help in my great need,
Queen of high Cruachan.'
'I obey your will
With speedy feet and a most thankful heart:
For you have been, O Aengus of the birds,

Our giver of good counsel and good luck.'
And with a groan, as if the mortal breath
Could but awaken sadly upon lips
That happier breath had moved, her husband turned
Face downward, tossing in a troubled sleep;
But Maeve, and not with a slow feeble foot,
Came to the threshold of the painted house
Where her grandchildren slept, and cried aloud,
Until the pillared dark began to stir
With shouting and the clang of unhooked arms.
She told them of the many-changing ones;
And all that night, and all through the next day
To middle night, they dug into the hill.
At middle night great cats with silver claws,
Bodies of shadow and blind eyes like pearls,
Came up out of the hole, and red-eared hounds
With long white bodies came out of the air
Suddenly, and ran at them and harried them.

The 'Maines' children dropped their spades, and stood
With quaking joints and terror-stricken faces,
Till Maeve called out, 'These are but common men.
The Maines' children have not dropped their spades
Because Earth, crazy for its broken power,
Casts up a show and the winds answer it
With holy shadows.' Her high heart was glad,
And when the uproar ran along the grass
She followed with light footfall in the midst,
Till it died out where an old thorn-tree stood.

Friend of these many years, you too had stood
With equal courage in that whirling rout;
For you, although you've not her wandering heart,
Have all that greatness, and not hers alone,
For there is no high story about queens
In any ancient book but tells of you;
And when I've heard how they grew old and died,
Or fell into unhappiness, I've said,
'She will grow old and die, and she has wept!'
And when I'd write it out anew, the words,

Half crazy with the thought, She too has wept!
Outrun the measure.
                                        I'd tell of that great queen
Who stood amid a silence by the thorn
Until two lovers came out of the air
With bodies made out of soft fire.
The one, about whose face birds wagged their fiery wings,
Said, 'Aengus and his sweetheart give their thanks
To Maeve and to Maeve's household, owing all
In owing them the bride-bed that gives peace.'
Then Maeve: 'O Aengus, Master of all lovers,
A thousand years ago you held high ralk
With the first kings of many-pillared Cruachan.
O when will you grow weary?'
                                        They had vanished;
But our of the dark air over her head there came
A murmur of soft words and meeting lips.

BAILE AND AILLINN
1903

Baile and Aillinn

ARGUMENT. Baile and Aillinn were lovers, but Aebgus, the Master of Love, wishing them to be happy in his own land among the dead, told to each a story of the other' death, so that their hearts were broken and they died.

I hardly hear the curlew cry,
Nor the grey rush when the wind is high,
Before my thoughts begin to run
On the heir of Uladh, Buan's son,
Baile, who had the honey mouth;
And that mild woman of the south,
Aillinn, who was King Lugaidh's heir.
Their love was never drowned in care
Of this or that thing, nor grew cold
Because their bodies had grown old.
Being forbid to marry on earth,
They blossomed to immortal mirth.

About the time when Christ was born,
When the long wars for the White Horn
And the Brown Bull had not yet come,
Young Baile Honey-Mouth, whom some
Called rather Baile Little-Land,
Rode out of Emain with a band
Of harpers and young men; and they
Imagined, as they struck the way
To many-pastured Muirthemne,
That all things fell out happily,

And there, for all that fools had said,
Baile and Aillinn would be wed.

They found an old man running there:
He had ragged long grass-coloured hair;
He had knees that stuck out of his hose;
He had puddle-water in his shoes;
He had half a cloak to keep him dry,
Although he had a squirrel's eye.

O wandering birds and rushy beds,
You put such folly in our heads
With all this crying in the wind,
No common love is to our mind,
And our poor Kate or Nan is less
Than any whose unhappiness
Awoke the harp-strings long ago.
Yet they that know all things but know
That all this life can give us is
A child's laughter, a woman's kiss.
Who was it put so great a scorn
In the grey reeds that night and morn
Are trodden and broken by the herds,
And in the light bodies of birds
The north wind tumbles to and fro
And pinches among hail and snow?

That runner said: 'I am from the south;
I run to Baile Honey-Mouth,
To tell him how the girl Aillinn
Rode from the country of her kin,
And old and young men rode with her:
For all that country had been astir
If anybody half as fair
Had chosen a husband anywhere
But where it could see her every day.
When they had ridden a little way
An old man caught the horse's head
With: 'You must home again, and wed
With somebody in your own land."

A young man cried and kissed her hand,
"O lady, wed with one of us";
And when no face grew piteous
For any gentle thing she spake,
She fell and died of the heart-break.'

Because a lover's heart's worn out,
Being tumbled and blown about
By its own blind imagining,
And will believe that anything
That is bad enough to be true, is true,
Baile's heart was broken in two;
And he, being laid upon green boughs,
Was carried to the goodly house
Where the Hound of Ulad sat before
The brazen pillars of his door,
His face bowed low to weep the end
Of the harper's daughter and her friend
For although years had passed away
He always wept them on that day,
For on that day they had been betrayed;
And now that Honey-Mouth is laid
Under a cairn of sleepy stone
Before his eyes, he has tears for none,
Although he is carrying stone, but two
For whom the cairn's but heaped anew.

We hold, because our memory is
So full of that thing and of this,
That out of sight is out of mind.
But the grey rush under the wind
And the grey bird with crooked bill
Have such long memories that they still
Remember Deirdre and her man;
And when we walk with Kate or Nan
About the windy water-side,
Our hearts can hear the voices chide.
How could we be so soon content,
Who know the way that Naoise went?
And they have news of Deirdre's eyes,

Who being lovely was so wise—
Ah! wise, my heart knows well how wise.

Now had that old gaunt crafty one,
Gathering his cloak about him,
Where Aillinn rode with waiting-maids,
Who amid leafy lights and shades
Dreamed of the hands that would unlace
Their bodices in some dim place
When they had come to the marriage-bed,
And harpers, pacing with high head
As though their music were enough
To make the savage heart of love
Grow gentle without sorrowing,
Imagining and pondering
Heaven knows what calamity;

'Another's hurried off,' cried he,
'From heat and cold and wind and wave;
They have heaped the stones above his grave
In Muirthemne, and over it
In changeless Ogham letters writ —
Baile, that was of Rury's seed.
But the gods long ago decreed
No waiting-maid should ever spread
Baile and Aillinn's marriage-bed,
For they should clip and clip again
Where wild bees hive on the Great Plain.
Therefore it is but little news
That put this hurry in my shoes.'

Then seeing that he scarce had spoke
Before her love-worn heart had broke.
He ran and laughed until he came
To that high hill the herdsmen name
The Hill Seat of Laighin, because
Some god or king had made the laws
That held the land together there,
In old times among the clouds of the air.

That old man climbed; the day grew dim;
Two swans came flying up to him,
Linked by a gold chain each to each,
And with low murmuring laughing speech
Alighted on the windy grass.
They knew him: his changed body was
Tall, proud and ruddy, and light wings
Were hovering over the harp-strings
That Edain, Midhir's wife, had wove
In the hid place, being crazed by love.

What shall I call them? fish that swim,
Scale rubbing scale where light is dim
By a broad water-lily leaf;
Or mice in the one wheaten sheaf
Forgotten at the threshing-place;
Or birds lost in the one clear space
Of morning light in a dim sky;
Or, it may be, the eyelids of one eye,
Or the door-pillars of one house,
Or two sweet blossoming apple-boughs
That have one shadow on the ground;
Or the two strings that made one sound
Where that wise harper's finger ran.
For this young girl and this young man
Have happiness without an end,
Because they have made so good a friend.

They know all wonders, for they pass
The towery gates of Gorias,
And Findrias and Falias,
And long-forgotten Murias,
Among the giant kings whose hoard,
Cauldron and spear and stone and sword,
Was robbed before earth gave the wheat;
Wandering from broken street to street
They come where some huge watcher is,
And tremble with their love and kiss.

They know undying things, for they
Wander where earth withers away,

Though nothing troubles the great streams
But light from the pale stars, and gleams
From the holy orchards, where there is none
But fruit that is of precious stone,
Or apples of the sun and moon.

What were our praise to them? They eat
Quiet's wild heart, like daily meat;
Who when night thickens are afloat
On dappled skins in a glass boat,
Far out under a windless sky;
While over them birds of Aengus fly,
And over the tiller and the prow,
And waving white wings to and fro
Awaken wanderings of light air
To stir their coverlet and their hair.

And poets found, old writers say,
A yew tree where his body lay;
But a wild apple hid the grass
With its sweet blossom where hers was,
And being in good heart, because
A better time had come again
After the deaths of many men,
And that long fighting at the ford,
They wrote on tablets of thin board,
Made of the apple and the yew,
All the love stories that they knew.

Let rush and bird cry out their fill
Of the harper's daughter if they will,
Beloved, I am not afraid of her.
She is not wiser nor lovelier,
And you are more high of heart than she,
For all her wanderings over-sea;
But I'd have bird and rush forget
Those other two; for never yet
Has lover lived, but longed to wive
Like them that are no more alive.

THE SHADOWY WATERS
1906

TO LADY GREGORY

I walked among the seven woods of Coole:
Shan-walla, where a willow-bordered pond
Gathers the wild duck from the winter dawn;
Shady Kyle-dortha; sunnier Kyle-na-no,
Where many hundred squirrels are as happy
As though they had been hidden by green boughs
Where old age cannot find them; Pairc-na-lee,
Where hazel and ash and privet blind the paths:
Dim Pairc-na-carraig, where the wild bees fling
Their sudden fragrances on the green air;
Dim Pairc-na-tarav, where enchanted eyes
Have seen immortal, mild, proud shadows walk;
Dim Inchy wood, that hides badger and fox
And marten-cat, and borders that old wood
Wise Biddy Early called the wicked wood:
Seven odours, seven murmurs, seven woods.
I had not eyes like those enchanted eyes,
Yet dreamed that beings happier than men
Moved round me in the shadows, and at night
My dreams were cloven by voices and by fires;
And the images I have woven in this story
Of *Forgael* and Dectora and the empty waters
Moved round me in the voices and the fires,
And more I may not write of, for they that cleave
The waters of sleep can make a chattering tongue
Heavy like stone, their wisdom being half silence.
How shall I name you, immortal, mild, proud shadows?
I only know that all we know comes from you,

And that you come from Eden on flying feet.
Is Eden far away, or do you hide
From human thought, as hares and mice and coneys
That run before the reaping-hook and lie
In the last ridge of the barley? Do our woods
And winds and ponds cover more quiet woods,
More shining winds, more star-glimmering ponds?
Is Eden out of time and out of space?
And do you gather about us when pale light
Shining on water and fallen among leaves,
And winds blowing from flowers, and whirr of feathers
And the green quiet, have uplifted the heart?

I have made this poem for you, that men may read it
Before they read of *Forgael* and Dectora,
As men in the old times, before the harps began,
Poured out wine for the high invisible ones.

The Harp of Aengus

Edain came out of Midhir's hill, and lay
Beside young Aengus in his tower of glass,
Where time is drowned in odour-laden winds
And Druid moons, and murmuring of boughs,
And sleepy boughs, and boughs where apples made
Of opal and ruby and pale chrysolite
Awake unsleeping fires; and wove seven strings,
Sweet with all music, out of his long hair,
Because her hands had been made wild by love.
When Midhir's wife had changed her to a fly,
He made a harp with Druid apple-wood
That she among her winds might know he wept;
And from that hour he has watched over none
But faithful lovers.

The Shadowy Waters
A Dramatic Poem

Person in the Poem

FORGAEL	AIRBRIC
SAILORS	DECTORA

The deck of an ancient ship. At the right of the stage is the mast, with a large square sail hiding a great deal of the sky and sea on that side. The tiller is at the left of the stage; it is a long oar coming through an opening in the bulwark. The deck rises in a series of steps hehind the tiller, and the stern of the ship curves overhead. When the play opens there are four persons upon the deck. Aibric stands by the tiller. Forgael sleeps upon the raised portion of the deck towards the front of the stage. Two Sailors are standing near to the mast, on which a harp is hanging.

First Sailor. Has he not led us into these waste seas
For long enough?

Second Sailor. Aye, long and long enough.

First Sailor. We have not come upon a shore or ship
These dozen weeks.

Second Sailor. And I had thought to make
A good round Sum upon this cruise, and turn—
For I am getting on in life—to something
That has less ups and downs than robbery.

First Sailor. I am so tired of being bachelor
I could give all my heart to that Red Moll
That had but the one eye.

Second Sailor. Can no bewitchment
Transform these rascal billows into women
That I may drown myself?

First Sailor. Better steer home,
Whether he will or no; and better still
To take him while he sleeps and carry him
And drop him from the gunnel.

Second Sailor. I dare not do it.
Were't not that there is magic in his harp,
I would be of your mind; but when he plays it
Strange creatures flutter up before one's eyes,
Or cry about one's ears.

First Sailor. Nothing to fear.

Second Sailor. Do you remember when we sank that galley
At the full moon?

First Sailor. He played all through the night.

Second Sailor.
Until the moon had set; and when I looked
Where the dead drifted, I could see a bird
Like a grey gull upon the breast of each.
While I was looking they rose hurriedly,
And after circling with strange cries awhile
Flew westward; and many a time since then
I've heard a rustling overhead in the wind.

First Sailor. I saw them on that night as well as you.
But when I had eaten and drunk myself asleep
My courage came again.

Second Sailor. But that's not all.
The other night, while he was playing it,
A beautiful young man and girl came up
In a white breaking wave; they had the look
Of those that are alive for ever and ever.

First Sailor. I saw them, too, one night. Forgael was playing,
And they were listening there beyond the sail.
He could not see them, but I held out my hands
To grasp the woman.

Second Sailor. You have dared to touch her?

First Sailor. O she was but a shadow, and slipped from me.

Second Sailor. But were you not afraid?

First Sailor. Why should I fear?

Second Sailor. 'Twas Aengus and Edain, the wandering lovers,
To whom all lovers pray.

First Sailor. But what of that?
A shadow does not carry sword or spear.

Second Sailor. My mother told me that there is not one
Of the Ever-living half so dangerous
As that wild Aengus. Long before her day
He carried Edain off from a king's house,
And hid her among fruits of jewel-stone
And in a tower of glass, and from that day
Has hated every man that's not in love,
And has been dangerous to him.

First Sailor. I have heard
He does not hate seafarers as he hates
Peaceable men that shut the wind away,
And keep to the one weary marriage-bed.

Second Sailor. I think that he has Forgael in his net,
And drags him through the sea.

First Sailor. Well, net or none,
I'd drown him while we have the chance to do it.

Second Sailor. It's certain I'd sleep easier o' nights
If he were dead; but who will be our captain,
Judge of the stars, and find a course for us?

First Sailor. I've thought of that. We must have Aibric with us,
For he can judge the stars as well as Forgael.
(*Going towards Aibric.*)

Become our captain, Aibric. I am resolved
To make an end of Forgael while he sleeps.
There's not a man but will be glad of it
When it is over, nor one to grumble at us.

Aibric. You have taken pay and made your bargain for it.

First Sailor. What good is there in this hard way of living,
Unless we drain more flagons in a year
And kiss more lips than lasting peaceable men
In their long lives? Will you be of our troop
And take the captain's share of everything
And bring us into populous seas again?

Aibric. Be of your troop! Aibric be one of you
And Forgael in the other scale! kill Forgael,
And he my master from my childhood up!
If you will draw that sword out of its scabbard
I'll give my answer.

First Sailor. You have awakened him.
(*To Second Sailor.*)

We'd better go, for we have lost this chance.
(*They go out.*)

Forgael. Have the birds passed us? I could hear your voice,
But there were others.

Aibric. I have seen nothing pass.

Forgael. You're certain of it? I never wake from sleep
But that I am afraid they may have passed,
For they're my only pilots. If I lost them
Straying too far into the north or south,
I'd never come upon the happiness
That has been promised me. I have not seen them
These many days; and yet there must be many
Dying at every moment in the world,
And flying towards their peace.

Aibric. Put by these thoughts,
And listen to me for a while. The sailors
Are plotting for your death.

Forgael. Have I not given
More riches than they ever hoped to find?
And now they will not follow, while I seek
The only riches that have hit my fancy.

Aibric. What riches can you find in this waste sea
Where no ship sails, where nothing that's alive
Has ever come but those man-headed birds,
Knowing it for the world's end?

Forgael. Where the world ends
The mind is made unchanging, for it finds
Miracle, ecstasy, the impossible hope,
The flagstone under all, the fire of fires,
The roots of the world.

Aibric. Shadows before now
Have driven travellers mad for their own sport.

Forgael. Do you, too, doubt me? Have you joined their plot?

Aibric. No, no, do not say that. You know right well
That I will never lift a hand against you.

Forgael. Why should you be more faithful than the rest,
Being as doubtful?

Aibric. I have called you master
Too many years to lift a hand against you.

Forgael. Maybe it is but natural to doubt me.
You've never known, I'd lay a wager on it,
A melancholy that a cup of wine,
A lucky battle, or a woman's kiss
Could not amend.

Aibric. I have good spirits enough.

Forgael. If you will give me all your mind awhile—
All, all, the very bottom of the bowl—
I'll show you that I am made differently,
That nothing can amend it but these waters,
Where I am rid of life—the events of the world—
What do you call it?—that old promise-breaker,
The cozening fortune-teller that comes whispering,
You will have all you have wished for when you have earned
Land for your children or money in a pot.-
And when we have it we are no happier,
Because of that old draught under the door,
Or creaky shoes. And at the end of all
How are we better off than Seaghan the fool,
That never did a hand's turn? Aibric! Aibric!
We have fallen in the dreams the Ever-living
Breathe on the burnished mirror of the world
And then smooth out with ivory hands and sigh,
And find their laughter sweeter to the taste
For that brief sighing.

Aibric. If you had loved some woman—

Forgael. You say that also? You have heard the voices,
For that is what they say—all, all the shadows—
Aengus and Edain, those passionate wanderers,
And all the others; but it must be love
As they have known it. Now the secret's out;
For it is love that I am seeking for,
But of a beautiful, unheard-of kind
That is not in the world.

Aibric. And yet the world
Has beautiful women to please every man.

Forgael. But he that gets their love after the fashion
Loves in brief longing and deceiving hope
And bodily tenderness, and finds that even
The bed of love, that in the imagination

Had seemed to be the giver of all peace,
Is no more than a wine-cup in the tasting,
And as soon finished.

Aibric. All that ever loved
Have loved that way—there is no other way.

Forgael. Yet never have two lovers kissed but they
believed there was some other near at hand,
And almost wept because they could not find it.

Aibric. When they have twenty years; in middle life
They take a kiss for what a kiss is worth,
And let the dream go by.

Forgael. It's not a dream,
But the reality that makes our passion
As a lamp shadow—no—no lamp, the sun.
What the world's million lips are thirsting for
Must be substantial somewhere.

Aibric. I have heard the Druids
Mutter such things as they awake from trance.
It may be that the Ever-living know it—
No mortal can.

Forgael. Yes; if they give us help.

Aibric. They are besotting you as they besot
The crazy herdsman that will tell his fellows
That he has been all night upon the hills,
Riding to hurley, or in the battle-host
With the Ever-living.

Forgael. What if he speak the truth,
And for a dozen hours have been a part
Of that more powerful life?

Aibric. His wife knows better.
Has she not seen him lying like a log,

Or fumbling in a dream about the house?
And if she hear him mutter of wild riders,
She knows that it was but the cart-horse coughing
That set him to the fancy.

Forgael. All would be well
Could we but give us wholly to the dreams,
And get into their world that to the sense
Is shadow, and not linger wretchedly
Among substantial things; for it is dreams
That lift us to the flowing, changing world
That the heart longs for. What is love itself,
Even though it be the lightest of light love,
But dreams that hurry from beyond the world
To make low laughter more than meat and drink,
Though it but set us sighing? Fellow-wanderer,
Could we but mix ourselves into a dream,
Not in its image on the mirror!

Aibric. While
We're in the body that's impossible.

Forgael. And yet I cannot think they're leading me
To death; for they that promised to me love
As those that can outlive the moon have known it,
Had the world's total life gathered up, it seemed,
Into their shining limbs—I've had great teachers.
Aengus and Edain ran up out of the wave—
You'd never doubt that it was life they promised
Had you looked on them face to face as I did,
With so red lips, and running on such feet,
And having such wide-open, shining eyes.

Aibric. It's certain they are leading you to death.
None but the dead, or those that never lived,
Can know that ecstasy. Forgael! Forgael!
They have made you follow the man-headed birds,
And you have told me that their journey lies
Towards the country of the dead.

Forgael. What matter
If I am going to my death?—for there,
Or somewhere, I shall find the love they have
promised.
That much is certain. I shall find a woman.
One of the Ever-living, as I think—
One of the Laughing People—and she and I
Shall light upon a place in the world's core,
Where passion grows to be a changeless thing,
Like charmed apples made of chrysoprase,
Or chrysoberyl, or beryl, or chrysolite;
And there, in juggleries of sight and sense,
Become one movement, energy, delight,
Until the overburthened moon is dead.
(*A number of sailors enter hurriedly.*)

First Sailor. Look there! there in the mist! a ship of spice!
And we are almost on her!

Second Sailor. We had not known
But for the ambergris and sandalwood.

First Sailor. No; but opoponax and cinnamon.

Forgael (*taking the tiller from Aibric*).
The Ever-living have kept my bargain for me,
And paid you on the nail.

Aibric. Take up that rope
To make her fast while we are plundering her.

First Sailor. There is a king and queen upon her deck,
And where there is one woman there'll be others.

Aibric. Speak lower, or they'll hear.

First Sailor. They cannot hear;
They are too busy with each other. Look!
He has stooped down and kissed her on the lips.

Second Sailor. When she finds out we have better men aboard
She may not be too sorry in the end.

First Sailor. She will be like a wild cat; for these queens
Care more about the kegs of silver and gold
And the high fame that come to them in marriage,
Than a strong body and a ready hand.

Second Sailor. There's nobody is natural but a robber,
And that is why the world totters about
Upon its bandy legs.

Aibric. Run at them now,
And overpower the crew while yet asleep!

(*The sailors go out.*)

(*Voices and the clashing of swords are heard from the other ship, which cannot be seen because of the sail.*)

A Voice. Armed men have come upon us! O I am slain!

Another Voice. Wake all below!

Another Voice. Why have you broken our sleep?

First Voice. Armed men have come upon us! O I am slain!

Forgael (*who has remained at the tiller*).
There! There they come! Gull, gannet, or diver,
But with a man's head, or a fair woman's,
They hover over the masthead awhile
To wait their friends; but when their friends have come
They'll fly upon that secret way of theirs.
One—and one—a couple—five together;

And I will hear them talking in a minute.
Yes, voices! but I do not catch the words.
Now I can hear. There's one of them that says,
'How light we are, now we are changed to birds!'
Another answers, 'Maybe we shall find
Our heart's desire now that we are so light.'
And then one asks another how he died,
And says, 'A sword-blade pierced me in my sleep.'
And now they all wheel suddenly and fly
To the other side, and higher in the air.
And now a laggard with a woman's head
Comes crying, 'I have run upon the sword.
I have fled to my beloved in the air,
In the waste of the high air, that we may wander
Among the windy meadows of the dawn.'
But why are they still waiting? why are they
Circling and circling over the masthead?
What power that is more mighty than desire
To hurry to their hidden happiness
Withholds them now? Have the Ever-living Ones
A meaning in that circling overhead?
But what's the meaning? (*He cries out.*) Why do you
  linger there?
Why linger? Run to your desire,
Are you not happy winged bodies now?

(*His voice sinks again.*)

Being too busy in the air and the high air,
They cannot hear my voice; but what's the meaning?

(*The sailors have returned. Dectora is with them.*)

Forgael (*turning and seeing her*).
Why are you standing with your eyes upon me?
You are not the world's core. O no, no, no!
That cannot be the meaning of the birds.
You are not its core. My teeth are in the world,
But have not bitten yet.

Dectora. I am a queen,
And ask for satisfaction upon these

Who have slain my husband and laid hands upon me.
(*Breaking loose from the sailors who are holding her.*)
Let go my hands!

Forgael. Why do you cast a shadow?
Where do you come from? Who brought you to this place?
They would not send me one that casts a shadow.
Dectora. Would that the storm that overthrew my ships,
And drowned the treasures of nine conquered nations,
And blew me hither to my lasting sorrow,
Had drowned me also. But, being yet alive,
I ask a fitting punishment for all
That raised their hands against him.

Forgael. There are some
That weigh and measure all in these waste seas—
They that have all the wisdom that's in life,
And all that prophesying images
Made of dim gold rave out in secret tombs;
They have it that the plans of kings and queens
But laughter and tears—laughter, laughter, and tears;
That every man should carry his own soul
Upon his shoulders.

Dectora. You've nothing but wild words,
And I would know if you will give me vengeance.

Forgael. When she finds out I will not let her go—
When she knows that.

Dectora. What is it that you are muttering—
That you'll not let me go? I am a queen.

Forgael. Although you are more beautiful than any,
I almost long that it were possible;
But if I were to put you on that ship,
With sailors that were sworn to do your will,
And you had spread a sail for home, a wind
Would rise of a sudden, or a wave so huge
It had washed among the stars and put them out,

And beat the bulwark of your ship on mine,
Until you stood before me on the deck—
As now.

Dectora. Does wandering in these desolate seas
And listening to the cry of wind and wave
Bring madness?

Forgael. Queen, I am not mad.

Dectora. Yet say
That unimaginable storms of wind and wave
Would rise against me.

Forgael. No, I am not mad—
If it be not that hearing messages
From lasting watchers, that outlive the moon,
At the most quiet midnight is to be stricken.

Dectora. And did those watchers bid you take me captive?

Forgael. Both you and I are taken in the net.
It was their hands that plucked the winds awake
And blew you hither; and their mouths have promised
I shall have love in their immortal fashion;
And for this end they gave me my old harp
That is more mighty than the sun and moon,
Or than the shivering casting-net of the stars,
That none might take you from me.

Dectora (*first trembling back from the mast where the harp is, and then laughing*). For a moment
Your raving of a message and a harp
More mighty than the stars half troubled me,
But all that's raving. Who is there can compel
The daughter and the granddaughter of kings
To be his bedfellow?

Forgael. Until your lips

Have called me their beloved, I'll not kiss them.

Dectora. My husband and my king died at my feet,
And yet you talk of love.

Forgael. The movement of time
Is shaken in these seas, and what one does
One moment has no might upon the moment
That follows after.

Dectora. I understand you now.
You have a Druid craft of wicked sound
Wrung from the cold women of the sea
A magic that can call a demon up,
Until my body give you kiss for kiss.

Forgael. Your soul shall give the kiss.

Dectora. I am not afraid,
While there's a rope to run into a noose
Or wave to drown. But I have done with words,
And I would have you look into my face
And know that it is fearless.

Forgael. Do what you will,
For neither I nor you can break a mesh
Of the great golden net that is about us.

Dectora. There's nothing in the world that's worth a fear.
(*She passes Forgael and stands for a moment looking into his face.*)
I have good reason for that thought.
(*She runs suddenly on to the raised part of the poop.*)
And now
I can put fear away as a queen should.
(*She mounts on to the hulwark and turns towards Forgael.*)
Fool, fool! Although you have looked into my face
You do not see my purpose. I shall have gone
Before a hand can touch me.

Forgael (folding his arms). My hands are still;
The Ever-living hold us. Do what you will,
You cannot leap out of the golden net.

First Sailor. No need to drown, for, if you will pardon us
And measure out a course and bring us home,
We'll put this man to death.

Dectora. I promise it.

First Sailor. There is none to take his side.

Aibric. I am on his side,
I'll strike a blow for him to give him time
To cast his dreams away.

(*Aibric goes in front of Forgael with drawn sword. Forgael takes the harp.*)

First Sailor. No other'll do it.

(*The sailors throw Aibric on one side. He falls and lies upon the deck. They lift their swords to strike Forgael, who is about to play the harp. The stage begins to darken. The Sailors hesitate in fear.*)

Second Sailor. He has put a sudden darkness over the moon.

Dectora. Nine swords with handles of rhinoceros horn
To him that strikes him first!

First Sailor. I will strike him first.
(*He goes close up to Forgael with his sword lifted.*)
(*Shrinking back.*) He has caught the crescent moon out of the sky,
And carries it between us.

Second Sailor. Holy fire
To burn us to the marrow if we strike.

Dectora. I'll give a golden galley full of fruit,
That has the heady flavour of new wine,
To him that wounds him to the death.

First Sailor. I'll do it.
For all his spells will vanish when he dies,
Having their life in him.

Second Sailor. Though it be the moon
That he is holding up between us there,
I will strike at him.

Others. And I! And I! And I!
(*Forgael* plays the harp.)

First Sailor (*falling into a dream suddenly*).
But you were saying there is somebody
Upon that other ship we are to wake.
You did not know what brought him to his end,
But it was sudden.

Second Sailor. You are in the right;
I had forgotten that we must go wake him.

Dectora. He has flung a Druid spell upon the air,
And set you dreaming.

Second Sailor. How can we have a wake
When we have neither brown nor yellow ale?

First Sailor. I saw a flagon of brown ale aboard her.

Third Sailor. How can we raise the keen that do not know
What name to call him by?

First Sailor. Come to his ship.
His name will come into our thoughts in a minute.
I know that he *died a thousand* years ago,
And has not yet been waked.
Second Sailor (*beginning to keen*). Ohone! O! O! O!
The yew-bough has been broken into two,
And all the birds are scattered.

All the sailors. O! O! O! O!

(*They go out keening.*)

Dectora. Protect me now, gods that my people swear by.
(*Aibric has risen from the deck where he had fallen. He has begun looking for his sword as if in a dream.*)

Aibric. Where is my sword that fell out of my hand
When I first heard the news? Ah, there it is!
(*He goes dreamily towards the sword, but Dectora runs at it and takes it up before he can reach it.*)

Aibric (*sleepily*). Queen, give it to me.

Dectora. No, I have need of it.

Aibric. Why do you need a sword? But you may keep it.
Now that he's dead I have no need of it,
For everything is gone.

A Sailor (*calling from the other ship*). Come hither, Aibric,
And tell me who it is that we are waking.

Aibric (*half to Dectora, half to himself*).
What name had that dead king? Arthur of Britain?
No, no—not Arthur. I remember now.
It was golden-armed Iollan, and he died
Broken-hearted, having lost his queen
Through wicked spells. That is not all the tale,
For he was killed. O! O! O! O! O! O!
For golden-armed Iollan has been killed.

(*He goes out.*)

(*While he has been speaking, and through part of what follows, one hears the wailing of the Sailors from the other ship. Dectora stands with the sword lifted in front of Forgael.*)

Dectora. I will end all your magic on the instant.
(*Her voice becomes dreamy, and she lowers the sword slowly, and finally lets it fall. She spreads out her hair. She takes off her crown and lays it upon the deck.*)

This sword is to lie beside him in the grave.
It was in all his battles. I will spread my hair,
And wring my hands, and wail him bitterly,
For I have heard that he was proud and laughing,
Blue-eyed, and a quick runner on bare feet,
And that he died a thousand years ago.
O; O! O! O!

(*Forgael* changes the tune.)

But no, that is not it.
I knew him well, and while I heard him laughing
They killed him at my feet. O! O! O! O!
For golden-armed Iollan that I loved.
But what is it that made me say I loved him?
It was that harper put it in my thoughts,
But it is true. Why did they run upon him,
And beat the golden helmet with their swords?

Forgael. Do you not know me, lady? I am he
That you are weeping for.

Dectora. No, for he is dead.
O! O! O! O! for golden-armed Iollan.

Forgael. It was so given out, but I will prove
That the grave-diggers in a dreamy frenzy
Have buried nothing but my golden arms.
Listen to that low-laughing string of the moon
And you will recollect my face and voice,
For you have listened to me playing it
These thousand years.

(*He starts up, listening to the birds. The harp slips from his hands, and remains leaning against the bulwarks behind him.*)

What are the birds at there?
Why are they all a-flutter of a sudden?
What are you calling out above the mast?
If railing and reproach and mockery
Because I have awakened her to love
By magic strings, I'll make this answer to it:
Being driven on by voices and by dreams

That were clear messages from the Ever-living,
I have done right. What could I but obey?
And yet you make a clamour of reproach.

Dectora (*laughing*). Why, it's a wonder out of reckoning
That I should keen him from the full of the moon
To the horn, and he be hale and hearty.

Forgael. How have I wronged her now that she is merry?
But no, no, no! your cry is not against me.
You know the counsels of the Ever-living,
And all that tossing of your wings is joy,
And all that murmuring's but a marriage-song;
But if it be reproach, I answer this:
There is not one among you that made love
By any other means. You call it passion,
Consideration, generosity;
But it was all deceit, and flattery
To win a woman in her own despite,
For love is war, and there is hatred in it;
And if you say that she came willingly

Dectora. Why do you turn away and hide your face,
That I would look upon for ever?

Forgael. My grief!

Dectora. Have I not loved you for a thousand years?

Forgael. I never have been golden-armed Iollan.

Vectora. I do not understand. I know your face
Better than my own hands.

Forgael. I have deceived you
Out of all reckoning.

Dectora. Is it not true
That you were born a thousand years ago,
In islands where the children of Aengus wind

In happy dances under a windy moon,
And that you'll bring me there?

Forgael. I have deceived you;
I have deceived you utterly.

Dectora. How can that be?
Is it that though your eyes are full of love
Some other woman has a claim on you,
And I've but half!

Forgael. O no!

Dectora. And if there is,
If there be half a hundred more, what matter?
I'll never give another thought to it;
No, no, nor half a thought; but do not speak.
Women are hard and proud and stubborn-hearted,
Their heads being turned with praise and flattery;
And that is why their lovers are afraid
To tell them a plain story.

Forgael. That's not the story;
But I have done so great a wrong against you,
There is no measure that it would not burst.
I will confess it all.

Dectora. What do I care,
Now that my body has begun to dream,
And you have grown to be a burning sod
In the imagination and intellect?
If something that's most fabulous were true
If you had taken me by magic spells,
And killed a lover or husband at my feet
I would not let you speak, for I would know
That it was yesterday and not to-day
I loved him; I would cover up my ears,
As I am doing now. (*A pause.*) Why do you weep?

Forgael. I weep because I've nothing for your eyes
But desolate waters and a battered ship.

Dectora. O why do you not lift your eyes to mine?

Forgael. I weep—I weep because bare night's above,
And not a roof of ivory and gold.

Dectora. I would grow jealous of the ivory roof,
And strike the golden pillars with my hands.
I would that there was nothing in the world
But my beloved that night and day had perished,
And all that is and all that is to be,
All that is not the meeting of our lips.

Forgael. You turn away. Why do you turn away?
Am I to fear the waves, or is the moon
My enemy?

Dectora. I looked upon the moon,
Longing to knead and pull it into shape
That I might lay it on your head as a crown.
But now it is your thoughts that wander away,
For you are looking at the sea. Do you not know
How great a wrong it is to let one's thought
Wander a moment when one is in love?
(*He has moved away. She follows him. He is looking out over the sea, shading his eyes.*)
Why are you looking at the sea?

Forgael. Look there!

Dectora. What is there but a troop of ash-grey birds
That fly into the west?

Forgael. But listen, listen!

Dectora. What is there but the crying of the birds?

Forgael. If you'll but listen closely to that crying
You'll hear them calling out to one another
With human voices.

Dectora. O, I can hear them now.
What are they? Unto what country do they fly?

Forgael. To unimaginable happiness.
They have been circling over our heads in the air,
But now that they have taken to the road
We have to follow, for they are our pilots;
And though they're but the colour of grey ash,
They're crying out, could you but hear their words,
'There is a country at the end of the world
Where no child's born but to outlive the moon.'
(*The sailors come in with Aibric. They are in great excitement.*)

First Sailor. The hold is full of treasure.

Second Sailor. Full to the hatches.

First Sailor. Treasure on treasure.

Third Sailor. Boxes of precious spice.

First Sailor. Ivory images with amethyst eyes.

Third Sailor. Dragons with eyes of ruby.

First Sailor. The whole ship
Flashes as if it were a net of herrings.

Third Sailor. Let's home; I'd give some rubies to a woman.

Second Sailor. There's somebody I'd give the amethyst eyes to.

Aibric (*silencing them with a gesture*).
We would return to our own country, *Forgael*,
For we have found a treasure that's so great
Imagination cannot reckon it.

And having lit upon this woman there,
What more have you to look for on the seas?

Forgael. I cannot—I am going on to the end.
As for this woman, I think she is coming with me.

Aibric. The Ever-living have made you mad; but no,
It was this woman in her woman's vengeance
That drove you to it, and I fool enough
To fancy that she'd bring you home again.
'Twas you that egged him to it, for you know
That he is being driven to his death.

Dectora. That is not true, for he has promised me
An unimaginable happiness.

Aibric. And if that happiness be more than dreams,
More than the froth, the feather, the dust-whirl,
The crazy nothing that I think it is,
It shall be in the country of the dead,
If there be such a country.

Dectora. No, not there,
But in some island where the life of the world
Leaps upward, as if all the streams o' the world
Had run into one fountain.

Aibric. Speak to him.
He knows that he is taking you to death;
Speak—he will not deny it.

Dectora. Is that true?

Forgael. I do not know for certain, but I know.
That I have the best of pilots.

Aibric. Shadows, illusions,
That the Shape-changers, the Ever-laughing Ones,
The Immortal Mockers have cast into his mind,
Or called before his eyes.

Dectora. O carry me
To some sure country, some familiar place.
Have we not everything that life can give
In having one another?

Forgael. How could I rest
If I refused the messengers and pilots
With all those sights and all that crying out?

Dectora. But I will cover up your eyes and ear,
That you may never hear the cry of the birds,
Or look upon them.

Forgael. Were they but lowlier
I'd do your will, but they are too high—too high.

Dectora. Being too high, their heady prophecies
But harry us with hopes that come to nothing,
Because we are not proud, imperishable,
Alone and winged.

Forgael. Our love shall be like theirs
When we have put their changeless image on.

Dectora. I am a woman, I die at every breath.

Aibric. Let the birds scatter, for the tree is broken,
And there's no help in words. (*To the sailors.*)
To the other ship,
And I will follow you and cut the rope
When I have said farewell to this man here,
For neither I nor any living man
Will look upon his face again.
(*The sailors go out.*)

Forgael (to Dectora), Go with him,
For he will shelter you and bring you home.

Aibric (*taking Forgael's hand*). I'll do it for his sake.

Dectora. No. Take this sword
And cut the rope, for I go on with *Forgael.*

Aibric (half falling into the keen).
The yew-bough has been broken into two,
And all the birds are scattered—O! O! O!
Farewell! farewell! (*He goes out.*)

Dectora. The sword is in the rope—
The rope's in two—it falls into the sea,
It whirls into the foam. O ancient worm,
Dragon that loved the world and held us to it,
You are broken, you are broken. The world drifts away,
And I am left alone with my beloved,
Who cannot put me from his sight for ever.
We are alone for ever, and I laugh,
Forgael, because you cannot put me from you.
The mist has covered the heavens, and you and I
Shall be alone for ever. We two—this crown—
I half remember. It has been in my dreams.
Bend lower, O king, that I may crown you with it.
O flower of the branch, O bird among the leaves,
O silver fish that my two hands have taken
Out of the running stream, O morning star,
Trembling in the blue heavens like a white fawn
Upon the misty border of the wood,
Bend lower, that I may cover you with my hair,
For we will gaze upon this world no longer.

Forgael (gathering Dectora's hair about him).
Beloved, having dragged the net about us,
And knitted mesh to mesh, we grow immortal;
And that old harp awakens of itself
To cry aloud to the grey birds, and dreams,
That have had dreams for father, live in us.

THE TWO KINGS
1914

King Eochaid came at sundown to a wood
Westward of Tara. Hurrying to his queen
He had outridden his war-wasted men
That with empounded cattle trod the mire,
And where beech trees had mixed a pale green light
With the ground-ivy's blue, he saw a stag
Whiter than curds, its eyes the tint of the sea.
Because it stood upon his path and seemed
More hands in height than any stag in the world
He sat with tightened rein and loosened mouth
Upon his trembling horse, then drove the spur;
But the stag stooped and ran at him, and passed,
Rending the horse's flank. King Eochaid reeled,
Then drew his sword to hold its levelled point
Against the stag. When horn and steel were met
The horn resounded as though it had been silver,
A sweet, miraculous, terrifying sound.
Horn locked in sword, they tugged and struggled there
As though a stag and unicorn were met
Among the African Mountains of the Moon,
Until at last the double horns, drawn backward,
Butted below the single and so pierced
The entrails of the horse. Dropping his sword
King Eochaid seized the horns in his strong hands
And stared into the sea-green eye, and so
Hither and thither to and fro they trod
Till all the place was beaten into mire.
The strong thigh and the agile thigh were met,
The hands that gathered up the might of the world,
And hoof and horn that had sucked in their speed

Amid the elaborate wilderness of the air.
Through bush they plunged and over ivied root,
And where the stone struck fire, while in the leaves
A squirrel whinnied and a bird screamed out;
But when at last he forced those sinewy flanks
Against a beech-bole, he threw down the beast
And knelt above it with drawn knife. On the instant
It vanished like a shadow, and a cry
So mournful that it seemed the cry of one
Who had lost some unimaginable treasure
Wandered between the blue and the green leaf
And climbed into the air, crumbling away,
Till all had seemed a shadow or a vision
But for the trodden mire, the pool of blood,
The disembowelled horse.
King Eochaid ran
Toward peopled Tara, nor stood to draw his breath
Until he came before the painted wall,
The posts of polished yew, circled with bronze,
Of the great door; but though the hanging lamps
Showed their faint light through the unshuttered windows,
Nor door, nor mouth, nor slipper made a noise,
Nor on the ancient beaten paths, that wound
From well-side or from plough-land, was there noise;
Nor had there been the noise of living thing
Before him or behind, but that far off
On the horizon edge bellowed the herds.
Knowing that silence brings no good to kings,
And mocks returning victory, he passed
Between the pillars with a beating heart
And saw where in the midst of the great hall
Pale-faced, alone upon a bench, Edain
Sat upright with a sword before her feet.
Her hands on either side had gripped the bench,
Her eyes were cold and steady, her lips tight.
Some passion had made her stone. Hearing a foot
She started and then knew whose foot it was;
But when he thought to take her in his arms
She motioned him afar, and rose and spoke:
'I have sent among the fields or to the woods

The fighting-men and servants of this house,
For I would have your judgment upon one
Who is self-accused. If she be innocent
She would not look in any known man's face
Till judgment has been given, and if guilty,
Would never look again on known man's face.'
And at these words he paled, as she had paled,
Knowing that he should find upon her lips
The meaning of that monstrous day.
Then she:
'You brought me where your brother Ardan sat
Always in his one seat, and bid me care him
Through that strange illness that had fixed him there.
And should he die to heap his burial-mound
And carve his name in Ogham.' Eochaid said,
'He lives?' 'He lives and is a healthy man.'
'While I have him and you it matters little
What man you have lost, what evil you have found.'
'I bid them make his bed under this roof
And carried him his food with my own hands,
And so the weeks passed by. But when I said,
"What is this trouble?" he would answer nothing,
Though always at my words his trouble grew;
And I but asked the more, till he cried out,
Weary of many questions: "There are things
That make the heart akin to the dumb stone."
Then I replied, "Although you hide a secret,
Hopeless and dear, or terrible to think on,
Speak it, that I may send through the wide world
For medicine." Thereon he cried aloud,
"Day after day you question me, and I,
Because there is such a storm amid my thoughts
I shall be carried in the gust, command,
Forbid, beseech and waste my breath." Then I:
"Although the thing that you have hid were evil,
The speaking of it could be no great wrong,
And evil must it be, if done 'twere worse
Than mound and stone that keep all virtue in,
And loosen on us dreams that waste our life,
Shadows and shows that can but turn the brain."

But finding him still silent I stooped down
And whispering that none but he should hear,
Said, "If a woman has put this on you,
My men, whether it please her or displease,
And though they have to cross the Loughlan waters
And take her in the middle of armed men,
Shall make her look upon her handiwork,
That she may quench the rick she has fired; and though
She may have worn silk clothes, or worn a crown,
She'll not be proud, knowing within her heart
That our sufficient portion of the world
Is that we give, although it be brief giving,
Happiness to children and to men."
Then he, driven by his thought beyond his thought,
And speaking what he would not though he would,
Sighed, "You, even you yourself, could work the cure!"
And at those words I rose and I went out
And for nine days he had food from other hands,
And for nine days my mind went whirling round
The one disastrous zodiac, muttering
That the immedicable mound's beyond
Our questioning, beyond our pity even.
But when nine days had gone I stood again
Before his chair and bending down my head
I bade him go when all his household slept
To an old empty woodman's house that's hidden
Westward of Tara, among the hazel-trees —
For hope would give his limbs the power — and await
A friend that could, he had told her, work his cure
And would be no harsh friend.
When night had deepened,
I groped my way from beech to hazel wood,
Found that old house, a sputtering torch within,
And stretched out sleeping on a pile of skins
Ardan, and though I called to him and tried
To shake him out of sleep, I could not rouse him.
I waited till the night was on the turn,
Then fearing that some labourer, on his way
To plough or pasture-land, might see me there,
Went out.

Among the ivy-covered rocks,
As on the blue light of a sword, a man
Who had unnatural majesty, and eyes
Like the eyes of some great kite scouring the woods,
Stood on my path. Trembling from head to foot
I gazed at him like grouse upon a kite;
But with a voice that had unnatural music,
"A weary wooing and a long," he said,
"Speaking of love through other lips and looking
Under the eyelids of another, for it was my craft
That put a passion in the sleeper there,
And when I had got my will and drawn you here,
Where I may speak to you alone, my craft
Sucked up the passion out of him again
And left mere sleep. He'll wake when the sun wakes,
Push out his vigorous limbs and rub his eyes,
And wonder what has ailed him these twelve months."
I cowered back upon the wall in terror,
But that sweet-sounding voice ran on: "Woman,
I was your husband when you rode the air,
Danced in the whirling foam and in the dust,
In days you have not kept in memory,
Being betrayed into a cradle, and I come
That I may claim you as my wife again."
I was no longer terrified — his voice
Had half awakened some old memory —
Yet answered him, "I am King Eochaid's wife
And with him have found every happiness
Women can find." With a most masterful voice,
That made the body seem as it were a string
Under a bow, he cried, "What happiness
Can lovers have that know their happiness
Must end at the dumb stone? But where we build
Our sudden palaces in the still air
Pleasure itself can bring no weariness.
Nor can time waste the cheek, nor is there foot
That has grown weary of the wandering dance,
Nor an unlaughing mouth, but mine that mourns,
Among those mouths that sing their sweethearts' praise,
Your empty bed." "How should I love," I answered,

"Were it not that when the dawn has lit my bed
And shown my husband sleeping there," I have sighed,
'Your strength and nobleness will pass away'?
Or how should love be worth its pains were it not
That when he has fallen asleep within my arms,
Being wearied out, I love in man the child?
What can they know of love that do not know
She builds her nest upon a narrow ledge
Above a windy precipice?" Then he:
"Seeing that when you come to the deathbed
You must return, whether you would or no,
This human life blotted from memory,
Why must I live some thirty, forty years,
Alone with all this useless happiness?"
Thereon he seized me in his arms, but I
Thrust him away with both my hands and cried,
"Never will I believe there is any change
Can blot out of my memory this life
Sweetened by death, but if I could believe,
That were a double hunger in my lips
For what is doubly brief."
                                        And now the shape
My hands were pressed to vanished suddenly.
I staggered, but a beech-tree stayed my fall,
And clinging to it I could hear the cocks
Crow upon Tara.
                                        King Eochaid bowed his head
And thanked her for her kindness to his brother,
For that she promised, and for that refused.
Thereon the bellowing of the empounded herds
Rose round the walls, and through the bronze-ringed door
Jostled and shouted those war-wasted men,
And in the midst King Eochaid's brother stood,
And bade all welcome, being ignorant.

THE GIFT OF HARUN AL-RASHID
1923

Kusta Ben Luka is my name, I write
To Abd Al-Rabban; fellow-roysterer once,
Now the good Caliph's learned Treasurer,
And for no ear but his.
                                        Carry this letter
Through the great gallery of the Treasure House
Where banners of the Caliphs hang, night-coloured
But brilliant as the night's embroidery,
And wait war's music; pass the little gallery;
Pass books of learning from Byzantium
Written in gold upon a purple stain,
And pause at last, I was about to say,
At the great book of Sappho's song; but no,
For should you leave my letter there, a boy's
Love-lorn, indifferent hands might come upon it
And let it fall unnoticed to the floor.
Pause at the Treatise of Parmenides
And hide it there, for Caiphs to world's end
Must keep that perfect, as they keep her song,
So great its fame.
                                        When fitting time has passed
The parchment will disclose to some learned man
A mystery that else had found no chronicler
But the wild Bedouin. Though I approve
Those wanderers that welcomed in their tents
What great Harun Al-Rashid, occupied
With Persian embassy or Grecian war,
Must needs neglect, I cannot hide the truth
That wandering in a desert, featureless
As air under a wing, can give birds' wit.

In after time they will speak much of me
And speak but fantasy. Recall the year
When our beloved Caliph put to death
His Vizir Jaffer for an unknown reason:
'If but the shirt upon my body knew it
I'd tear it off and throw it in the fire.'
That speech was all that the town knew, but he
Seemed for a while to have grown young again;
Seemed so on purpose, muttered Jaffer's friends,
That none might know that he was conscience-struck —
But that's a traitor's thought. Enough for me
That in the early summer of the year
The mightiest of the princes of the world
Came to the least considered of his courtiers;
Sat down upon the fountain's marble edge,
One hand amid the goldfish in the pool;
And thereupon a colloquy took place
That I commend to all the chroniclers
To show how violent great hearts can lose
Their bitterness and find the honeycomb.
'I have brought a slender bride into the house;
You know the saying, "Change the bride with spring."
And she and I, being sunk in happiness,
Cannot endure to think you tread these paths,
When evening stirs the jasmine bough, and yet
Are brideless.'

'I am falling into years.'

'But such as you and I do not seem old
Like men who live by habit. Every day
I ride with falcon to the river's edge
Or carry the ringed mail upon my back,
Or court a woman; neither enemy,
Game-bird, nor woman does the same thing twice;
And so a hunter carries in the eye
A mimic of youth. Can poet's thought
That springs from body and in body falls
Like this pure jet, now lost amid blue sky,
Now bathing lily leaf and fish's scale,
Be mimicry?'

'What matter if our souls
Are nearer to the surface of the body
Than souls that start no game and turn no rhyme!
The soul's own youth and not the body's youth
Shows through our lineaments. My candle's bright,
My lantern is too loyal not to show
That it was made in your great father's reign.

'And yet the jasmine season warms our blood.'

'Great prince, forgive the freedom of my speech:
You think that love has seasons, and you think
That if the spring bear off what the spring gave
The heart need suffer no defeat; but I
Who have accepted the Byzantine faith,
That seems unnatural to Arabian minds,
Think when I choose a bride I choose for ever;
And if her eye should not grow bright for mine
Or brighten only for some younger eye,
My heart could never turn from daily ruin,
Nor find a remedy.'
'But what if I
Have lit upon a woman who so shares
Your thirst for those old crabbed mysteries,
So strains to look beyond Our life, an eye
That never knew that strain would scarce seem bright,
And yet herself can seem youth's very fountain,
Being all brimmed with life?'
'Were it but true
I would have found the best that life can give,
Companionship in those mysterious things
That make a man's soul or a woman's soul
Itself and not some other soul.'
'That love
Must needs be in this life and in what follows
Unchanging and at peace, and it is right
Every philosopher should praise that love.
But I being none can praise its opposite.
It makes my passion stronger but to think
Like passion stirs the peacock and his mate,

The wild stag and the doe; that mouth to mouth
Is a man's mockery of the changeless soul.'
And thereupon his bounty gave what now
Can shake more blossom from autumnal chill
Than all my bursting springtime knew. A girl
Perched in some window of her mother's house
Had watched my daily passage to and fro;
Had heard impossible history of my past;
Imagined some impossible history
Lived at my side; thought time's disfiguring touch
Gave but more reason for a woman's care.
Yet was it love of me, or was it love
Of the stark mystery that has dazed my sight,
Perplexed her fantasy and planned her care?
Or did the torchlight of that mystery
Pick out my features in such light and shade
Two contemplating passions chose one theme
Through sheer bewilderment? She had not paced
The garden paths, nor counted up the rooms,
Before she had spread a book upon her knees
And asked about the pictures or the text;
And often those first days I saw her stare
On old dry writing in a learned tongue,
On old dry faggots that could never please
The extravagance of spring; or move a hand
As if that writing or the figured page
Were some dear cheek.
Upon a moonless night
I sat where I could watch her sleeping form,
And wrote by candle-light; but her form moved.
And fearing that my light disturbed her sleep
I rose that I might screen it with a cloth.
I heard her voice, 'Turn that I may expound
What's bowed your shoulder and made pale your cheek'
And saw her sitting upright on the bed;
Or was it she that spoke or some great Djinn?
I say that a Djinn spoke. A livelong hour
She seemed the learned man and I the child;
Truths without father came, truths that no book
Of all the uncounted books that I have read,

Nor thought out of her mind or mine begot,
Self-born, high-born, and solitary truths,
Those terrible implacable straight lines
Drawn through the wandering vegetative dream,
Even those truths that when my bones are dust
Must drive the Arabian host.
The voice grew still,
And she lay down upon her bed and slept,
But woke at the first gleam of day, rose up
And swept the house and sang about her work
In childish ignorance of all that passed.
A dozen nights of natural sleep, and then
When the full moon swam to its greatest height
She rose, and with her eyes shut fast in sleep
Walked through the house. Unnoticed and unfelt
I wrapped her in a hooded cloak, and she,
Half running, dropped at the first ridge of the desert
And there marked out those emblems on the sand
That day by day I study and marvel at,
With her white finger. I led her home asleep
And once again she rose and swept the house
In childish ignorance of all that passed.
Even to-day, after some seven years
When maybe thrice in every moon her mouth
Murmured the wisdom of the desert Djinns,
She keeps that ignorance, nor has she now
That first unnatural interest in my books.
It seems enough that I am there; and yet,
Old fellow-student, whose most patient ear
Heard all the anxiety of my passionate youth,
It seems I must buy knowledge with my peace.
What if she lose her ignorance and so
Dream that I love her only for the voice,
That every gift and every word of praise
Is but a payment for that midnight voice
That is to age what milk is to a child?
Were she to lose her love, because she had lost
Her confidence in mine, or even lose
Its first simplicity, love, voice and all,
All my fine feathers would be plucked away

And I left shivering. The voice has drawn
A quality of wisdom from her love's
Particular quality. The signs and shapes;
All those abstractions that you fancied were
From the great Treatise of Parmenides;
All, all those gyres and cubes and midnight things
Are but a new expression of her body
Drunk with the bitter sweetness of her youth.
And now my utmost mystery is out.
A woman's beauty is a storm-tossed banner;
Under it wisdom stands, and I alone —
Of all Arabia's lovers I alone —
Nor dazzled by the embroidery, nor lost
In the confusion of its night-dark folds,
Can hear the armed man speak.